World Economy changes and challenges

Timely Reports to Keep
Journalists, Scholars and the Public
Abreast of Developing Issues, Events and Trends

Editorial Research Reports
Published by Congressional Quarterly Inc.
1414 22nd Street, N.W.
Washington, D.C. 20037

About the Cover

The cover was designed by Staff Artist Belle Burkhart.

Editor, Hoyt Gimlin
Managing Editor, Sandra Stencel
Editorial Assistants, Laurie De Maris, Elizabeth Furbush
Production Manager, I. D. Fuller
Assistant Production Manager, Maceo Mayo

Library of Congress Cataloging in Publication Data

Main entry under title:

Editorial research reports on world economy, changes and challenges.

Reports originally appeared in Editorial research reports.
Bibliography: p.
Includes index.
1. Economic history — 1971-   — Addresses, essays, lectures. I. Congressional Quarterly, inc. II. Title: World economy, changes and challenges.
HC59.E39   1983   330.9'04   83-7333
ISBN 0-87187-266-8

Contents

Foreword

Perhaps more than ever before, Americans are looking abroad for answers to their economic woes. Foreign trade increasingly becomes more vital to this nation's well-being. The United States seeks new markets in Japan and Europe, especially for farm products, and at the same time it devises ways to protect such basic industries as automobiles and steel from Japanese and European exports. Tensions have arisen with Japan over trade policies and with Europe over Reagan administration attempts to control scientific information in industrial projects affecting America's allies. It is information which Washington says would aid Russia's quest for high technology to benefit a sagging Soviet economy and bolster the country militarily.

Indeed, "high tech" has become the watchword of America's economic gurus, who say that retaining the nation's leadership in such high technology fields as computers and satellite-aided telecommunications are the hope for tomorrow. While scenarios of a high-tech future are being written for industry generally, present-day problems with a global dimension beset the American financial community. A world debt crisis has made the U.S. banking system vulnerable to economic disasters in faraway places. With the recent decline in world petroleum prices, some of yesterday's "oil rich" countries are stalling their creditors, frantically scrambling for new loans to pay off old ones.

Despite potential damage to credit institutions, and thus the world economy, diminishing oil prices do provide a note of optimism that has long been absent in global economics. It was nearly 10 years ago, in the fall of 1973 that the Organization of Oil Exporting Countries (OPEC) began boosting petroleum prices skyward. Economists attribute many of the world's economic difficulties of the past decade to the staggering costs thrust upon fuel-importing countries, including the United States.

The nine Reports that make up this book examine such problems as trade, the debt crisis, Japanese relations, scientific information and others in detail. Together, they provide the reader an overview of the changes occurring in the world economy today, and the challenges facing it in the midst of a global recession.

Hoyt Gimlin
Editor

Washington, D.C.
April 1983

Worldᴅᴇʙᴛ Crisis

by

William Sweet

**Jan. 21
1 9 8 3**

WORLD DEBT CRISIS

I N A quiet but significant reversal of U.S. policy, Treasury Secretary Donald T. Regan announced in early December that the Reagan administration would support large increases in the International Monetary Fund's lending resources.[1] The shift in the U.S. position cleared the way for the world's leading industrial nations to reach preliminary agreements on a "substantial" increase in IMF quotas *(see p. 17)*.[2] Just three months earlier, when the IMF and World Bank held their annual meeting in Toronto, the United States stood virtually alone in opposing a 50 to 100 percent increase in IMF quotas. President Reagan told the delegates that the "magic of the marketplace" would take care of world debt problems.

The reasons why Reagan and Regan reversed U.S. policy are not hard to find. During the final months of 1982, first Mexico and then Brazil — the world's two largest debtor countries — plunged into deep financial troubles that made it impossible for them to meet debt repayment schedules. As a result, international rescue operations of unprecedented scope had to be arranged on an emergency basis. Partly because of the large-scale involvement of U.S. commercial banks in lending to Mexico and Brazil, the Reagan administration took a leading part in the operations, commiting sizable U.S. resources to the two countries *(see p. 5)*.

The Mexican and Brazilian bailouts, coming on top of a number of lesser but still serious repayment crises, have raised urgent questions about whether international institutions and arrangements are adequate to prevent a collapse of the world monetary system. They also have provoked a lot of controversy about whether the banks themselves are to some extent responsible for the crises, whether they deserve to be penalized and whether they could be penalized without bringing on a financial panic.

---

[1] Regan also suggested that an international monetary conference, similar to the 1944 Bretton Woods conference, be convened to address the debt crisis. In July 1944, delegates from 44 countries met at Bretton Woods, the New Hampshire resort, to design the postwar monetary system. They agreed to establish the International Monetary Fund (IMF), to assist countries with balance of payments problems, and the International Bank for Reconstruction and Development (the World Bank), to finance specific projects. Regan's idea of holding an international monetary conference reportedly has met with a cool reception abroad.

[2] At meetings in Paris and Frankfurt in mid-December and in Paris on Jan. 18, 1983.

Most monetary officials, including Federal Reserve Chairman Paul Volcker, take the position that the orderly servicing of debt and monetary stability require the governments of the industrial nations to stand firm behind troubled Third World debtors and their creditor banks.[3] In the opinion of almost all financial experts, the industrial countries just cannot afford to allow Third World debtors to default on the hundreds of billions of dollars they have borrowed from private banks in the United States, Europe and Japan. Treasury Secretary Regan articulated the prevailing view in hearings held by the House Banking, Finance and Urban Affairs Committee on Dec. 21: "Were we not to solve [the world debt problem] we could have a worldwide depression through defaults in many nations. . . . I think it's avoidable, but it's going to take care."

Responsibility of U.S. Banks in Dispute

Congress must approve any increases in U.S. contributions to the IMF and some members are not convinced that the debt situation is absolutely urgent. Influential members of the banking committees have voiced the suspicion that all the talk about a debt crisis is just a ploy to get the government to help private banks out of a mess of their own making. Some members find it hard to understand why the U.S. government should come to the aid of foreign debtors without a moment's hesitation, although it usually goes through prolonged agonies over whether to bail out failing enterprises at home.

In hearings before the Joint Economic Committee on Nov. 24, Sen. William Proxmire, D-Wis., the ranking minority member of the Senate Banking Committee, accused Volcker of having a "double standard." Proxmire asked Volcker why he was encouraging banks to keep lending money to troubled Third World debtors, in the name of "orderly" debt servicing, when he was not urging banks "to lend to American farmers, home builders and other small businesses."

At the Dec. 21 House Banking Committee hearings, Committee Chairman Fernand J. St Germain, D-R.I., told Treasury Secretary Regan that he was not prepared to support an increase in IMF quotas, which he referred to as a bailout for the major banks. After St Germain's position was criticized in a Dec. 27 editorial in *The Washington Post*, Rep. Charles E. Schumer, D-N.Y., wrote a letter to the paper saying that "if we do not impose some reasonable penalty on the banks, there will

---

[3] Syndicated columnists Rowland Evans and Robert Novak have reported that Volcker was instrumental in persuading the Reagan administration to change its position on IMF quotas. Sources told them that Volcker "left no doubt," in a meeting with White House officials on Oct. 28, "that the sky was falling." See their column in *The Washington Post*, Dec. 12, 1982.

Most Indebted Countries

Country	Total Private Debt (in millions)	Debt to U.S. Banks (in millions)
Mexico	$64,395	$24,925
Brazil	55,300	18,886
Venezuela	27,249	11,046
Argentina	25,305	8,612
South Korea	19,994	8,621
Chile	11,757	6,259
Yugoslavia	9,967	2,476
Indonesia	8,155	2,531
Algeria	7,728	1,308
Israel*	6,126	2,202
Egypt*	5,350	1,494
Turkey*	3,956	1,478
India*	1,577	499

*Public debt exceeds private debt.

Source: Figures for total private debt from the Bank for International Settlements; figures for debt to U.S. banks from U.S. Federal Reserve Board.

be nothing [to prevent] their placing the financial system in jeopardy the next time an uncreditworthy borrower promises to pay extraordinarily high interest rates in exchange for an unsafe loan." [4]

House and Senate Democrats have not been the only ones to question the bankers' role in the debt situation. Lawrence Rout, *The Wall Street Journal's* correspondent in Mexico City, has described their role in the Mexican crisis as "a classic example of international banking gone awry." In an article on the paper's editorial page, Rout said the Mexican situation "illustrates the herd instincts of bankers, and how all-consuming competition among them can, at best, permit, and at worst, push a government to mismanage its economy.... Mexico is a case study of the 'merry-go-round' philosophy that often infects commercial banks' dealings with foreign countries. Credit-worthiness isn't judged by a country's ability to repay loans, but by its ability to get more loans to service existing debt." [5]

Massive Bailouts for Mexico and Brazil

The seeds of Mexico's problems were sown nearly 10 years ago, when reports began to spread of newly discovered Mexican oil reserves that might rival Saudi Arabia's.[6] Largely on the strength of the country's prospective oil wealth, commercial

---

[4] See *The Washington Post,* Jan. 1, 1983.
[5] See *The Wall Street Journal,* Oct. 22, 1982.
[6] See "Mexican-U.S. Relations," *E.R.R.,* 1977 Vol. II, p. 717.

banks in the United States, Europe and Japan lent Mexico tens of billions of dollars during the following years. Much of the money went to fund oil development projects, which could be expected in time to generate enough hard-currency export revenue to repay the loans.[7] But a lot of the money also went to fund public sector deficits, social welfare programs and public enterprises of sometimes dubious viability.

Mexico's situation began to deteriorate in 1980-81, when a world oil glut depressed prices, causing Mexican export revenues to start dropping from anticipated levels. At the same time, world prices for many other commodities exported by Mexico fell sharply because of sagging demand in the recession-ridden industrial countries, while soaring interest rates greatly added to the cost of servicing Mexico's accumulating foreign debt.[8]

The Mexican crisis came to a head last August, following the second massive devaluation of the peso in less than a year. It became apparent that Mexico would be unable to meet payments on its foreign debt, which was estimated to be somewhere between $75 billion and $90 billion. In response, the U.S. government took the lead in arranging a package of measures to save Mexico from default.

In August, the Reagan administration agreed to lend Mexico $1 billion in advance payments for oil destined for the strategic reserve and $1 billion in subsidized agricultural credits — this on top of a $700 million line of credit with the Federal Reserve that Mexico has at its disposal. U.S. commercial banks, which had lent Mexico about $25 billion, agreed to forego repayments of $10 billion in principal for 90 days, pending negotiation of an IMF credit. Together with 12 other industrialized countries, the United States arranged at the end of August to lend Mexico $1.85 billion, which was channeled through the Bank for International Settlements (BIS) in Basel *(see box, p. 9)*. The U.S. Treasury put up nearly half the BIS loan, drawing on its Exchange Stabilization fund, which is ordinarily reserved for the buying and selling of currencies to stabilize the dollar's exchange rate. Two days before Christmas, the IMF agreed to lend Mexico $4 billion.[9]

---

[7] Hard currencies, like the U.S. dollar, the West German mark, the British pound, French franc and Japanese yen, can be readily used in international commerce to pay bills and liquidate debts.

[8] Most large internationally syndicated loans are made at interest rates that float with international rates. Generally they are tied to the London Interbank Offer Rate (LIBOR), which is the rate banks overseas pay for U.S. dollar deposits.

[9] More precisely, the IMF credit was SDR 3.6 billion. IMF transactions are always reported in terms of "special drawing rights" (SDRs), an artificially created reserve currency and unit of account, which is based on a weighted composite of the dollar, mark, pound, franc and yen.

By the time the final touches were being put on Mexico's bailout package, the United States was deeply involved in making similar arrangements for Brazil, another debtor nation severely affected by low commodity prices and high interest rates. Brazil's total external debt is probably about $90 billion, and its debts to private U.S. banks come to nearly $19 billion.[10]

On Dec. 1, President Reagan announced that the United States would lend Brazil $1.23 billion in short-term credits from

Jim Wells Photographers
Donald T. Regan

the Treasury's Exchange Stabilization Fund.[11] A week later, at a meeting in Frankfurt, West Germany, Treasury Secretary Regan agreed with the finance ministers of Britain, France and the Federal Republic to arrange a $1.5 billion BIS loan for Brazil, in which the U.S. share would be $500 million. In mid-December, Brazil received a $500 million loan from the IMF's compensatory financing facility and it negotiated a $4.6 billion, three-year standby credit with the IMF, which awaits the approval of the fund's executive board.[12] On Dec. 20, the president of Brazil's central bank told representatives of 125 banks, meeting at New York's Plaza Hotel, that Brazil would need about $9.6 billion in new and rolled-over credits to get through 1983.

Among bankers, regulators and independent economists, Brazil's difficulties have been almost as shocking as Mexico's. Since Brazil is a major importer of oil, it was always assumed that the country would have serious problems in the 1970s and 1980s. But bankers generally expected Brazil to weather the problems, partly because of the high growth rates it achieved after the oil shock of 1973-74, and partly because of its stable military regime. Bankers have considered Brazil's financial management superb, and even after oil prices took another giant leap upward in 1979-80, they rated the country a good credit risk.

Poland, Argentina and Others in Arrears

If Brazil and Mexico were the only major debtors in arrears, the situation might be described as disconcerting, but not necessarily critical. However, several other major debtors also have fallen far behind in their payments, and others soon may. Last

---

[10] The uncertainty in the estimate for the total arises from controversy over the size of Brazil's short-term debt. The Brazilian government has estimated it as $11 billion, but other sources have said it may be as high as $30 billion.

[11] Later in the month, the Treasury put up another $300 million for Brazil.

[12] Compensatory financing loans are granted, without conditions, to countries that have suffered from an unavoidable drop in export earnings. Standby credits are given only under conditions that generally require the borrower to adopt austerity measures.

spring, at the time of the British-Argentine war over the Falkland Islands, it became apparent that Argentina — Latin America's third largest debtor — would be unable to service its debt on schedule. Just months before that, the banks got word that Poland, which is Eastern Europe's biggest debtor, would be unable to meet its payments.

While the amount owed U.S. banks by Poland is less than $2 billion, a relatively small amount, the country's total debt to the West comes to about $26 billion. When Poland fell into arrears in 1981, it dashed a cherished theory among bankers that Russia, for the sake of détente, would never allow one of its clients to fall into bad graces with the West. With the collapse of this so-called "umbrella theory," all of Eastern Europe's debt — currently about $87 billion — began to seem vulnerable. Not long after Poland fell into arrears, Romania had to begin rescheduling its debt repayments, and bankers started to worry about the economic outlook in East Germany, Hungary and Yugoslavia as well.[13]

In a system that depends on the maintenance of confidence among a very large number of creditor banks — over 500 in the case of Poland, 200 with Romania — the emergence of serious problems in a leading debtor country can easily undermine the status of other debtors and unleash a fury of loan denials and debt referrals. Once it became evident that Poland was in trouble, it got harder for other Eastern European countries to borrow, and once that happened, some of them found it still more difficult to service existing debts. The same thing happened in Latin America around the middle of last year, after Argentina stopped meeting its repayment schedule. Lending to the other big Latin American borrowers dried up, which helped precipitate the Mexican and Brazilian crises.

Argentina has been a favored country among international bankers since 1976, when a military junta overthrew the country's Peronist government. Between 1978 and 1982, Argentina's external debt grew almost threefold to about $36 billion — much of it short-term debts to commercial banks. At the end of June 1982, Argentina owed banks in the United States about $8.6 billion, and 40 percent of that was due in a year or less.

Last September, rumors that Argentina might repudiate its debt sent gold prices to an 11-month high in New York and Hong Kong. The rumors proved unfounded, but it has been an

---

[13] Since Yugoslavia is not a Soviet client, bankers have never regarded it with the complacency associated with the umbrella theory. But the U.S. bank exposure is bigger in Yugoslavia than in the East Bloc countries, and bankers may count on help from the U.S. government in the event of a pinch. Hungary and Romania, though Russian satellites, also are members of the IMF. Poland opened discussions with the IMF in 1981, but talks were suspended after the crackdown on the Solidarity trade union in December of that year.

Growing Role of Basel Settlements Bank

In several of the bailout operations undertaken in recent months, the Bank for International Settlements (BIS) in Basel, Switzerland, has played a role almost equal to the International Monetary Fund (IMF) in coordinating emergency action. Partly because it is relatively small, the BIS sometimes can act faster than the more cumbersome IMF. It has long served as a somewhat informal and highly confidential meeting place for central bankers, and an agreement negotiated under its auspices in 1975 — the so-called "concordat" — is supposed to detail how central banks are to govern the international activities of commercial banks in their jurisdictions.

Founded in 1930 to help manage the collection of German World War I reparations, the BIS is a peculiar private-public hybrid. It technically is privately held, and it reportedly turns a tidy profit for investors; but 29 central bankers — mainly from Western Europe and the East Bloc — sit on the board of governors. Among other activities, the BIS manages the European Monetary System and gathers the world's most comprehensive statistics on private international lending.

While the BIS is under pressure from both debtors and creditors to become increasingly active in crisis management, it seems most unlikely that it will displace the IMF as the world's preeminent central banking institution. The BIS itself has discouraged overly ambitious speculation about its future.

open secret for nearly a year that Argentina is in arrears, and its financial officials currently are negotiating with its 11 leading bank creditors for a $1.1 billion short-term bridge loan, $1.5 billion in five-year credits, and a plan to refinance principal payments on the public and private sector debt due in 1982 and 1983. The Argentine government has reached an agreement in principle with the IMF for a $1.8 billion loan and it has been discussing a credit of $500 million to $750 million with the BIS.

Debt reschedulings are not unusual and, ordinarily, they are not unwelcome to bankers.[14] Bankers charge their debtors high front-end fees for the privilege of having their debts refinanced, and generally the borrowers pay a stiff penalty in terms of higher interest rates as well. The latest round of reschedulings are no exception, and in the short run at least, they may prove quite profitable to the banks. There is danger, though, that the tougher terms will make it even harder for countries like Mexico to get their houses in order.

[14] There have been 53 official debt reschedulings involving 20 countries since 1956, according to a 1982 report by the Group of 30 entitled "Risks in International Lending." The Group of 30 is a committee of top experts on international finance, chaired by H. Johannes Witteveen, the former managing director of the IMF. The committee meets twice a year to discuss international developments, and its work is supported by a small professional staff.

Some of the countries that have had to reschedule their debts in years past have managed to boost hard-currency earnings, under the discipline of austerity programs, and are now able to service their debts. Turkey, which had to reschedule $3.2 billion in 1980, made payments of $2.1 billion in 1982 on its $20.5 billion foreign debt. The Peruvian government, having rescheduled $518 million in 1978, says it will not have to renegotiate repayments in 1983 provided it is able to raise new international loans.

For every Turkey or Peru, however, there is another country that is still on the ropes or beginning to stumble. Zaire, which international bankers have referred to as a "basket case" for years, still has serious financial problems. Chile, a major recipient of commercial loans ever since the Allende regime was overthrown in 1973, went into an economic nose dive last year. It has just received IMF approval for a loan of $882.5 million. Ecuador, a relatively prosperous oil exporter that has been stung, like Mexico, by lower petroleum prices, announced in October that it would have to renegotiate payments on its public foreign debt. Even among the wealthiest countries of Western Europe, there are signs of strain. Concern is mounting, for example, about Denmark's ability to keep servicing its $15 billion foreign debt; Standard & Poor's has added the country to its "CreditWatch" list.[15]

To enumerate the most troubled debtor nations by no means exhausts the list of borrowers that are in trouble or could be soon. "Behind the front line of giants among the debtor countries," a financial weekly recently pointed out, "are large numbers of smaller countries in Latin America, Eastern Europe and Africa [which] either are or soon will be in a similar squeeze. While they pose, individually, less of a threat to the safety of international banking, a default by any one of them would suffice to seriously damage what confidence is left in the stability of the international credit structure."[16]

Scope and Concentration of World Debts

How much international credit is at risk, overall? Absolutely up-to-date and comprehensive statistics on world debt are unavailable, but several reputable authorities collect and publish data regularly, and by piecing the various sources together, it is possible to arrive at reasonable, sound estimates for the debt total. By any account, it is a staggering number.

The IMF, in its 1982 economic report, projected that long-term external debt, both public and private, would surpass $500

---

[15] France's foreign debt is estimated at $45 billion, Belgium's at $15 billion, Spain's at $13 billion, Portugal's at $10 billion, Ireland's at $8 billion and Greece's at $7 billion.
[16] *Rundt's Weekly Intelligence,* Dec. 20, 1982, p. 2.

billion by the end of the year.[17] The Bank for International Settlements, in its latest survey of commercial banks, estimated that private debt, short-term as well as long-term, came to $395.5 billion as of end-June 1982. The most recent Federal Reserve survey indicated that the debt to U.S. banks from borrowers in Africa, Asia, Eastern Europe and Latin America came to about $130 billion at the end of last June. If the IMF data on public and private long-term debt are combined with the BIS figures on private short-term borrowing, the total debt of countries in Africa, Asia, Eastern Europe and Latin America would appear to be between $700 billion and $800 billion.[18]

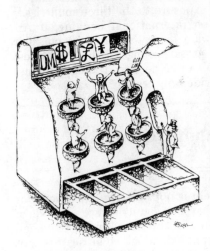

Since 1980, the developing countries have seen prices for their commodity exports drop to the lowest levels in 25 years; real per capita growth has come to a "virtual standstill" in the Third World; levels of international reserve currencies have fallen sharply since 1978, relative to import levels; and on top of having more debt outstanding than ever before, "a larger proportion is coming due in the short term."[19] While the oil-poor developing countries have registered some improvement in their balance of payments on current account (exports and imports of goods and services), they continue to run a yearly deficit in excess of $50 billion.

Last year, according to the IMF's 1982 report, the debt servicing payments of the non-OPEC developing countries exceeded $100 billion for the first time.[20] In 1981, the average debt service ratio of these countries — the ratio of their debt repayments to earnings from exports of goods and services — exceeded 20 percent for the first time. By an old rule of thumb, this is the maximum level considered safe by bankers. While the ratio for the non-OPEC developing countries in 1981 was over 20 percent *on average,* some of the countries saw their ratios go much higher.

In 1982, according to estimates prepared by Morgan Guar-

---

[17] IMF, "World Economic Outlook," 1982, Table 30, p. 170.
[18] Discrepancies in the ways the two organizations define their reporting areas and collect data make it impossible to be more precise.
[19] William G. Gasser and David L. Roberts, "Bank Lending to Developing Countries," *Federal Reserve Bank of New York Quarterly Review,* autumn 1982.
[20] IMF, *op. cit.,* Table 33, p. 173.

anty Trust, Argentina's debt service ratio approximated 179 percent; Mexico's 129 percent; Ecuador's 122 percent; Brazil's 122 percent; and Chile's 116 percent.[21] In other words, even if these five countries had spent every cent they earned from exports of goods and services to repay their debts in 1981, they still would have been unable to meet all repayments without borrowing more money.

As of the end of June 1982, Argentina, Brazil and Mexico accounted for 40 percent of the foreign debt owed to U.S. commercial banks. The nine largest U.S. banks reportedly have made loans equal to 130 percent of their total equity to these three countries, and their total loan loss reserves are said to equal just 12 percent of their exposure to the three countries.[22] According to one authority on international banking, if Argentina, Mexico and Brazil were to pay no interest on their foreign debts for a year, "the gross earnings of the five largest U.S. banks would decline by about 75 percent, [though] the net after-tax effect would be considerably less." [23]

World Economic Context

A HIGH concentration of debt is not necessarily irrational or unjustified, considering that big countries are capable of handling larger debt repayments.[24] And even among the small circle of very heavy borrowers, individual countries are not necessarily affected the same way by global economic changes. For example, of the 13 countries identified as the Third World's most heavily indebted nations in 1981, five are oil exporters, which stand to gain if petroleum prices rise, and six are manufacturing exporters, which stand to lose.[25]

Still, most macroeconomic factors affect most developing countries the same way, and for the coming year at least, the outlook is not very encouraging. With oil prices and interest rates now trending downward, economic activity, import demand and commodity prices ought to pick up somewhat. But virtually all economic forecasts anticipate very little or no

---

[21] See Morgan Guaranty Trust, *World Financial Markets*, October 1982, p. 5.
[22] See Jay Palmer, "The Debt Bomb Threat," *Time*, Jan. 10, 1983, p. 43.
[23] Pedro-Pablo Kucynski, "Latin American Debt," *Foreign Affairs*, winter 1982-83, p. 359. Kuzynski is president of First Boston International.
[24] See Robert Solomon, *The International Monetary System, 1945-1981* (1982), p. 329.
[25] Algeria, Argentina, Brazil, Egypt, India, Indonesia, Israel, Korea, Mexico, Spain, Turkey, Venezuela and Yugoslavia accounted for nearly two-thirds of the Third World's debt in 1981, according to the World Bank's "World Debt Tables," December 1981, p. xvii. In the new edition that is due out this month, Chile replaces Spain in the top 13.

growth among the highly industrialized countries in 1983. Even if production did increase more strongly than anybody now expects, recent experience indicates that this might be a short-lived and mixed blessing. More likely than not, another round of oil price hikes would bring the recovery to a standstill, and the developing countries would find themselves even worse off than before. Every time the world has gone through this kind of cycle in the last 10 years, the Third World's debt crisis has deepened.

When the OPEC states first quadrupled the price of oil at the end of 1973-74, there were predictions that world monetary arrangements might collapse.[26] Experts warned that a protracted imbalance of payments, as between the oil exporters and oil importers, would slow economic growth in the industrialized countries, bankrupt the oil-poor developing countries and throw the world into a massive recession or depression. Concern was especially acute about the stability of the commercial banks, which were using short-term deposits from the OPEC countries to make long-term loans to oil importers. It was feared that an abrupt and massive withdrawal of OPEC funds could bring the system down.

As it happened, the world economy limped through 1974 and 1975, and during the following years oil prices stabilized and then fell gently. The OPEC countries proved in general to be conservative investors, and there were no precipitous withdrawals or transfers of funds.

Then, in 1979-80, there was another burst of oil price hikes, and this time — in contrast to 1973-74 — the developing countries most affected were already deeply in debt to commercial banks. The result was a nasty double bind for the banks. If they continued to make new loans to the oil-poor countries, some would soon reach levels of indebtedness considered unsafe by normal banking standards. But if they stopped making new loans, they might throw countries into economic chaos and jeopardize the repayment of existing debt.[27]

In early 1980, bankers and bank regulators started to make uncharacteristically nervous statements in public. Otmar Emminger, the prestigious former head of West Germany's central bank, expressed the fear that the world financial system could "have a great fall." Initially, however, leading bankers were inclined to think they could cope with the crisis and even profit from it, provided they hung together and set the toughest possible terms in loan negotiations. It was only last summer,

---

[26] See "Arab Oil Money," *E.R.R.*, 1974 Vol. I, pp. 363-381 and "World Financing Under Stress," *E.R.R.*, 1975 Vol. I, pp. 287-305.
[27] See "Third World Debts," *E.R.R.*, 1980 Vol. II, pp. 541-560.

13

with the outbreak of the Mexican crisis, that they began to lose their nerve. Rimmer de Vries, chief international economist at Morgan Guaranty Trust, is reported to have said that the Mexican crisis was "like an atomic bomb being dropped in the world financial system." [28]

Bargaining Strength of Debtors, Lenders

Since World War II, there has been a fairly standard international procedure for dealing with countries, like Mexico, that fall into severe balance of payments problems. Commercial banks would suspend lending; an IMF team would be sent in to design an austerity program for the delinquent country; once the country accepted the program, the IMF would extend a stabilization credit; and when the country's economic situation improved, lending would resume. Often, the imposition of an austerity program would provoke riots, and sometimes even revolution. But so long as the international financial community stood united against the indebted country, the standard operating procedure worked reasonably well.

In the debt crisis that erupted last year, the usual procedures have been followed up to a point, and to a point the debtor countries have adopted the kind of stabilization measures favored by the IMF.[29] But with so many large, very heavily indebted countries lined up against the banks, the bargaining position of the debtors is much stronger than it used to be. There is a maxim, long revered among bankers, to the effect that if you owe a bank a great deal of money, you're the bank's slave; but if you owe the bank a truly gigantic amount of money, the bank is your slave. Leaders of the debtor countries are beginning to sense, it seems, that they have enslaved the banks, and in the recent debt negotiations, they have tended to act accordingly.

The Mexican government did not hesitate to freeze dollar deposits in Mexico and nationalize the country's banks, even as it was approaching the big international banks with urgent pleas for help. When Brazilian financial officials presented their proposals for refinancing the country's debt to bankers last December, there was a good deal of grumbling about their "take it or leave it" attitude. Poland got considerably more favorable terms in its second round of rescheduling talks than it did in the

---

[28] Quoted in *Time*, Jan. 10, 1983. Asked to confirm the quote, de Vries's first reaction was to exclaim, "Did I say that?" Upon reflection, he said he compared the Mexican crisis to nuclear war in the following sense: It was something everybody knew could happen but never really expected to happen.

[29] The Mexican government, for example, has said it will make a concerted effort to curb corruption and cut public sector deficits. Wage increases are to be held to about half the inflation rate, which is running at close to 100 percent per annum. As a result of the peso's depreciation, which has dropped by roughly 80 percent vis-à-vis the dollar since the beginning of 1982, the cost of imports is much higher.

Top IMF Borrowers

Country	Total Loan (millions)	Month of Agreement	Month of Expiration
India	$5,500.00	Nov. 81	Nov. 84
Mexico	3,960.00	Dec. 82	Dec. 85
Yugoslavia	1,828.20	Jan. 81	Dec. 83
Turkey	1,375.00	June 80	June 83
Romania	1,212.75	June 81	June 84
Pakistan	1,010.90	Dec. 81	Nov. 83
Peru	715.00	June 82	June 85
Chile	550.00	Jan. 83	Jan. 85
Ivory Coast	532.95	Feb. 81	Feb. 84
Jamaica	525.47	April 81	April 84

Source: International Monetary Fund

first, even though its economy is in worse shape than before. Romania had barely finished rescheduling its 1982 debt when it "informed" banks it would have to refinance the principal coming due in 1983 as well.

How far would the debtors be prepared to go, if push came to shove? Would some go so far as to repudiate their debts? To many financial experts, such threats seem utterly implausible, since a country that renounced its debt would have to be prepared to go without any international credit for many years to come. Peter Kenan, a professor of international economics at Princeton University, has said that if a country repudiated its debt, "it would be 50 years before it could borrow again." [30]

Walter Wriston, the chairman of Citibank, has often been quoted as saying that lending to countries is the safest kind of lending because countries, unlike corporations, do not go out of business and disappear.[31] But while countries do not disappear in the geographic or cultural sense, as a general rule, governments do change, and sometimes they change radically. While well established governments may appreciate the risks of repudiating debts, revolutionary mobs may not, and by the time they learn their lesson, a lot of damage can get done.

The Iranian hostage crisis was a clear example of a revolutionary government taking power and showing little regard for its future standing in the community of nations. In the end Iran's international creditors came out of the crisis with their funds intact, but they owed their good fortune largely to the fact that Iranian assets frozen at the order of President Carter in U.S.

[30] Quoted in *The New York Times,* Jan. 10, 1983.
[31] See *Time,* Jan. 10, 1983.

15

banks more than covered Iran's outstanding loans.[32] Still, the settlement of the crisis on terms favorable to the banks showed just how strong the incentives are for even the most fanatic government to restore its standing in the financial community.

The same kind of pressures apply to creditors. Last year, when Poland fell into arrears, many Americans thought it might be a good idea to penalize the country's military rulers by declaring the country in default on its debts. The AFL-CIO and Defense Secretary Caspar W. Weinberger, among others, thought the U.S. government should encourage the banks to foreclose on their loans. But bankers around the world pointed out that a default declaration could easily trigger a financial panic. Because of cross-default provisions contained in most international loan agreements, if any one bank or group of banks declares a borrower in default, all outstanding loans are automatically considered in default immediately. In a situation like this, there could be a sudden wave of bad loan write-offs, precipitous drops in reported earnings at the banks affected, plunges in stock values, etc. Because of such considerations, apparently, President Reagan overruled those who wanted to declare Poland in default.

Global Rescue Measures

THE IMF, under the relatively aggressive leadership of its French managing director, Jacques de Larosière, has placed increased emphasis on keeping all channels of international credit flowing. It has been the IMF's traditional role to impose discipline on debtor countries, but ever since the Mexican crisis broke out, de Larosière has worked hard to discipline the creditor banks as well.

In the negotiations connected with a large IMF credit for Argentina, for example, de Larosière told the country's bank creditors that the IMF could proceed with the loan only if they put up $1.5 billion in new credits. Without written assurances from the banks, he told the bank creditors last December, he would be unable to ask the IMF's executive board for an Argentine credit at a meeting scheduled for Jan. 26. Last November, de Larosière informed Mexico's 1,400 bank creditors that they would have to roll over $20 billion in Mexican credits maturing between August 1982 and end-1984 before the IMF would agree to provide the country with a loan.

[32] See "Settling International Claims," *E.R.R.*, 1981 Vol. I, pp. 149-168.

Richard N. Cooper, a professor of international economics at Harvard, has said we may be witnessing the creation "of a true world central bank." [33] Whether that turns out to be the case or not could depend on whether or how soon the IMF's lending resources are increased. Because of the recent loan agreements with Mexico and Brazil, and the large credits pending for a number of other countries, the fund's resources are said to be stretched somewhat thinly.

At a meeting in Paris on Jan. 18, representatives of the 10 largest industrial countries agreed in principle to increase IMF quotas substantially — probably to about $100 billion from the current level of $67 billion. The "G-10" representatives also agreed to increase the "General Arrangements to Borrow" from $6.8 billion to about $19 billion. The GAB is a lending pool made up of currencies from the G-10 countries, which the IMF administers. Like the Treasury's Exchange Stabilization Fund, its traditional use has been for the purchase and sale of currencies to stabilize foreign exchange rates, but it may also be used now for temporary credit relief.

IMF Photo
Jacques de Larosière

A meeting of the IMF's Interim Committee that was scheduled for April has been advanced to Feb. 10-11, 1983, so that the increases in lending resources can be approved expeditiously. Even then, the quota increases must be ratified by member governments, and there is concern that the fund may run short on resources before monies from members arrive. De Larosière recently flew to Saudi Arabia to try to secure a large loan for the IMF, and there is serious speculation that the IMF may raise money in the commercial markets.

Proposed Innovations in Financial Arena

Some financial specialists have argued that it is not enough to rely on organizations like the International Monetary Fund and the Bank for International Settlements *(see box, p. 9)*, and that new methods of dealing with the debt problem are required. At the behest of William S. Ogden, vice chairman of the Chase Manhattan Bank, representatives of 35 international banks recently agreed to establish a clearinghouse to monitor international credit and collect information on debtors. This new organization, the Institute of International Finance, is to be based in Washington.

[33] Quoted by Clyde H. Farnsworth in *The New York Times*, Jan. 9, 1983.

Norman A. Bailey, a former investment banker who currently is senior director of national security planning for the president's National Security Council, has suggested the "creation of an instrument that could be called an exchange participation note." These "equity-like" notes would "constitute claims on some prudent level of current and future foreign exchange earnings of selected debtor countries." They would be issued by the central banks of the debtor countries and they would be offered to "their private and official lenders on a pro rata basis to replace the existing amortization schedules. The central banks of the debtor countries would accept final responsibility for repaying all external debts, public and private, and would act as collection and paying agents." [34]

Felix G. Rohatyn, the head of New York City's Municipal Assistance Corporation ("Big Mac"), has proposed the creation of a new Reconstruction Finance Corporation that could supply capital to troubled banks as a lender of last resort. In the event a bank was threatened with bankruptcy by a major default, Rohatyn's "RFC" would "have the authority to acquire preferred stock" and thus "relieve the danger" and "permit an orderly settlement of the bank's obligations." [35]

Status of U.S. Banks

THE WORLD debt crisis came to a head at a time when the U.S. banking system already was under severe strain, partly as a result of high inflation and high interest rates, partly as a result of government deregulation and partly for other economic and institutional reasons.[36] Significant structural changes have taken place in the system during the past two years, as evidenced by a wave of mergers between financial and quasi-financial institutions, a crisis in the savings and loan industry and the meteoric growth of money market funds. As the partitions between the various segments of the system have come down, banks have become much more competitive with each other in going after deposits and loan business.

Under the circumstances, investors easily get skittish about individual institutions, and relatively small events can set off

[34] Norman A. Bailey, "A Safety Net for Foreign Lending," *Business Week*, Jan. 10, 1983, p. 17.

[35] Felix G. Rohatyn, "The State of the Banks," *The New York Review of Books*, Nov. 4, 1982, p. 6.

[36] See "Banking Deregulation," *E.R.R.*, 1981 Vol. II, pp. 573-592.

big shock waves. Early last summer, the failure of Oklahoma City's Penn Square Bank got a great deal of attention, mainly because several leading banks had to write off millions of dollars in bad loans that Penn Square had involved them in. Largely as a result of the Penn Square debacle, Chicago's Continental Illinois Bank and Chase Manhattan reported net losses in the second quarter of 1982 — their first quarterly losses since the Great Depression. The prices of their stocks promptly "dropped like tellers' wickets at closing time." [37]

Also last year, Moody's lowered its bond ratings for nine leading bank holding companies from triple-A to double-A. Moody's already had dropped its ratings for several other bank holding companies, and the only leading bank company that still retains the top Moody's rating is Morgan Guaranty.[38] In reporting the lowered ratings last March, Moody's cited a large number of factors, including the banks' "significantly [larger] exposure to less developed countries." [39]

Sensitivity About Public Disclosure Issue

With bank stocks volatile, federal regulators have been agonizing about how much information the banks should be required to disclose to investors about their foreign loans. Last summer, after the Securities and Exchange Commission (SEC) asked banks to report exceptionally big exposures, their stock prices dropped. But Federal Reserve Chairman Volcker is said to have relaxed his agency's reporting requirements so that banks with problematic loans to countries like Mexico and Brazil would not necessarily have to list those loans as nonperforming assets. A spokesman for the Federal Reserve would not verify that the reporting requirements had been changed. But in a Nov. 16 speech to the New England Council in Boston, Volcker said: "Where new loans facilitate the adjustment process in troubled countries and enable a country to strengthen its economy and service its international debt in an orderly manner, new credits should not be subject to supervisory criticism."

In the relatively closed world of international banking and bank regulation, public information has always been regarded with a good deal of suspicion. Many bankers apparently believe that information tends to feed irrational speculation, and the less of it there is out in the public domain, the better off everybody is. So long as everything went well, and banks regularly reported growing earnings quarter after quarter, year after

---

[37] Jerry Edgerton, "Bargains in Battered Bank Stocks," *Money*, November 1982, p. 167.
[38] Standard & Poor's, on the other hand, has reduced bond ratings from AAA to AA+ for just three bank holding companies: BankAmerica, Citicorp and Northwest Bancorporation. International debts were not a factor in these re-ratings.
[39] See *Moody's Bond Survey*, March 22, 1982, p. 2467.

year, regulators and politicians were inclined to let bankers pretty much take care of their own affairs. But now that the bankers are coming to Washington for help, and now that federal agencies are putting up billions of dollars to keep the biggest Third World debtors from going under, bankers may find that they will have to be a bit more open about their books. In the bankers' cozy world, this will not be easy to accept, but there may be no alternative.

Selected Bibliography

Books

Aronson, Jonathan David, *Money and Power: Banks and the World Monetary System,* Sage Publications, 1977.

Faith, Nicholas, *Safety in Numbers,* Viking 1982.

Salamon, Robert, *The International Monetary System, 1945-1981,* Harper & Row, 1982.

Sampson, Anthony, *The Money Lenders: Bankers and a World in Turmoil,* The Viking Press, 1981.

Articles

Cline, William R., "Mexico's Crisis: The World's Peril," *Foreign Policy,* winter 1982-83.

Gasser, William J. and David L. Roberts, "Bank Lending to Developing Countries: Problems and Prospects," *Federal Reserve Bank of New York Quarterly Review,* autumn 1982.

Kucynski, Pedro-Pablo, "Latin American Debt," *Foreign Affairs,* winter 1982-83.

Volcker, Paul L., "The Recycling Problem Revisited," *Challenge,* July-August 1980.

Zevin, Robert B., "Producing Something from Nothing," *The Atlantic,* July 1982.

Reports and Studies

Bank for International Settlements, "The Maturity Distribution of International Bank Lending," Basel, December 1982.

Editorial Research Reports: "Third World Debts," 1980 Vol. II, p. 541; "World Financing Under Stress," 1975 Vol. I, p. 287.

Federal Reserve System, Federal Financial Institutions Examination Council, "Country Exposure Lending Survey: June 1982," Washington, Dec. 6, 1982.

Hardy, Chandra S., "Rescheduling Developing Country Debts, 1956-81: Lessons and Recommendations," Overseas Development Council, Washington, 1982.

World Bank, "World Debt Tables," December 1979, December 1981 and January 1983 editions.

Illustration on cover and p. 11 by George Rebh.

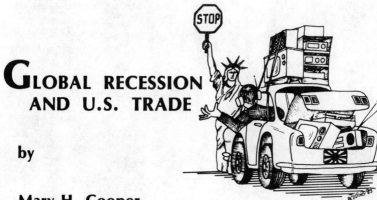

GLOBAL RECESSION AND U.S. TRADE

by

Mary H. Cooper

Mar. 4
1 9 8 3

GLOBAL RECESSION AND U.S. TRADE

FOR THE first two years of the Reagan administration, the overriding domestic issue was the state of the economy. The focus of concern changed, however, as the deepening recession brought with it a significant drop in the rate of inflation that had preoccupied Americans during the previous administration. With the rise of business failures over the past two years, concern has shifted to the plight of the unemployed. Critics of the administration point first to domestic economic policy and the "supply-side" theory on which it rests. But increasingly, labor leaders and their political allies in the Democratic Party are looking abroad for answers to the nation's economic woes. They maintain that America's trading partners and traditional allies, by applying aggressive export policies and limiting U.S. imports to their own markets, are in effect exporting domestic unemployment to the United States.

Reagan's critics say that what this country needs to get its ailing industries back on their feet and American workers back on the job is a more realistic trade policy than the "free-trade" approach favored by the administration. The trade issue, almost unheard of in recent years, promises to be at the forefront of congressional debate in 1983 and could be a decisive factor in the outcome of the 1984 presidential race.

Rising Trade Deficit and Unemployment

Although the U.S. economy is less dependent upon foreign trade for its health than those of most industrialized nations, a number of domestic industries rely heavily on export of their products for survival, while others are particularly vulnerable to imported products with which they must compete on the domestic market. As U.S. Trade Representative William E. Brock III recently pointed out: "In recent years four out of five of the new U.S. jobs in manufacturing have been created by international trade. One out of every three acres planted by American farmers is producing crops for export. Two trillion dollars of goods and services currently are being traded internationally and the potential for growth is unlimited." [1]

In spite of a 15.6 percent drop in oil imports last year, the

---

[1] Testifying before the Senate Finance Committee, Jan. 25, 1983.

United States registered a record trade deficit of $42.7 billion for 1982, after posting a $39.7 billion deficit the previous year.[2] While the trade statistics indicated a lack of growth on both sides, with a 7 percent decline in imports and a 9 percent fall in exports, the overall deficit underscored the plight of export-dependent industries.

Over the past decade Americans have been able to pay their foreign oil bills largely thanks to a significant rise in agricultural exports, which quadrupled between 1973 and 1979 to over $40 billion.[3] In 1982, however, agricultural exports, while maintaining a comfortable surplus over imports, fell to $21.4 billion from $26.6 billion in 1981. The reasons for this decline, said Jim Donald, chairman of the Department of Agriculture's World Food and Agricultural Outlook and Situation Board, were "very weak world economic conditions, along with the strength of the dollar." Due to the increased value of the dollar over nearly all major currencies in 1982, U.S. agricultural commodities tended to be priced higher in overseas markets than competitive products from other countries.

Other analysts point as well to the U.S. embargo on grain sales to the Soviet Union, imposed in 1980 in response to the Soviet invasion of Afghanistan, as a crucial factor in diverting foreign buyers to other, more reliable, grain suppliers, in particular Argentina and Canada. At the same time, favorable weather conditions among grain exporting nations and weakening demand due to the recession have caused sizable surpluses of grain stocks, further depressing prices for these commodities, which account for almost half of all U.S. agricultural exports.

In addition to declining exports, many sectors of the U.S. economy face steep competition from imported goods. Chief among these is the auto industry, which continued to lose its share of the domestic car market in 1982, when the value of auto imports rose to $20.6 billion from $18.4 billion the year before. Last year imports accounted for 27.9 percent of all cars sold in the United States. If the current trend continues, said Gene Kasraiss, legislative representative of the United Auto Workers (UAW), imports could account for 35-40 percent of the U.S. automobile market by the end of the 1980s. This, he said, would have a disastrous effect on jobs. Some 300,000 UAW members are already out of work.

---

[2] U.S. Department of Commerce, "Summary of U.S. Export and Import Merchandise Trade," Jan. 28, 1983. These deficit figures include the value of insurance and freight. When calculated on a balance-of-payments basis, the 1982 trade deficit was $36.1 billion.

[3] Sandra S. Batie and Robert G. Healy, "The Future of American Agriculture," *Scientific American*, February 1983, p. 45.

Another basic industry troubled by the recession and foreign competition is the steel industry.[4] While iron and steel imports fell by $1.3 billion between 1981 and 1982 to $9.9 billion — partly as a result of last year's agreement with European producers to limit exports to the United States — domestic steel mills operated at only 40 percent capacity and reported a staggering 50 percent unemployment rate for the year.

In the United States, the recession that began in mid-1981 has not only lasted longer than any previous downturn in the postwar period, but has also outlived most economic forecasters' predictions. The results have included a record postwar unemployment rate of 9.7 percent (12 million workers) in 1982, as well as a 1.8 percent drop in the real gross national product (GNP) — the nation's output of goods and services adjusted for inflation — from 1981 to 1982, the largest yearly decline since the end of World War II.

While falling demand for U.S. exports is largely attributable to the dampening effects of the worldwide recession, much of the blame for the declining trade balance is placed on the

overvaluation of the dollar on foreign exchange markets. Lawrence B. Krause, senior fellow in economics at the Brookings Institution in Washington, D.C., estimates that blame for the trade deficit lies "50-50 between the recession and the strong dollar." Other economists, including C. Fred Bergsten, director of the Institute for International Economics, place even greater emphasis on the dollar's role.[5] According to Treasury Department statistics, the dollar appreciated 20.4 percent from the beginning of 1981 through January 1983 against the currencies of the 23 other countries belonging to the Organization for Economic Cooperation and Development (OECD).[6] With each successive appreciation of the dollar's value, U.S. exports become more costly to overseas buyers and less competitive with similar goods produced abroad. Dollar appreciation also makes domestically produced goods less attractive than imports to American consumers.

---

[4] See "Rebuilding the Nation's Steel Industry," *E.R.R.*, 1982 Vol. I, pp. 169-188.
[5] The non-profit research institute is located at 11 Dupont Circle, N.W., Washington, D.C. 20036. Bergsten was a Treasury Department official during the Carter administration.
[6] The OECD, headquartered in Paris, gathers information regarding economic policies and problems of its 24 member nations: Australia, Austria, Belgium, Canada, Denmark, Finland, France, Great Britain, Greece, Iceland, Ireland, Italy, Japan, Luxembourg, the Netherlands, New Zealand, Norway, Portugal, Spain, Sweden, Switzerland, Turkey, the United States, and West Germany.

Conflicts Among Primary Trading Blocs

With the contraction of economic growth and exports brought on by the global recession, numerous conflicts have erupted among the principal trading blocs, which are locked in increasingly fierce competition to maintain their overseas markets while protecting their domestic ones. Japan, the strongest of these, incurred a surplus of nearly $30 billion last year in its trading with the United States and the European Economic Community (EEC) — $19 billion with the United States alone. It is an embarrassment of riches for Japan, which is accused by its trading partners of building its surplus by unfairly excluding many of their goods from the Japanese market.[7]

The Japanese Ministry of International Trade and Industry maintains that the trade imbalance is due to factors other than tariffs or non-tariff barriers such as import quotas and stiff quality-control standards.[8] It points out that the Japanese economy is also troubled by rising unemployment and a slowdown of its basic industries, including steel and autos.[9] Japan's exports in fact fell by more than 13 percent in the second half of 1982, their biggest postwar decline. Japanese officials, fearing isolation by Japan's trading partners, point to recent tariff cuts on over 300 imported items, but U.S. and EEC officials respond that Japan has not gone far enough toward removing its trade barriers.

While previous conflicts between the United States and Japan have centered on Japanese textiles, color television sets and steel, current problem areas are Japanese auto exports and U.S. access to Japanese markets, especially for sales of citrus fruits and beef. Although Japan agreed in 1981 to export no more than 1.68 million autos a year to the United States *(see p. 31)*, they still account for one-fourth of the new car sales in America and Detroit has asked for further restrictions. On the other hand, the American suggestion that Japan open its markets to a greater share of U.S. beef and citrus products has provoked mass demonstrations in the streets of Tokyo by Japanese farmers who protest that the Japanese market already absorbs about half of all U.S. exports of these items.

Western European countries are also pressing for greater access to Japanese markets. France, in particular, has retaliated

---

[7] For background, see "Tensions in U.S.-Japanese Relations," *E.R.R.*, 1982 Vol. I, pp. 251-272.

[8] See "Japan's Import Barriers: An Analysis of Divergent Bilateral Views," Japan Economic Institute of America, Inc., 1981. The institute, located at 1000 Connecticut Ave., N.W., Washington, D.C. 20036, is a research and publications organization funded by the Japanese Foreign Ministry, that provides information on the Japanese economy and U.S.-Japan relations.

[9] *Japan Economic Survey*, January 1983, pp. 10-11. *Japan Economic Survey* is published by the Japan Economic Institute of America.

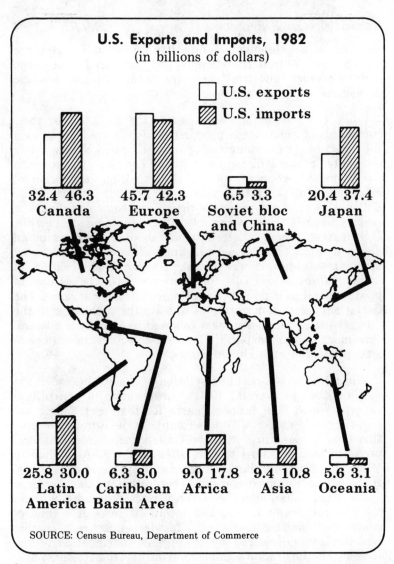

U.S. Exports and Imports, 1982
(in billions of dollars)

☐ U.S. exports
▨ U.S. imports

32.4 46.3
Canada

45.7 42.3
Europe

6.5 3.3
Soviet bloc
and China

20.4 37.4
Japan

25.8 30.0
Latin
America

6.3 8.0
Caribbean
Basin Area

9.0 17.8
Africa

9.4 10.8
Asia

5.6 3.1
Oceania

SOURCE: Census Bureau, Department of Commerce

by erecting non-tariff barriers of its own to Japanese products. The French government now requires that all Japanese videotape recorders be processed through a small, provincial customhouse and that all documents and instruction manuals accompanying imports be translated into French.

For its part, Japan now finds itself increasingly vulnerable to competition from the newly industrialized countries of Hong Kong, Singapore, South Korea and Taiwan, which are following Japan's example of promoting an export-dependent economy by specializing in such labor-intensive industries as steel and textiles. But even these "new Japans," with their 10 percent average economic growth in the 1970s, are finding that the global recession and subsequent contraction of world markets are preventing them from transforming their industrial bases to the high-technology industries necessary to their future economic development.

While the 10 member countries of the EEC[10] focus their complaints of unfair trade practices on Japan, they are in turn the object of similar complaints from the United States. While the United States still enjoyed a $5.3 billion trade surplus with the combined economies of the EEC in 1982, its margin of advantage shrank in that year from its 1981 surplus of $9 billion. U.S. steelmakers accuse their European counterparts of seeking to solve their own problems[11] by dumping steel on the U.S. market, where it accounts for about 25 percent of all domestic sales. This has been made possible, they say, by government subsidies of the industry, which enable European manufacturers to sell their products abroad at below cost of production, thus making U.S. steel uncompetitive at home. The Carter administration's attempt to solve the problem with the "trigger-price" mechanism was followed in 1982 by a bilateral agreement to limit exports of certain categories of European steel products to the United States.[12]

While 1982 saw a partial resolution of the steel dispute, the battle still rages over the EEC's subsidization of agricultural exports, which U.S. farmers blame for their own falling exports on world markets. To this complaint the Europeans reply that their trade deficit with the United States in agricultural products has continued to rise, after reaching $6.8 billion in 1980. They attribute the American decline in world agricultural trade not to European subsidies but rather to the increased value of the dollar, high U.S. interest rates, reduced U.S. grain sales to the Soviet Union, and record harvests at a time of contracting overseas markets.[13] This deepening trade conflict was further underscored by European condemnation of the Reagan administration's imposition of sanctions against European subsidiaries of U.S. companies selling equipment to the Soviet Union for use in construction of the Siberian gas pipeline *(see box, p. 29)*.

(see box, p. 29)

---

[10] Great Britain, France, West Germany, Italy, the Netherlands, Belgium, Luxembourg, Ireland, Denmark, and Greece.

[11] About 230,000 European steelworkers, or one-half the work force, have lost their jobs since the mid-1970s, the EEC's ambassador to Washington, Sir Roy Denman, said in an address to the U.S. Chamber of Commerce, Sept. 15, 1982.

[12] The "trigger-price" mechanism, introduced in late 1977, established a minimum price for which steel imports could be sold on the U.S. market. Sale of imports below the "trigger-price" allowed U.S. steelmakers to initiate anti-dumping suits against the offending producers. The Reagan administration agreed in August 1982 to drop all pending anti-dumping suits in exchange for EEC quotas on steel exports to the United States.

[13] The "EC's Common Agricultural Policy - Debunking Some Common Myths," *European Community News,* Jan. 18, 1983. *European Community News* is published by the European Community Information Service, 2100 M St. N.W., Washington, D.C. 20037.

Controversy Over Siberian Gas Pipeline

The Export Administration Act, first enacted in 1940, gave U.S. presidents the authority to limit exports for defense or foreign policy reasons. While the act has been repeatedly modified to reduce the number of export items that the president may ban at any time, presidential application of the law has provoked controversy in recent years. President Carter twice banned exports to the Soviet Union for political reasons, once in 1978 after the imprisonment of Soviet dissident Anatoly Scharansky and again, in retaliation for the Soviet invasion of Afghanistan in December 1979, when he imposed an embargo on U.S. grain sales to the Soviet Union.

By far the most controversial application of the Export Administration Act was President Reagan's ban on U.S. exports for use in the construction of the Siberian gas pipeline linking the vast natural gas reserves east of the Ural Mountains with markets in energy-poor Western Europe. The sanctions were originally imposed in December 1981 in retaliation for the military crackdown in Poland. They prohibited U.S. companies from exporting oil and gas drilling equipment to the Soviets and were expanded in June 1982 to include foreign subsidiaries of U.S. firms as well as independent companies producing equipment under license from U.S. firms.

The sanctions were roundly condemned by America's European allies, who accused the administration of violating international law in forcing foreign firms to break previous contracts with the Soviet Union, as well as by U.S. firms that had provided licenses to the affected European companies. Reagan finally removed the sanctions on Nov. 13, 1982, and came to an agreement with the NATO allies on a blueprint to study the entire question of East-West trade and its implications for Western security. The study is being conducted by the OECD and Cocom, the NATO organization responsible for determining the potential strategic value of exports to the Soviet Union.

Sluggish growth in the industrialized nations has also depressed demand for the commodities produced by the less developed countries (LDCs) of the Third World, whose lack of industrial development makes them dependent upon export of raw materials such as iron ore, copper and bauxite. With the exception of the oil-exporting countries, these less developed nations are faced with a staggering combined external debt of about $500 billion, which they are unable to repay for lack of export-generated income.[14] Unable to export commodities, the LDCs have reduced imports, 40 percent of which come from the industrialized nations. For the U.S. economy, which has directed one-third of its exports to Third World nations *(see box, p. 27)*, the effect of the debt crisis in these countries has been further deepening of its own trade deficit.

[14] For background, see "World Debt Crisis," *E.R.R.*, 1983 Vol. I, pp. 47-64.

Events Leading to the GATT Ministerial

Responding to the fall in the volume of world trade and the rise in protectionist sentiment among U.S. trading partners, Reagan administration officials — notably Trade Representative Brock and Commerce Secretary Malcolm Baldrige — began to call for the strengthening of U.S. and international trade rules. By March 1982, over 250 "reciprocity" bills had been introduced in Congress to establish rules limiting or barring imports from countries whose trade barriers to U.S. exports were stricter than U.S. rules on imports from those countries. Brock, citing the growing importance of the services sector of the economy (65 percent of GNP), also began to call for inclusion of this sector in the international agreements governing international trade overseen by the General Agreement on Tariffs and Trade (GATT), whose rules cover only merchandise and commodity trade *(see box, p. 35)*.

It was in this atmosphere that the 88 members of GATT, for the first time in nine years, held a ministerial level meeting in Geneva on Nov. 24-29, 1982. Convened largely at the insistence of the United States, the meeting had an ambitious agenda: to further liberalize international trading rules, to impose the same regulations already applied to manufactured goods to the services sector, to stem the wave of protectionist measures imposed by member governments, and to liberalize trade restrictions in agricultural products.

But the GATT ministerial meeting served principally to underscore the growing rift among the main trading blocs, especially between the United States and the EEC over agricultural policy *(see p. 34)*. In their final declaration, the participants agreed only to "resist protectionist pressures" and to "refrain from taking or maintaining any measures inconsistent with GATT." Such issues as expanding GATT rules to include trade in services and liberalizing trade in agricultural goods were relegated to further study. While Brock, who led the U.S. delegation to the Geneva meeting, gave the ministerial a "grade of C" at its conclusion, he recently said that "given the economic atmosphere in which the ministerial took place, perhaps our most important achievement was in keeping the GATT system together and moving in a positive direction." [15]

Labor Seeking Protection From Imports

To the Reagan administration's appeal for "free trade," spokesmen for ailing U.S. businesses and labor unions respond with calls for "fair trade." The AFL-CIO's 1983 platform contained an entire section on the trade issue, in which the

---

[15] Testimony before the Senate Finance Committee, Jan. 25, 1983.

"simplistic dialogue of 'free trade' vs. 'protectionism' " was condemned. Since other governments routinely intervene in the flow of trade, it stated, so too "the United States needs clear limits on certain imports until the nation's future is assured."

The document went on to describe the confederation's chief trade priorities for the year: temporary restrictions on "harmful imports"; enactment of a "domestic content" law that would compel foreign automakers selling to American consumers to build up to 90 percent of each auto in the United States or face import quotas; and to win assurances that a greater portion of U.S. raw materials will be processed domestically before exportation.[16] "Reciprocity should have some teeth in it ...," stated AFL-CIO President Lane Kirkland. "We ought to play by the same ground rules as our competitors and negotiate from that basis." [17]

The UAW is pressing for passage of a domestic content bill again this year, despite the fact that the Japanese agreed Feb. 12 to continue their voluntary restraints on auto exports to the United States for one more year, to March 31, 1984. The House passed a domestic content bill last December, but only after adding a weakening provision that would invalidate the legislation if it were found to violate the General Agreement on Tariffs and Trade. Sponsors will attempt to drop that provision this year, and will probably succeed in getting the measure through the House. But the Senate, which did not vote on the measure last year, is still considered unlikely to pass such a bill. Senate Republicans tend to agree with the White House that it is a bad piece of legislation that would aid autoworkers at the expense of other sectors of the economy.

The domestic content bill was just one of the measures introduced in the 97th Congress to protect U.S. industries from further erosion due to imports. On Oct. 1, Congress passed a law to encourage creation of export trading companies, previously barred by antitrust laws, to facilitate small business exporting.[18] A "reciprocity" bill, devised under the leadership of Sen. John C. Danforth, R-Mo., sought to impose trade restrictions on countries that limited access of U.S. exports to their markets. While neither this nor other reciprocity bills passed last year, similar legislation will be introduced in the 98th Congress *(see p. 37),* where some members appear to be softening their traditionally staunch backing of free-trade policies under pressure from their home districts, especially those hard hit by factory closings and rising unemployment.

---

[16] "Jobs: The Agenda for Recovery," *AFL-CIO News,* Jan. 8, 1983.
[17] Interview in *AFL-CIO News,* Jan. 22, 1983.
[18] See "Small Business: Trouble on Main Street," *E.R.R.,* 1983 Vol. I, pp. 78-80.

Protection vs. Free Trade

PARALLELS can be drawn between the international economic problems of today and those that prevailed after World War I. That period, too, was marked by intense competition from foreign-made goods, and the result was the same — mounting pressure for protection of American jobs. Tariff rates were raised in 1922 to the highest levels in years, thus making it difficult for the European allies to repay their war debts. It is generally agreed that the tariff policies of the 1920s contributed to the Depression of the 1930s.

As early as 1921 the Baltimore *Evening Sun* warned: "A tariff wall that keeps foreign goods out may also keep American goods in; that unless we buy from the outside we cannot sell to the outside." But most Americans ignored such prophets of doom. "The American people . . . ," wrote historian Thomas A. Bailey, "continued to believe that imports were basically bad." [19] This prejudice toward imports was embodied in the Smoot-Hawley Tariff of 1930,[20] which raised tariffs on imported durable goods to a record high level of 59 percent by 1932.

The Smoot-Hawley tariff greatly darkened the already gloomy international economic picture.

> Foreign exporters, unable to sell their products in America, could not build up dollar credits with which to buy American automobiles and other items. . . . Many nations, either for self-protection or as a reprisal, jacked up their rates or erected spite fences. Britain abandoned her historic free-trade policy, and bound the parts of her empire, including Canada, more closely to herself in imperial preference arrangements. Other nations engaged in boycotts of American goods, and in various ways sought to quarantine the United States economically. The result was an intensification of narrow economic isolation and a worsening of that financial and political chaos which finally spawned Adolf Hitler.[21]

A turnabout in American tariff policy was inaugurated with the Reciprocal Trade Agreements Act of 1934. The movement toward lower tariffs was led by Secretary of State Cordell Hull, a Tennessean committed to the position long popular in the South that low tariffs were good for the country. The 1934 act gave the president authority to negotiate trade agreements with individual countries and greatly reduced duties in return for similar concessions on their part. By incorporating "most-

---

[19] Thomas A. Bailey, *A Diplomatic History of the American People* (1969), p. 656.
[20] A measure sponsored by Sen. Reed Smoot, R-Utah, and Rep. Willis C. Hawley, R-Ore.
[21] Bailey, *op. cit.*, p. 665.

favored-nation" clauses in these agreements, reductions negotiated with one country would be extended to others. By 1947, Hull and his successors had negotiated agreements with 29 nations, thereby achieving a substantial reduction on duties affecting 70 percent of America's imports.

After World War II the United States took the lead in trying to establish a broader approach to tariff reduction and trade liberalization. It was largely due to American initiative that 23 countries signed the General Agreement on Tariffs and Trade in 1947 *(see box, p. 35).*

Structural Changes in the World Economy

Although GATT represents a multilateral attempt to mediate differences among the contracting nations over changing trade patterns, many observers believe more attention should be paid to the structural changes that have brought them about, in order that a more coherent and effective trade strategy may be elaborated for the future. For example, there has been an enormous impact on trade from the postwar reindustrialization of Western Europe and Japan, the emergence of newly industrialized nations and the lack of industrial development in the LDCs.

Before the oil shocks of the mid-1970s, postwar international trade had grown about 7 percent a year, thanks in part to the removal of barriers under the various GATT negotiations. The undisputed winner in this situation was of course the United States, which claimed in the economic boom years of the 1950s and 1960s about one-fourth of the world market in manufactured goods, and 95 percent of all domestic sales of autos, steel and consumer electronics in 1960. By 1979, in contrast, the U.S. world market share had fallen to approximately 17 percent, and domestic manufacturers could claim only a 79 percent share of auto sales, 86 percent of steel products, and less than half of consumer electronics goods sold domestically.[22]

While domestic industry was ceding some of its power to Japan and, increasingly, to the newly industrialized nations of East Asia, the services sector began to grow. As early as the mid-1950s, the number of American workers employed in the services sector began to exceed those in the blue-collar industries. As a result of this deindustrialization process, seven out of every 10 non-agricultural workers in the United States are currently employed in the services sector. At the same time, the growing role of the Third World nations in the world economy has increased its interdependent nature. In 1982 alone, the less

---

[22] John Naisbitt, *Megatrends: Ten New Directions Transforming Our Lives* (1982), pp. 55-56.

developed countries bought over 40 percent of American exports and over one-quarter of total OECD exports.

Trade Prospects in 1980s

WHILE the predictability of economic trends has been shown, especially in 1982, to be spotty at best, economic forecasters are almost unanimous in their assessment that the current recession has just about "bottomed out" in the United States. But although domestic business activity is expected to pick up in 1983, the problems in export-dependent industries are likely to continue for some time, as countries that import U.S. products continue to be plagued by high unemployment and slow growth. Since unemployment in the United States is expected to remain high in 1983, perhaps peaking in the first half of the year, industries already hurt by imports will likely continue to experience difficulties throughout the year.

Another factor impeding U.S. export activity will be the strong dollar, although some forecasters predict that interest rates should continue their current downward trend, weakening the dollar against major currencies before the year is out. Lawrence B. Krause of the Brookings Institution, for example, predicts that the dollar's depreciation will mean that the U.S. trade picture will improve by 1984. Others take a more pessimistic view. The U.S. ambassador to the Federal Republic of Germany, Arthur F. Burns, fears that "political tensions on account of economic difficulties may well continue to trouble the alliance." [23]

According to Agriculture Department estimates, agricultural exports should sustain a $20.6 billion surplus in fiscal 1983, following the previous year's fall to $23.7 billion from fiscal 1981's $26.6 billion surplus. While he sees some hope in falling interest rates, Jim Donald maintains that "it will take a while to cut back on stocks" and that agricultural sales abroad will depend on the pace of recovery in the rest of the world.

New Disputes Over Agricultural Exports

Continued differences between the United States and its allies are expected to dominate the Western economic summit to be held in May in Williamsburg, Va.[24] Especially troublesome

---

[23] Address before the Deutsche Atlantische Gesellschaft, Bonn, Dec. 9, 1982.

[24] The major industrialized nations — the United States, Canada, Japan, West Germany, Great Britain, France and Italy — participate in the economic summits, held annually since 1975 to discuss problems in coordinating each country's economic policy.

GATT's Role in World Trade

The General Agreement on Tariffs and Trade (GATT), initially signed by 23 countries on Oct. 30, 1947, currently has 88 members which together account for 80 percent of world trade. In addition to these "contracting parties," many other countries comply informally with GATT regulations. The Agreement contains rules on both tariff and non-tariff barriers to trade across national boundaries, as well as specific tariff concessions for the individual nations. These have been modified in seven successive "rounds" of negotiations aimed at reducing barriers on a reciprocal basis. The best known of these were the Kennedy Round (1964-1967) and the Tokyo Round (1973-1979), which resulted in an overall 39 percent reduction in tariffs on manufactured goods.

The main provisions of GATT rules can be summarized as follows:

Member nations must confer "most-favored-nation" status to all other members, allowing equal access to all on their domestic markets.

Once tariffs have been removed or reduced by negotiation, they must not be reimposed in the form of compensatory domestic taxes.

Where imports are shown to threaten domestic industries producing similar items, member nations may impose anti-dumping or countervailing duties to offset this damage. Similarly, an "escape clause" permits the suspension or modification of tariff concessions when a surge in imports threatens domestic industries. GATT rules do not, however, prohibit competing nations from retaliating against those invoking the "escape clause" if consultations do not produce compensatory action on the part of the nation invoking the clause.

Import quotas are permitted only for agricultural or fishery products when necessary to protect domestic production-control programs and to avoid balance-of-payments crises.

GATT lacks power to enforce its rules because Congress refused to allow the U.S. government to participate in its proposed administrative bodies, which consequently never came into being. The 300-member GATT secretariat, based in Geneva, provides a forum for the airing of disputes among contracting nations, allowing GATT to perform a mediating role in world trade.

is the conflict between the United States and the European countries over agricultural exports. The dispute intensified in January when the Reagan administration arranged to subsidize the export of wheat flour to Egypt, a market previously dominated by subsidized EEC flour sales.

The subsidy was a clear indication that the administration has somewhat softened its free-trade philosophy *(see p. 37)*.

Problems in export-dependent industries are likely to continue for some time.

But officials are clearly reluctant to declare an all-out trade war.[25] Agriculture Secretary John R. Block told the House Foreign Affairs Committee on Feb. 15, "I don't think we should go around picking off markets in the world indiscriminately. However, if you find that a market that was ours has been taken away ... we have no other choice but to compete." Secretary of State George P. Shultz told the Senate Foreign Relations Committee the same day that if subsidies are commonly used to market agricultural products, "the net result will not be good, and we will be in effect giving products away."

The United States also finds itself involved in a dispute over agricultural exports with the People's Republic of China, which on Jan. 19 suspended all imports of U.S. cotton, soybeans and chemical fibers this year in retaliation for the administration's refusal to allow imports of Chinese textiles to exceed the 1.5 percent growth rate permitted China's competitors for the U.S. market — Taiwan, South Korea and Hong Kong. With bilateral trade totaling $5.2 billion last year, the breach in negotiations could lead to a further erosion of the U.S. trade picture, but the administration gave in to pressure from the domestic textile industry, which has idled some 200,000 workers since the beginning of the recession. Another source of attrition in the bilateral trade relationship regards U.S. policy on high-technology exports to Peking, which the Reagan administration has thus far failed to define and which was not clarified during Secretary of State Shultz' first official trip to Peking in early February.[26]

Greater success was claimed by the administration from the

[25] See *Congressional Quarterly Weekly Report*, Feb. 19, 1983, pp. 380-382.
[26] For background, see "Trade with China," *E.R.R.*, 1980, Vol. II, pp. 887-903.

outcome of the January visit to Washington by Japanese Prime Minister Yasuhiro Nakasone who, while declining to reduce current import restrictions on U.S. beef and citrus products, introduced shortly before his departure from Tokyo reform measures reducing tariffs and liberalizing customs procedures, product standards and testing criteria affecting some 60 percent of U.S. products exported to Japan.[27] President Reagan was unable to produce much in the way of tangible evidence of noticeable change in the Japanese attitudes on import quotas. But the visit did relieve some of the political tensions between the two countries, which could lead to further improvements in trade relations in the coming months. Citing domestic unrest over growing economic troubles, Nakasone appeared to have gained recognition in Washington that any substantive liberalizing measures in trade policy must await parliamentary elections this summer in order for Nakasone, himself elected in November 1982, to consolidate his political position.

One of the few areas of agreement between the United States and its industrialized trading partners is over the threat posed to international trade by the growing external debt of the less developed countries. In a striking policy reversal, the administration agreed in mid-January to support an increase in the special emergency fund that the International Monetary Fund makes available to borrowing nations to help repay their debts. While considerable opposition to increased funding is expected from members of Congress concerned about ballooning budget deficits, the move by the administration, which had previously espoused the notion that Third World development could best be handled by the "magic of the marketplace," is an indication of the heightened level of concern in official circles.

Reagan's Position; Outlook in Congress

The events of the past two years have had an impact on the administration's trade policy. But while the president has had to bend somewhat to protectionist pressures from voters and members of Congress, he remains basically committed to a free-trade policy. This was made clear in the economic report Reagan sent to Congress Feb. 2, in which he said he was "committed to a policy of preventing the enactment of protectionist measures in the United States."

> While the United States may be forced to respond to the trade distorting practices of foreign governments through the use of strategic measures, such practices do not warrant indiscriminate protectionist actions, such as domestic content rules for automobiles sold in the United States [Reagan said]. Widespread protectionist policies would hurt American consumers by raising

---

[27] See *Japan Economic Institute Report*, Jan. 21, 1983, pp. 1-2.

prices of the products they buy, and by removing some of the pressures for cost control and quality improvement that result from international competition. Moreover, protectionism at home could hurt the workers, farmers and firms in the United States that produce goods and services for export, since it would almost inevitably lead to increased protectionism by governments abroad.

Reagan's position is not likely to quell critics' calls for more specific measures aimed at protecting domestic industries and workers in urgent need of help. A domestic content bill has already been reintroduced in the House, and although its prospects in the Senate remain uncertain *(see p. 31)*, debate on the bill is likely to be even more heated than last year. The 98th Congress is also considering other controversial trade issues. For example, the recent request by a Florida-based machine tool manufacturer, Houdaille Industries Inc., that investment tax credits be denied to American companies that buy machine tools from Japan, has prompted debate over the advisability of formulating an official governmental industrial policy similar to Japan's export policy.[28]

The reciprocity bill introduced last year under the sponsorship of Sen. Danforth will be reintroduced in 1983. While Ambassador Brock condemns the "dollar for dollar" interpretation of reciprocity espoused by many critics of U.S. trade policy, the milder wording of the Danforth initiative, which would strengthen the president's authority to negotiate trade agreements and to retaliate against unfair trading practices, has been praised by Brock, in that it respects the administration's definition of correct trade policy as one creating "a global trading system in which benefits are mutually shared and concessions are mutually made." [29]

The Export Administration Act, due to expire Sept. 30, is likely to be renewed in 1983, with some possible changes. The law, which authorizes the president to limit exports for foreign policy or defense reasons, may be modified to permit the export of Alaskan oil to Japan, a topic discussed during Prime Minister Nakasone's Washington visit. Business interests, hurt by the Siberian pipeline sanctions, are pressing for the relaxation of the terms of the current law and for a provision honoring the sanctity of existing contracts. But some within the administration are asking for further export restrictions under the law.

Also up for renewal in September is funding authorization for the Export-Import Bank. President Reagan, in his Jan. 25 State

---

[28] See *Congressional Quarterly Weekly Report*, Jan. 29, 1983, pp. 211-214.
[29] Trade policy briefing, Jan. 24, 1983.

U.S. Trade Barriers

The creation of the General Agreement on Tariffs and Trade in 1947 *(see box, p. 35)* led to the reduction of direct tariffs by the 23 original member nations. But, ironically, it also led to an increase in the number of non-tariff barriers in many countries. The United States, which had led the effort to liberalize international trade, was among the countries erecting trade barriers to protect domestic industries. For example, the Buy American Act of 1933 and its successive amendments give preference to domestic companies for all government procurement contracts. Antidumping duties, imposed against importers of products sold in the United States for less than domestic prices, have recently been applied against European steel imports.

Countervailing duties, or surcharges on products whose export has been facilitated by government subsidy, are yet another non-tariff barrier imposed by the U.S. government. Quantitative ceilings include both unilateral import quotas and "voluntary" agreements extracted from trading partners whose exports harm domestic industry, under threat of actual import quotas should they fail to cooperate. Japan's "voluntary" auto export limit *(see p. 26)* falls into this category. Other obstacles to free trade currently applied by the United States and its trading partners include customs valuations and industrial quality standards, which are often so complex as to constitute true trade barriers.

of the Union message, seemed to reverse his previously stated intention of reducing the bank's funding by proposing an increase in its authority to guarantee loans to developing countries buying U.S. exports.

Aside from the immediate implications of trade-related legislation likely to be discussed in 1983, the entire debate on international trade is certain to influence the campaign for the 1984 presidential election. Even now, when President Reagan has yet to declare publicly whether or not he intends to run for a second term, his Democratic critics and potential opponents are gearing up for battle over trade policy. Former Vice President Walter F. Mondale, considered the leading Democratic contender in this early phase of the campaign, has already come down on the side of strict reciprocity laws. He also favors using a well-funded Export-Import Bank "to match the export subsidies of our trade competitors, product for product, dollar for dollar." [30] President Reagan is also being challenged on trade policy by conservatives within his own party. Speaking for this group, conservative commentator Kevin Phillips took the administration to task for failing to formulate a coherent trade policy.[31]

---

[30] Article by Mondale published in *The New York Times,* Nov. 8, 1982.
[31] Article published in *The Washington Post,* Jan. 23, 1983. Phillips is the author of *The Emerging Republican Majority* (1969) and *Post-Conservative America* (1982).

In coming months, the issue of "protectionism" vs. "free trade" will continue to unfold in congressional debate. Its outcome will depend to a large extent on the pace of economic recovery and the prospects for employment of American workers. In the absence of an overall policy with established priorities for the direction of the U.S. economy and its role in international trade, domestic industries hurt by a falling share of the domestic market, as well as those whose exports fail to compete effectively on world markets, seem likely to continue pressing for special concessions from Washington.

Selected Bibliography

Books

Cohen, Stephen D., *The Making of United States International Economic Policy,* Praeger Publishers, 1977.

Kindleberger, Charles P., *International Economics* (5th edition), Richard D. Irwin, Inc., 1973.

Metzger, Stanley D., *Lowering Nontariff Barriers: U.S. Law, Practice, and Negotiating Objectives,* Brookings, 1974.

Naisbitt, John, *Megatrends: Ten New Directions Transforming Our Lives,* Warner Books, 1982.

Tariffs, Quotas & Trade: The Politics of Protectionism, Institute for Contemporary Studies, 1979.

Articles

AFL-CIO News, selected issues.

Batie, Sandra S. and Robert G. Healy, "The Future of American Agriculture," *Scientific American,* February 1983.

"Black Ships Are Coming?" *Forbes,* Jan. 31, 1983.

European Community News, selected issues.

Japan Economic Survey, selected issues.

Kissinger, Henry A., "Saving the World Economy," *Newsweek,* Jan. 24, 1983.

Reports and Studies

Bergsten, C. Fred, "The Outlook for the Dollar," Institute for International Economics, December 1982.

Brock, William E. III, "Assessment of the GATT Ministerial Meeting," statement before the Senate Finance Committee, Jan. 25, 1983.

Burns, Arthur F., "Economic Health of the Western Alliance," address to the Deutsche Atlantische Gesellschaft, Dec. 9, 1982.

Editorial Research Reports: "World Debt Crisis," 1983 Vol. I, p. 47; "Tensions in U.S.-Japanese Relations," 1982 Vol. I, p. 251; "Trade with China," 1980 Vol. II, p. 887; "Trade Talks and Protectionism," 1979 Vol. I, p. 23.

Japan Economic Institute of America, "Japan's Import Barriers: An Analysis of Divergent Bilateral Views," 1981.

Cover illustration by Staff Artist Robert Redding; illustration on p. 25 by George Rebh; photograph on p. 36 by Lykes Lines.

CONTROLLING SCIENTIFIC INFORMATION

by

Jean Rosenblatt

July 9
1982

CONTROLLING SCIENTIFIC INFORMATION

T HE U.S. government has become increasingly concerned that advanced technology being developed and used by Western countries is finding its way to the Soviet Union and especially Soviet weaponry. While there is evidence that this is, indeed, happening *(see box, p. 49)*, the government's recent effort to prevent it by controlling the international exchange of scientific information is causing alarm in science, academia and industry. It is also causing problems with America's allies, most notably over a Russian natural gas pipeline to Europe *(see p. 57)*.

Government fears about technology transfer were made public in a 1976 report by the Department of Defense's Defense Science Board. The report, known as the Bucy Report,[1] concluded that the United States was losing its technological and economic lead over its adversaries by giving them information crucial to the development of militarily critical technologies and recommended stricter controls on the flow of information out of the country.

Since then government agencies have claimed authority under existing controls to prevent publication of certain kinds of research and technical data, to bar foreign scholars from university research projects and symposia, and to impose secrecy on inventions related to making and breaking codes. These and similar actions raise complicated questions with far-reaching implications about who should control information in the interests of national security, what should be controlled, and to what extent.

Industry and the academic community have made it clear that they do not want to help the Soviet Union gain access to militarily sensitive information. However, industry fears that undue control of information will hurt its position overseas and therefore the United States in the world market. Academics fear that excessive control will limit what can be taught and to whom. Such control, they argue, belies the constitutional right of freedom of expression and ultimately damages the creative process that produces technological innovation. Government officials, on the other hand, say that while they do not want to hobble technology, some formal restraint is necessary.

---

[1] For J. Fred Bucy, president of Texas Instruments Inc., who headed the study group that produced the report.

The current debate has not erupted in a vacuum. For years the government has been protecting technological information generated by federal workers and government-sponsored projects.[2] At issue now is the government's recent efforts to extend its control to non-government researchers whose projects do not directly relate to national security.

Effort to Control Cryptography Research

Government-imposed security is expanding especially in cryptography, the making and breaking of codes. Until relatively recently codes have been in the domain of the military services, the intelligence community and the diplomatic corps. Now the era of nationwide communications systems such as electronic funds transfer and computer storage banks filled with confidential data about businesses and individuals has created the need to protect that information with codes.[3] Major advances are being made in cryptography by researchers not tied to military or intelligence activities. The civilian interest in developing secure and convenient cryptographic systems has apparently come into conflict with the government's interest in protecting national security.

Stephen Unger, a professor of computer science at Columbia University, relates that in 1977 the Institute of Electrical and Electronics Engineers scheduled a symposium at which important research papers on cryptography were to be presented. The papers told of ways to conceal contents of messages and authenticate their authorship. Before the symposium was held, the institute received a letter from a member, Joseph Meyer, warning that the papers might subject it and the authors to prosecution under the Arms Export Control Act of 1976 *(see p. 50)*. Although he did not say so in his letter, Meyer turned out to be employed by the National Security Agency, the government agency that intercepts and deciphers communications of foreign governments and protects secret communications of the U.S. government.[4]

The symposium was held and no government action was taken. Moreover Adm. Bobby Inman, who was then NSA direc-

---

[2] See, for example, "Universities and the Government," *E.R.R.*, 1968 Vol. I, pp. 21-40; "Directions of Policy Research," *E.R.R.*, 1975 Vol. II, pp. 725-744; and "Politics of Science," *E.R.R.*, 1978 Vol. I, pp. 381-400.

[3] The problem of industrial espionage was highlighted when on June 22, the FBI charged 18 men, including several high-ranking Japanese business executives from Hitachi Ltd., of paying an undercover agent several hundred thousand dollars to steal technical data on new IBM computers. The Japanese immediately denied any wrongdoing but are dismayed at this country's use of undercover agents, which they believe is unfair. Observers have noted that intelligence-gathering is common among computer manufacturers and that the line between the legality and illegality of such practices is often thin.

[4] See "The Growing Threat of Government Secrecy," *Technology Review*, February-March, 1982. The article was adapted from a paper prepared for the American Association for the Advancement of Science's Committee on Scientific Information and Responsibility. Unger is a member of the committee.

tor, denied that the agency tried to suppress scholarly work in cryptography. He said Meyers' letter was not written on behalf of NSA. But there have been other incidents that Unger cites as causes of concern. One was an attempt by the University of Wisconsin at Milwaukee to patent an encryption device — a device used to convert messages into code — invented by George Davida, an associate professor of electrical engineering and computer science. Six months after the application was filed, in October 1977, the U.S. Patent and Trademark Office — prompted by the NSA — informed Davida that he would be subject to a $10,000 fine and two years in prison if the principles of his device were revealed to anyone other than federal agents.

About the same time, three Seattle engineers — David Miller, Carl Nicolai and William Raike — received a similar secrecy order concerning a voice scrambler they had tried to patent. Both cases created a public controversy. Davida's secrecy order was rescinded in June 1978 and the order on the scrambler was lifted later that year. Inman said the order on Davida's patent application was a bureaucratic error, but he did not explain why the other secrecy order was lifted.

NSA suggested in 1975 that the National Science Foundation give it sole funding authority over government-supported cryptography research.[5] The foundation rejected the proposal but in 1977, when the issue was raised again, agreed to add NSA staff members to the reviewers of cryptographic research proposals. In 1980, Leonard Adleman, a cryptography researcher at the Massachusetts Institute of Technology and the University of Southern California, was told that the foundation would not fully renew his grant because parts of his proposal "impinged" on national security. NSA then said it wanted to fund Adleman's research, but he rejected the offer. Eventually the foundation restored his entire grant.

Scientists' Opposition; Voluntary Restraint

Critics of government control of cryptography research contend that new ideas being developed are not an American monopoly and that the security of coding systems does not depend on concealing the methodology but on concealing the keys necessary for decoding. Another argument is that national security would actually be threatened by excessive secrecy in cryptography research. It is reasoned that new types of fraud are based on the manipulation of data in computer storage banks or intercepting coded information.[6] Thus industry needs

---

[5] The National Science Foundation is a government agency that provides about 28 percent of the federal support for basic and applied research that goes to academic institutions. Proposals are accepted on the basis of peer review.
[6] See "Computer Crime," *E.R.R.*, 1978 Vol. I, pp. 1-20.

to develop strong encryption systems. Anything that would hamper such development would endanger important information and allow disruption by foreign agents.

To deal with the conflict the American Council on Education, with the NSA's encouragement, formed the Public Cryptography Study Group. It is composed of experts from NSA and academia. Their job is to explore the problem of unclassified research in cryptography and its implications for both national security and academic freedom. The group recommended a voluntary review program, on a two-year trial basis, in which authors would submit their papers to the NSA for an opinion before publishing them, though the final decision on what to publish and when would rest with the authors. This program has been in existence since last fall, though not all researchers use it.

The study group concluded that a mandatory review program was unnecessary and would be counterproductive. According to Martin Hellman, a cryptographer at Stanford University, the voluntary program should work well "because at present there are no real controls on us, and so the NSA will have to behave reasonably to gain support." [7] As of April about 35 research papers had been submitted for review, according to Daniel Schwartz, a former NSA general counsel. Only a few had raised problems, and in those cases the authors agreed to make minor changes.

Other Research Targeted for Controls

The Department of Defense would like to monitor other areas of unclassified research through export-control regulations, now under revision *(see p. 52)*. In 1980, the director of the department's Very High Speed Integrated Circuits (VHSIC) program[8] told scientists working for the program through universities that any devices and data they developed under the program would be subject to the International Traffic in Arms Regulations, administered by the State Department in consultation with Defense, and the Export Administration regulations, administered by the Department of Commerce. A memo from the director attempting to define what was to be controlled said, in part:

> Controlled technical data do not include information normally considered to be basic science, such as information related to

---

[7] Quoted by Paul Wallich in "Cryptography: Voluntary Controls Seem to Work," in *Spectrum*, May 1982, p. 66. The *Spectrum* is a magazine published by the Institute of Electrical and Electronics Engineers.

[8] Integrated circuits are used in a variety of electronic products, including computers and videogames. The VHSIC program's goal is to accelerate the application of integrated circuits into weapon systems.

materials properties, physical and chemical reactions, fundamental physical limitations, stress analysis, statistical inference, device physics, and other such products of basic research. ... The distinction that is being made is between basic research and process, or utilization, technology. The former are not subject to controls, while the latter are.

The memo also stated, "In the case of basic research supported by the VHSIC program, although such research and its results are not generally controlled, it is the preference of the Program Office that only U.S. citizens and immigrant aliens who have declared their intention of becoming citizens participate. Where this preference cannot be accommodated, the contractor should be directed to the Program Office for resolution."[9]

The wording of this memo raises questions about definition of terms. For example, the distinction between basic and applied research is not always easy to make. In a field such as biotechnology, many scientists claim that no distinction can be made. In addition, the concept of technical data is not defined in export-control regulations. "These terms are defined only as one goes merrily down the river and over the dam," commented Harold Relyea, a government specialist with the Congressional Research Service. The memo also proposed restrictions that, according to MIT President Paul E. Gray, "disregard both the international character of U.S. universities and the difficulties such institutions would have in confining participation in and access to research to U.S. citizens and immigrant aliens." [10]

Last year, for example, the State Department informed Cornell University that a Hungarian engineer must not participate in private seminars or discussions but limit his study of electronics to the classroom. Nor was he to receive pre-publication copies of research papers. Because of these conditions his visit was cancelled. At Stanford University, the State Department questioned the research program of several visiting Chinese scholars working in computer science. The State Department

[9] Quoted by Paul E. Gray in "Technology Transfer at Issue: The Academic Viewpoint," *Spectrum*, May 1982, pp. 66-67.
[10] *Ibid.*, p. 67.

suggested that there be "no access to the design, construction, or maintenance data relevant to individual items of computer hardware. . . . This office should be advised prior to any visits to any industrial or research visits." [11]

Trend to Control Unclassified Information

Three other incidents have focused attention on the trend toward increased government control of unclassified information and have caused concern in the scientific community. One was the 1981 publication of a Defense brochure called "Soviet Military Power," which asserts that the Russians' military advantage over the United States has been aided partly by American scientists through exchanges, meetings and "professional and open literature." In October 1981, William D. Carey, executive officer of the American Association for the Advancement of Science (AAAS), wrote a letter to Frank Carlucci, deputy secretary of defense, criticizing the statements. Conferences, symposia and scientific literature, he said, "constitute the primary infrastructure of U.S. and worldwide communication in science, and without them the U.S. technology base would go stale very quickly."

> The Defense Department [Carey added] should know, by this time, how scientific practice is conducted and how necessary unimpaired communication in science is to advancing the state of the art and improving our own essential capabilities. . . . Our own military power will be diminished, not enhanced, if the wellheads of scientific communication are sealed and new knowledge confined in silos of secrecy and prior restraint.[12]

Carlucci, in reply to Carey, gave examples of scientific exchanges with the Soviet Union that have not been reciprocal and evidence of how the Russians are misusing scholarly exchanges *(see box, p. 49)*. Carlucci concluded: "By the very nature of our open and free society, we recognize that we will never be able to halt fully the flow of militarily critical technology to the Soviet Union. Nevertheless, we believe that it is possible to inhibit this flow without infringing upon legitimate scientific discourse." [13]

The second incident occurred in January 1982, at a symposium held by the American Association for the Advancement of Science on striking a balance between scientific freedom and the government's need to protect national security. Admiral Inman warned scientists that "there will be pressure for legislation to stop the hemorrhage of the nation's technologies." In

---

[11] Quoted by Stephen Unger, *op. cit.*, p. 33.
[12] See "Scientific Exchanges and U.S. National Security," *Science*, Jan. 8, 1982, pp. 139-140.
[13] *Ibid.*, p. 141.

U.S.-Soviet Student Exchanges

Over a 10-year period, mostly in the 1960s, according to Assistant Secretary of Defense Stephen Bryen, the Soviet Union and Eastern bloc countries may have acquired up to 40 percent of the design skills for their antitank weapons from the "open U.S. literature, mostly unclassified research papers and patent information."* Bryen also said that by using U.S. sources the Russians have developed antitank weapons sooner than they would have otherwise.

In his reply to William Carey's letter criticizing statements made in the Defense brochure "Soviet Military Power," Defense official Frank Carlucci said that the Russians were misusing scholarly exchanges as well as our open literature. He said that while the United States sends young graduate students, most of them doing work in the humanities, to Moscow State University and Leningrad State University, the Soviet Union sends older, experienced technical people, some from military research institutes. They attend any of about 100 U.S. universities and "are granted academic freedom and, with almost automatic government approval, can travel practically at will," Carlucci added in his letter. "American students in the Soviet Union are much more isolated and restricted in their travel and professional contacts."

Russian scholars sent to the United States are often involved in applied military research. Carlucci said a Soviet student named S. A. Gubin studied fuel-air explosives in 1976-77 under an American professor, who happened to be a consultant to the U.S. Navy on fuel-air military explosive devices. While here, Gubin ordered several unclassified documents from the U.S. National Technical Information Service. Gubin eventually returned to the Soviet Union to work on developing fuel-air explosive weapons, Carlucci wrote.

A widely publicized incident occurred in 1980 when several Eastern bloc scientists were barred from attending conferences on bubble memory, lasers and electro-optical systems — technologies with direct military applications. The denials were precipitated by the revelation that a Hungarian physicist had provided the Soviet Union with information on magnetic bubble memories gained as a result of his frequent visits to U.S. laboratories.

* Quoted by Lois Ember in *Chemical and Engineering News*, April 5, 1982, p. 16.

"terms of harm to the national interest," he said, "it makes little difference whether . . . data are copied from technical journals in a library or given away by a member of our society to an agent of a foreign power." [14] Inman proposed that the voluntary prepublication review system being tried in cryptography be ex-

[14] Quoted by Christopher Paine in "Admiral Inman's Tidal Wave," *The Bulletin of the Atomic Scientists*, March 1982, p. 3.

tended to computers, electronic gear and techniques, lasers, crop projections and manufacturing processes.

Finally, this year President Reagan signed an executive order on security classification that omits the requirement set during the Carter administration that decisions imposing secrecy must be weighed against the public's right to know. The revised order states that "if there is reasonable doubt about the need to classify ... the information shall be considered classified." [15] Mary Cheh, a law professor at George Washington University in Washington, D.C., told Editorial Research Reports that the order makes it not only easier to classify information but also to keep it classified.

All previous executive orders on security classification — by Presidents Truman, Eisenhower, Nixon and Carter — "deliberately set out to reduce what was classified, to sharpen and clarify classification standards, and to reduce the number of people with the authority to classify," according to Allen Adler, an attorney with the Center for National Security Studies in Washington, D.C.[16]

Current Government Controls

A RANGE of government controls, some under revision, form the basis of recent government efforts to restrict the flow of unclassified technical data beyond the United States. The Commerce Department is responsible for not only promoting trade but also prohibiting the export of militarily sensitive technologies under the Export Administration Regulations (EAR) and a Commodity Control List. Except for munitions and related technical data, which are controlled by a separate law, all exports, including technical data, are restricted or prohibited unless authorized by a Commerce Department license or regulation. Technical information is defined as "any kind that can be used, or adapted for use, in the design, production, manufacture, utilization or reconstruction of articles or materials" that appear on the Commodity Control List.[17]

Under the Arms Export Control Act of 1976, the State

[15] Quoted by Dorothy Nelkin in "Intellectual Property: The Control of Scientific Information," *Science,* May 14, 1982, p. 707.

[16] Quoted by Gina Kolata in "Technology Transfer: New Controls Urged," *Science,* Feb. 5, 1982, p. 635.

[17] Quoted by Mary Cheh in "Government Control of Private Ideas" (p. 7), a paper prepared for the annual meeting of the American Association for the Advancement of Science, 1982.

Information Controls

Export Administration Act of 1979. Through Export Administration Regulations (EAR) and a Commodity Control List, the Commerce Department controls sensitive technologies, except for munitions and related technical data.

Arms Export Control Act of 1976. The State Department controls munitions and related technical data through International Traffic in Arms Regulations (ITAR) and a Munitions List.

Atomic Energy Act of 1954. All information on nuclear weapons and nuclear energy is considered a government secret until declassified.

Inventions and Secrecy Act of 1951. Secrecy orders are issued on inventions if publication of the patent is judged harmful to national security. Upon issuance of a secrecy order, the invention becomes a government secret for one year. Secrecy orders are renewable each year.

Executive order on security classification. If there is a reasonable doubt about the need to classify, information is considered classified. This reverses the trend toward reducing the amount of classified information and sharpening and clarifying classification standards.

Department keeps a Munitions List and, by way of the International Traffic in Arms Regulations (ITAR) established by that act, requires a license for the import or export of any item on the list. As in the Commodity Control List, technical data are included in the Munitions List. The definition of technical data under the law is so broad that scientists have concluded that export regulations could extend to new developments in metallurgy, signal detection techniques and all aspects of computer technology. A Defense official was quoted as saying that ITAR, "if enforced to the letter, would cover virtually everything done in the U.S."[18]

While both EAR and ITAR have been invoked to exclude Soviet and Eastern bloc scientists from meetings in the United States and to monitor the activities of foreign graduate students — even to ban them from certain courses — use of these controls has generally been limited. In a paper delivered at the same symposium at which Admiral Inman caused a stir, Professor Mary Cheh noted that the government is aware that a broad interpretation of export control regulations would violate the First Amendment guarantee of free speech.[19] The government has also disclaimed any intention of using the regulations as a general monitor of unclassified scientific research, and no one

---

[18] *Ibid.*, p. 8.

[19] In 1978 the Justice Department sent a memorandum to Frank Press, science adviser to President Carter, concluding that ITAR, if broadly applied, would be unconstitutional.

has ever been prosecuted for publishing articles on technical data included on the Munitions List or the Commodity Control List.

Finally, under both sets of regulations, information in the public domain is exempt from controls. Academics have wondered, however, how new ideas can get into the public domain if the government can use export controls to prohibit communication or publication of ideas. Narrowing their scope is one answer, and both the Commerce and State Departments' rules are being revised to accomplish this. Stephen Bryen, assistant secretary of defense for international economics, trade and security policy, commented on the government's side of the dilemma: "We don't want to intrude unnecessarily on the free exchange of ideas. It's counterproductive. On the other hand, we don't like to see some of our best applied research going out the door where it can come back to haunt us." [20]

According to Harold Relyea of the Congressional Research Service, a member of the American Association for the Advancement of Science's Committee on Scientific Freedom and Responsibility, revision of ITAR is so difficult and time-consuming that the State Department has given it a "back-burner status." Relyea said in a recent interview: "We probably will not see modifications of these regulations for a couple of years — at least not until the end of next year." Commerce's new export regulations may be proposed as soon as this summer.

A group of government agencies is also putting together a Militarily Critical Technologies List (MCTL) that will identify technology essential to an advanced military capability. This will in turn be used as a basis for revising Commerce's Commodity Control List. A draft proposal of the MCTL, issued in 1980, met with severe criticism by industry. The list is voluminous — "about as thick as a Manhattan phone directory — hardly a list," commented Relyea. And it is classified, which limits its usefulness to anyone outside government. "Industry fears that it won't know what it can ship, for example, until it goes to a local bureaucrat, who checks to see whether the item is on the MCTL. One danger is that the bureaucracy will not always be aware of the state of the art in a given field and will be honor-bound by the list."

'Born-Classified' Concept of Information

Another control, the Atomic Energy Act of 1954, was used in 1979 to try to restrict unclassified information in one of the most widely publicized cases of such government intervention.

---

[20] Quoted by Lois R. Ember in "Secrecy in Science: A Contradiction in Terms?" *Chemical and Engineering News*, April 5, 1982, p. 11.

The government invoked the act seeking to prohibit publication of an article called "The H-Bomb Secret: How We Got It, Why We're Telling It" in *The Progressive,* a magazine published in Madison, Wis.[21]

Under provisions of the act, almost all information on nuclear energy and nuclear weapons is considered restricted and a government secret as soon as it is conceived. It is "born classified." The broad scope of these provisions has been limited by the fact that the government has given security clearance to a large number of people, has declassified much of the information that would otherwise have been considered restricted, and has generally applied the provisions only to restricted information generated by government employees or under government sponsorship.

But when *The Progressive* was ready to publish the H-bomb article the Department of Energy, given an advance copy of the article, declared that it contained restricted data and asked the magazine to revise it. When the editor refused, the government obtained a restraining order from a U.S. district court in Wisconsin. The magazine appealed the order, saying "prior restraint" on publishing violated the First Amendment. Before the appeals process was completed a Madison newspaper published a similar article. The Justice Department then dropped the case, saying it was moot. *The Progressive* eventually published the article.

Although the article was based on material in the public domain, the government had argued that the information in reworked form was not declassified, was therefore restricted and was presented in a way that would help other countries build hydrogen bombs.

A bill amending the Arms Export Control Act has been introduced in the past two Congresses by Rep. Charles E. Bennett, D-Fla., and would extend the born-classified concept to militarily critical ideas and technologies. The current bill, H.R. 109, strengthens the controls on the export of information about items on the Munitions List established by the act. Specifically, the bill authorizes the secretary of defense, in consultation with the secretaries of state and energy, to issue regulations specifying what kinds of information should not be disclosed, based on considerations of national interest. This information would be "born classified." The defense secretary does not now have this authority.

---

[21] For background on the case and the law, see "Atomic Secrecy," *E.R.R.,* 1979 Vol. II, pp. 641-660.

H.R. 109 has been referred to the Subcommittee on International Security and Scientific Affairs of the House Foreign Affairs Committee. No hearings have been held and none are anticipated. Many members of Congress oppose the bill because they think Defense should have a secondary role to the State and Commerce departments in cases where a technology has both military and commercial applications. Others in Congress think that the Commerce Department, in particular, is so keen to promote trade that it ignores national security considerations. The consensus is that H.R. 109 is too extreme to get far in Congress but the fact that it was introduced twice is an object of concern to its opponents. The council of the Association for Computing Machinery has adopted a resolution denouncing H.R. 109 and its underlying philosophy. The resolution was also endorsed by IEEE's Computer Society.

Secrecy Ordered on Patent Applications

A bill that did become law, in 1951, is the Invention and Secrecy Act. It was under this law that secrecy orders were issued on George Davida's encryption device and the voice scrambler invented by three Seattle engineers. It stipulates that all patent applications submitted to the Commerce Department's Patent and Trademark Office must be reviewed by a security team to determine whether they contain information related to national security. Applications that do are referred to the appropriate defense agency, which then decides whether the patent's disclosure would be harmful to national security. If so, the patent office issues an order rendering the information a government secret. Secrecy orders last for a year but can be renewed.

About 300 new secrecy orders are issued each year, but most cover patent applications from within the government or from government-sponsored projects. The law provides for an appeals process and for compensation for damages caused by secrecy or as payment for the government's use of an invention. According to law professor Mary Cheh, legal experts believe that if challenged on First Amendment grounds, the law would be declared unconstitutional, an infringement of freedom of speech.

Other Western countries also have some controls on technology transfer. The Coordinating Committee on Export Controls (CoCom) consists of countries in the North Atlantic Treaty Organization (NATO) minus Iceland and plus Japan. CoCom keeps a list of products that cannot be sold to Eastern bloc countries without approval but the expertise behind the products often goes unmonitored. In addition, the United States embargoes some items that other CoCom members do not, which may damage the position of some U.S. companies in world markets. Even if the Militarily Critical Technologies List, for example, is eventually revised to please all concerned, including industry, there is no assurance that CoCom members will apply it. "The degree of CoCom cooperation is going to be critical," said Jean Caffiaux, vice president of the Electric Industries Association.[22] But industry leaders do not think it likely that cooperation will be forthcoming.

It is difficult to determine the effectiveness of current export-control regulations. A Defense official acknowledged that keeping U.S. technology from the Russians for any length of time is probably impossible. "The purpose is to make it difficult for the Soviets," he said. "If they can save a ruble by begging, borrowing, or stealing the technology, that's one more ruble they can spend on their own research."[23]

Attempts to Strike a Balance

AMERICAN expertise in certain areas of military and commercial technology is lagging behind that of Japan and West Germany, according to informed opinion. The Soviet Union, once nearly 10 years behind the United States in electronics, is believed to have come at least halfway toward closing that gap. Advocates of stronger controls maintain that our military and industrial position will be even further eroded if the United States continues virtually to give away the results of its research. This country should at least, they say, delay the spread of information directly related to some military production processes.

Yet there is a question about how well the Soviet Union can apply whatever expertise it gains through technology transfer and about the costs to the United States in expanding its export-control system in light of the Russians' capability. According to Thane Gustafson, a political science researcher for the Rand Corp., the Russians' ability to learn from foreign technology is high only in areas where their skills are high. For this reason, Gustafson approves a control system of case-by-case evaluation, much like the one this country uses now.

In an article on U.S. export controls and Soviet technology adapted from his book *Selling the Russians the Rope* (1981),

---

[22]Quoted by Paul Wallich in "Technology Transfer at Issue: The Industry Viewpoint," *Spectrum*, May 1982, p. 72.
[23] *Ibid.*, p. 70.

Gustafson wrote, "History teaches that the control of technology transfer is at best a rear-guard action, achievable (and then only briefly) at the cost of regulations and secrecy that carry harmful side-effects. . . . Regulation, however well-intentioned, introduces screens and filters between the perception of an opportunity for innovation and the inspiration and incentive to take advantage of it. Consequently, if the national purpose is to maintain the U.S. technological lead, our first concern should be to be good innovators ourselves." [24] In other words, the benefits of controls are uncertain and the potential costs are high.

Academicians agree that excessive regulation would undermine the advancement of science and technology. Publication restraints, for example, would interfere with the cross-fertilization crucial to any creative process, including scientific research. Requiring clearance before a paper could be read or published would also discourage people from working in heavily regulated fields, particularly in universities where publication is important for career advancement. Some observers note that universities will just have to learn to live with constraints if they want to do research in sensitive areas. MIT President Gray argues that many faculty members would simply not undertake sensitive research. "If this occurs," he wrote, "both the university and the nation will suffer, and there will soon be fewer ideas and developments worth protecting." [25]

Stringent controls, it is argued, would sacrifice the important non-military need for information — for example, in cryptography — to protect the security of this country's rapidly expanding information systems network. "Work in cryptography is especially sensitive to restraint," argues Mary Cheh, "since cryptosystems must be constantly upgraded and changed as the information systems they protect change or are compromised." [26]

This argument reflects the concern that excessive information controls would damage the U.S. economy. Some industry leaders see the Reagan administration's move to tighten export controls as ironic, in light of its pledge to reduce government's role in business by eliminating excessive regulation. For companies with foreign subsidiaries, information could not flow freely between different parts of the same company. Tight controls would also constrict the flow of information between academia and industry. Peter J. Denning, head of Purdue University's computer science department, said at the AAAS symposium in

[24] Thane Gustafson, "U.S. Export Controls and Soviet Technology," *Technology Review*, February-March 1982, p. 35, and *The Bulletin of the Atomic Scientists*, March 1982, p. 5.
[25] Paul E. Gray, *op. cit.*, p. 64.
[26] Mary Cheh, *op. cit.*, p. 27.

Soviet Pipeline

America's attempt to block the building of a natural gas pipeline from the Soviet Union to Western Europe has set the Reagan administration at odds with several of this country's European allies and some of its own industrial leaders.

Russia had planned to build the pipeline with Western credits and technology but the administration, in retaliation for what it regarded as Soviet complicity in Poland, last December suspended a $175 million contract that General Electric had obtained from Russia to supply equipment.* It has sought to persuade Western European countries to withhold technological and financial aid, but so far with little success.

The administration is concerned that the Soviet Union is buying high-technology equipment for "the Soviet military machine," in the words of Assistant Secretary of Commerce Lawrence J. Brady. In a speech he made in San Francisco on Jan. 13, Brady said that Vladimir Lenin "prophesied that the capitalists would gladly sell the rope with which they would be hung. The Siberian pipeline represents such a rope."

U.S. industry representatives, regarding the embargo as a lost chance in the Russian market, challenge the belief that Western technology sold to the Soviets will necessarily be used to benefit their war machine. Rand Corp. researcher Thane Gustafson contends that the "effects of internal Soviet obstacles [to applying our technology] ... dwarf those of the most stringent embargo the Western powers might devise."**

Western European governments are reported to be incensed on two grounds: That it is unwarranted U.S. interference in their affairs, and that the United States is trying to apply the embargo provisions to European subsidiaries of American companies.

British Prime Minister Margaret Thatcher, considered an ideological ally of President Reagan, nevertheless strongly criticized the U.S. embargo in an address to the House of Commons on July 1. "The question is whether one very powerful nation can prevent existing contracts from being fulfilled," she said. "I think it is wrong to do that."

She added: "I think it is harmful ultimately to American interests because so many people will say there is no point in making a contract to secure materials, machinery and equipment from the U.S. if at any time they can just cancel that contract."

In the meantime, Russia has announced that it will build large compressor stations for the pipeline which originally would have been purchased in the United States. The Frankfurter *Allgemeine Zeitung,* a leading West German newspaper, commented editorially on June 25: "The Siberian pipeline will be completed next year, regardless of whether the West will supply the promised parts."

---

* See "Soviet Economic Dilemmas," *E.R.R.*, 1982 Vol. I, pp. 130-132.
** "U.S. Export Controls and Soviet Technology," *Technology Review,* February-March 1982, p. 35.

January: "It is no accident that the computing field has been free of government regulation and has an impressive record of accomplishment.... If you want to win the Indy 500 race you build the fastest car. You don't throw nails on the track." [27]

Focus on Defining Issues and Terminology

The polarized positions first taken by government and academia have eased into a dialogue in which both sides are trying to clarify the issues and define terms. Academia, industry and government seem to agree that they "must be willing to sit down together," in the words of chief IBM scientist Lewis Branscomb, "and look for practical policies on technical data exports that are compatible with a national commitment to technical excellence, effective protection for sensitive military information, and the tradition of open scholarship in our universities." [28]

As part of that effort several organizations are studying the issues and meeting with government officials. The Committee on Science, Engineering and Public Policy of the National Academy of Sciences began a year-long study this spring to explore the potential impact of information controls on unclassified scientific and technological research, both basic and applied. The panel's preliminary findings are due in September and its final report will probably be issued by the end of this year.

The Department of Defense is working with the Association of American Universities to develop guidelines for disseminating information from Defense-sponsored research in specific areas. Francis B. Kapper, director of military-technology sharing at Defense, believes that university researchers may have to accept some prior restraint in the publication of research in militarily sensitive areas. But his boss, Richard DeLauer, undersecretary of defense for research and engineering, does not advocate prior restraints unless they are part of a contractual relationship.

To try to avoid an adversarial relationship with universities, Defense is seeking their guidance. It also plans to provide universities with a clearer picture of national security concerns and criteria for recognizing militarily sensitive technologies. To accomplish these goals, DeLauer set up a university-defense forum, with himself and Stanford University President Donald Kennedy as co-chairman. The forum intends to work on several issues affecting the Defense-university relationship, with technology transfer and export controls its first priority.

[27] Quoted by Christopher Paine, *op. cit.*, p. 6.
[28] Quoted by Ivars Peterson in "Controlling Technology Exports: Security vs. Knowledge," *Science News*, March 20, 1982, p. 206.

The Commerce Department's main effort is in revising its export regulations to define more precisely what kinds of technical data it should control and to clarify the types of U.S. exporters subject to control. The State Department is reviewing scientific exchange programs, including ones sponsored by the National Academy of Sciences.

To get a clearer picture of what scientists and engineers think about national security and secrecy in science, the AAAS is polling 100 leading representatives of that group. But Harold Relyea, a member of its Committee on Scientific Freedom and Responsibility, said in a recent interview that "until something emerges in the form of new regulations or legislative proposals — which could be in years or tomorrow — the debate is going to wander all over the back lot. Different voices will speak about different issues and there won't be much focus."

For example, according to Dorothy Nelkin, a professor in Cornell University's program on science, technology and society, scientists are seeking greater military support of research but are angered by national security restraints. "They emphasize the useful application of basic research," she wrote, "but then draw distinctions to avoid external control. Good reasons underlie each response but such contradictions may make science more vulnerable to control." [29]

The consensus is that resolution of any differences between those advocating less or more secrecy controls leans toward greater restraint. But at this time no one is sure how balanced this course will be and what role the scientific community can play in defining the scope of the controls.

---

[29] Dorothy Nelkin, *op. cit.*, p. 708.

Selected Bibliography

Books

Gustafson, Thane, *Selling the Russians the Rope,* Rand Corp., 1981.
Noble, David, *America by Design,* Knopf, 1977.
Wise, David, *The Politics of Lying: Government Deception, Secrecy, and Power,* Random House, 1973.

Articles

Bok, Sissela, "Secrecy and Openness in Science: Ethical Considerations," *Science, Technology and Human Values,* winter 1982.
Ember, Lois R., "Secrecy in Science: A Contradiction in Terms?" *Chemical and Engineering News,* April 5, 1982.
Gray, Paul E., "Technology Transfer at Issue: The Academic Viewpoint," *Spectrum,* May 1982.
Paine, Christopher, "Admiral Inman's Tidal Wave," *The Bulletin of the Atomic Scientists,* March 1982.
Science, selected issues.
Unger, Stephen H., "The Growing Threat of Government Secrecy," *Technology Review,* February/March 1982.
Wallich, Paul, "Technology Transfer at Issue: The Industry Viewpoint," *Spectrum,* May 1982.

Reports and Studies

Cheh, Mary, "Government Control of Private Ideas," prepared for the annual meeting of the American Association for the Advancement of Science, 1982.
Defense Science Board, U.S. Department of Defense, "An Analysis of Export Control on U.S. Technology — a DOD Perspective," 1976, and "Report of the Defense Science Board Task Force on University Responsiveness to National Security Requirements," 1982.
U.S. House of Representatives Committee on Government Operations, "The Government's Classification of Private Ideas," Government Printing Office, 1980.

Cover illustration by Staff Artist Robert Redding; p. 47 drawing by George Rebh

TENSIONS IN U.S.- JAPANESE RELATIONS

by

Marc Leepson

Apr. 9
1982

Editor's Note: Prime Minister Yasuhiro Nakasone came into office Nov. 26, 1982, promising to improve trade and defense relations with the United States. A month later his government announced a reduction in import duties on 47 farm commodities and 28 industrial items. The reductions — which included import taxes on foreign cigarettes but not on beef and citrus fruits — went into effect April 1, 1983. The U.S. Department of Commerce announced that the American trade deficit with Japan was nearly $19 billion in 1982, and protection legislation that did not pass Congress in 1982 has been reintroduced.

In a visit to the United States in January 1983, Nakasone, underscored his commitment to enlarge Japan's defense efforts. He pleased his hosts but caused consternation in his homeland by saying he would turn Japan into "an unsinkable aircraft carrier." Nakasone also has promised to work to eliminate Article IX *(see p. 76)* from Japan's constitution, and to increase defense spending to more than one percent of Japan's gross national product.

TENSIONS IN U.S.-
JAPANESE RELATIONS

I T'S APRIL in the nation's capital and the city's famed cherry trees are in full bloom. The original trees were a gift of friendship from Japan in 1912. But this year the beauty of the cherry blossoms has been overshadowed by the acrimonious debate over Japan's burgeoning trade imbalance with the United States. Japan exported $37.6 billion worth of merchandise — mostly manufactured goods — to the United States last year. U.S. exports to Japan in 1981 — mostly agricultural products and other raw materials — totaled $21.8 billion *(see box, p. 72)*.

This $15.8 billion trade deficit *(see box, p. 67)* comes at a time when the United States is in an economic recession that has hit its automobile industry particularly hard. Japanese automakers, on the other hand, are enjoying unparalleled success — much of it in the United States. Over 21 percent of the cars sold in the United States last year were made in Japan. Little wonder that Japan's trading policies have placed severe strains on U.S.-Japan ties. "Japanese-American relations are more troubled today than at any time since World War II," said international attorney Isaac Shapiro, expressing a sentiment shared by many.[1]

The trade issue that has received most attention in the United States is the difficulty U.S. manufacturers have had penetrating the Japanese market. Business and government officials and members of Congress have complained loudly about the barriers foreign businesses face in Japan. These include Japan's vigorous inspection of foreign-made goods and agricultural products and a distribution system that is bewildering to many foreigners.

At least 10 bills have been introduced in Congress that would require retaliatory action against nations that do not provide equal access to their markets.[2] According to U.S. Deputy Trade Representative David R. Macdonald, these so-called "reciprocity" bills would ensure that the United States had "access to other countries' markets to sell those products we produce and

---

[1] Testifying, March 9, 1982, before the House Foreign Affairs Subcommittee on Asian and Pacific Affairs. Shapiro, who was president of the Japan Society in New York from 1970-77, is an American who has lived in Japan and written widely about Japan and Japanese-American relations for publications in both countries.
[2] See *Congressional Quarterly Weekly Report*, March 27, 1982, pp. 703-74.

export most efficiently, in return for allowing other countries to export to the U.S. market those products they produce most efficiently." [3]

One reciprocity bill that has been receiving a lot of attention on Capitol Hill was introduced by Sen. John C. Danforth, R-Mo., chairman of the Senate International Trade Subcommittee. Danforth's bill, among other things, would require an annual report from the administration for each U.S. trading partner detailing any policy or practice that denies the United States trade opportunities substantially equivalent to those offered by the United States. The measure also would require the president to inform Congress of the trade-distorting impact on U.S. commerce of any of the identified barriers in the report. The president would be required to propose actions necessary to correct any imbalance if initial efforts to obtain redress failed.

Even though the bill does not single out any country or make presidential action mandatory, Japanese officials see the measure as an overt protectionist act directly aimed at their importing methods. But U.S. Trade Representative William E. Brock III, testifying before Danforth's subcommittee March 24, said the Reagan administration is committed to the concept of free trade and is firmly against protectionist legislation. Although the president is pushing Japan to give American companies more access to its domestic market, Brock said the administration would not support any law "which will force U.S. trade policy to require bilateral, sectoral, or product-by-product reciprocity." He said such a law would give a "distorted view of reciprocity," and "could undermine an already vulnerable multilateral trading system, trigger retaliation abroad, further deprive the United States of export markets and erode, if not eliminate, our role as the world leader in liberalizing international trade."

In a March 10 interview with Editorial Research Reports, Brock responded to Japanese allegations that reciprocity is tantamount to protectionism. "Insofar as this administration is concerned, reciprocity cannot and will not become a euphemism for protectionism," Brock said. "What [Congress is] seeking is equal access in this case with the Japanese market to the extent that they have full access to ours. I think it is a fact of life that business relationships have to be mutually beneficial. . . ."

Japan's Non-Tariff Barriers to Trade

The reciprocity debate has not focused on tariffs, the surcharges that countries place on imported goods. Japan's tariffs,

---

[3] Testifying, March 1, 1982, before the House Foreign Affairs Subcommittee on Asian and Pacific Affairs.

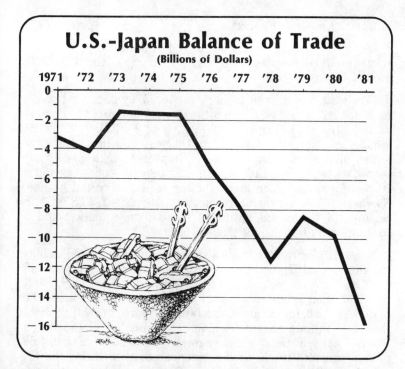

U.S.-Japan Balance of Trade
(Billions of Dollars)

| 1971 | '72 | '73 | '74 | '75 | '76 | '77 | '78 | '79 | '80 | '81 |

like those of most industrialized nations, are today at their lowest levels in modern history. This is due primarily to the work of the General Agreement on Tariffs and Trade (GATT), the 86-nation international agency that, among other things, discourages protectionist quotas and high tariffs *(see box, p. 74)*.

The current friction between the United States and Japan is primarily the result of "government regulations other than tariffs that directly alter the volume of composition of international trade. . . ." [4] In the case of Japan, these non-tariff barriers include the many and varied rules and regulations used by Japanese customs agents, as well as Japan's complicated distribution system. Merchandise is distributed in Japan from manufacturer to retailer through a complex web of buyers, wholesalers and other intermediaries. The system, which dates from the mid-19th century, is based on longtime personal links and is difficult for most foreigners to break into.

U.S. trade officials point to the Japanese cigarette industry as a particularly egregious example of that nation's non-tariff barriers. American-made cigarettes accounted for less than 2 percent of the Japanese market in 1981, compared to about 20 percent of sales in some European countries. One reason American cigarette manufacturers have found it difficult to sell in

---

[4] Richard E. Caves and Ronald W. Jones, *World Trade and Payments* (1981), p. 246.

Japan is the Japan Tobacco and Salt Public Corp. (JTS), a government monopoly that tightly controls the cigarette market.

JTS must buy all the tobacco produced by Japan's 113,000 small tobacco growers, a commitment that supports the domestic industry at the expense of importers. JTS also limits the number of licensed retail outlets that can sell imported cigarettes, allows only new brands of imported cigarettes to advertise on television, and imposes a 57 percent excise tax and a 20 percent distribution and handling fee on imported brands. *Business Week* magazine recently characterized JTS as "an example of the closed nature of the Japanese market and a continuing irritant in our trade relations." [5]

Non-tariff barriers to trade also exist in other nations, including the United States. For years this country has negotiated what are termed "voluntary export agreements" on sugar, textiles and other goods on a country-by-country basis. During the period 1977-80, for example, the Japanese agreed to sell no more than 1.75 million color television sets annually in the United States. Last year the Japanese agreed to ship no more than 1.68 million cars and trucks to the American market during the 12-month period beginning April 1, 1981. The Japanese government announced on March 29, 1982, that it would keep its automobile export limit at 1.68 million units for the next year.

Japanese Response to American Pressure

The U.S. clamor for market access has not gone unnoticed in Japan. In November 1981, the Japanese agreed to put into effect in April 1982 tariff cuts on semiconductor parts that had been scheduled to go into effect in fiscal years 1983 and 1984. Prime Minister Zenko Suzuki late last year set up a committee on International Economic Measures within his ruling Liberal Democratic Party to examine some of the remaining barriers to imports. The committee announced on Jan. 22, 1982, that Japan would eliminate 67 non-tariff barriers and set up an ombudsman's office to handle individual complaints on trade matters from abroad. Among other things, the Japanese will simplify testing procedures for certain types of automobiles, accept animal test data from abroad on medicines and cosmetics, and relax certain safety standards for electrical appliances.

The Japanese government considered these actions broad and far-reaching. But analysts in this country and in Europe — where Japan also has a large and growing trade surplus — believe Japan did not go far enough. According to Harvard University Professor Ezra F. Vogel, the 67 "concessions are

---

[5] Issue of March 22, 1982, p. 42.

Figuring the Trade Deficit

Question: What was the U.S. trade deficit with Japan in 1981?
- a) $13.4 billion
- b) $15.8 billion
- c) $18.0 billion

Answer: All of the above.

Each of the three figures has been used as the "official" difference in trade between Japan and the United States. The $13.4 billion figure was arrived at by the Japanese Ministry of Finance by adding in the cost of insurance and freight to U.S. imports, but not to Japanese exports.

The $18 billion deficit figure, which is often used by U.S. officials and members of Congress, is compiled by doing the reverse of what the Japanese do: by counting insurance and freight costs on Japanese imports, but not on U.S. exports.

The $15.8 billion deficit figure is the U.S. Department of Commerce's official total. It is figured without insurance and freight costs for both Japanese imports and U.S. exports. This report uses the $15.8 billion figure.

---

perceived abroad as so inadequate that Tokyo risks a trade war." [6] David Macdonald, the U.S. deputy trade representative, said the concessions were "largely a compilation of measures that already had been undertaken by various Japanese government agencies, and were very narrowly focused on standards and import procedures. They do not appear to represent a genuine effort by ministries to make the hard political decisions which are needed."

Despite the largely negative U.S. reaction to those concessions, Japanese and American trade officials have continued high-level negotiations throughout the first three months of 1982. After meetings in Tokyo on March 9 and 10, the head of the Japanese delegation, Hiromu Fukada, director-general of the Economic Affairs Bureau of the Japanese Foreign Ministry, announced that his nation recognized "the need for visible, forward-looking measures that will be understood by the American people." Observers interpreted that statement to mean that Japan would soon take additional steps to open its markets.

Japanese Foreign Minister Yoshio Sakurauchi, on a visit to Washington two weeks later, said Japan was considering decontrolling some farm import quotas and simplifying inspection procedures for tobacco imports. After a meeting with President Reagan March 22, Sakurauchi said, "Japan and the United States enjoy a very basic friendship. Upon this I have mentioned to the president we will make more efforts to solve the

---

[6] Writing in *The New York Times*, March 9, 1982. Vogel, who directs the program on U.S.-Japanese relations at Harvard, is the author of *Japan as Number One* (1979).

trade imbalance." Trade analysts think Japan will implement new policies before the economic summit meeting scheduled for June in Paris, and that negotiations over beef and citrus fruit imports could begin in October, six months ahead of schedule.

Trade Opportunities for U.S. Companies

Opinion is divided in this country over what effect the opening of Japan's markets will have on the U.S. economy. David Macdonald said in Tokyo March 9 that the elimination of Japanese non-tariff barriers would probably reduce the U.S. trade deficit "in the range of $5 to $10 billion." But others believe the figure would be much lower. Author Daniel Yergin estimated that eliminating the remaining non-tariff barriers would lead to an increase of only $800 million to $1 billion in U.S. exports to Japan. "This is not an insignificant number by any means," Yergin said, "but it is still less than 5 percent of Japan's overall surplus with the United States." [7]

As for the concept of reciprocity, there is evidence that American business leaders are not overly enthusiastic about it. An "informal sampling of business leaders" taken recently by *Fortune* magazine found "no one openly in favor of reciprocity legislation; most businessmen seemed fearful of retaliation." [8] A House Ways and Means subcommittee report released late last year concluded: "While we concede that Japan's trade barriers threaten the free world trading system, we believe that our prime focus should be on ways to make the U.S. economy more competitive." [9] The report called for improvements in American management techniques, labor-management relations, productivity and quality control. According to Harvard Professor Ezra Vogel, "American companies must work harder to achieve global competitiveness. They must, for example, train more people capable of doing business in the Japanese language and developing close relationships with Japanese businessmen and officials. And, of course, Washington must actively support these efforts."

The Japanese take the position that American businessmen have not worked hard enough to tailor their products to the Japanese market. "Forty years ago the American army and navy penetrated the Japanese islands physically," said Naohiro Amaya, a trade adviser to the Japanese government. "We ... shuddered at the vitality and guts of the American soldier.... Now, they are complaining about the difficulty of getting into

---

[7] Writing in *The Washington Post*, March 23, 1982. Yergin is a lecturer at Harvard's Kennedy School of Government.

[8] Richard I. Kirkland Jr., "Washington's Trade War of Words," *Fortune*, April 5, 1982, p. 38.

[9] House Ways and Means Subcommittee on Trade, "Report on Trade Mission to the Far East," Dec. 21, 1981, p. xiii.

the Japanese market. I think we wish them to revitalize their vitality and guts. . . . What is important is to study the Japanese market and study what the consumers are wishing to have. . . . If they appeal to the consumers, there is no doubt that they can get penetration into the Japanese market." [10]

William E. Brock III

Trade Representative Brock agreed with that statement — to an extent. "It is accurate to say that too few American businesses have made a real effort," Brock told Editorial Research Reports. "An awful lot have, and a number have been successful. Others have made an effort and have not been successful because of a variety of barriers. And far too many have simply not made an effort at all or have not persisted in it. . . . We've talked so much about Japanese barriers that I'm afraid some business people have said that it's not worth making the effort. That's not an accurate evaluation. There are sectors where the opportunity exists today and has not been fully seized."

A number of American companies have done well in Japan. The chemical giant E. I. Du Pont de Nemours Co. reported sales of $700 million in Japan in 1981, a 20 percent increase over the previous year. *Business Week* estimated that Texas Instruments (TI) Inc., the semiconductor manufacturer, sold $130 million worth of goods in Japan in 1981, a 9 percent rise over 1980. "TI recognized the market very early, and it started its operation with good people," said one industry observer in Tokyo. "They sent the first team over here, not a second team." [11]

Masumi Esaki, a special envoy to the United States on trade matters, recently listed other U.S. firms that have been successful in Japan. These include International Business Machine Corp., which supplies 40 percent of the computer market in Japan; Caterpillar Tractor Co. (32 percent of the Japanese tread-type tractor market); Warner-Lambert Co. (70 percent of the razor blade market); Japan Procter & Gamble Co. (85 percent of paper diapers); Garrett Corp. (64 percent of turbochargers); Borg-Warner Corp. (54 percent of automatic transmissions); Ford Motor Co. (36 percent of automatic transmissions); S. C. Johnson & Son, Inc. (30 percent of floor waxes and 20-30 percent of car waxes); Coca-Cola Co. (33 percent of

---

[10] Appearing on "The MacNeil/Lehrer Report," PBS-TV, March 3, 1982.
[11] Quoted in *Business Week*, Feb. 15, 1982, p. 62.

soft drinks); and Kimberly-Clark Corp. and Scott Paper Co. (34 percent of the tissue paper market).[12]

Japan's Economic Prospects

THE CENTRAL FACTS in any discussion about Japanese trade are that nation's acute shortage of natural resources and its constantly growing industrialization. "Because of Japan's narrow and poorly endowed geographic base, this industrialization has brought with it a heavy dependence on foreign sources of energy and raw materials and therefore an equal dependence on foreign markets for industrial exports to pay for necessary imports," wrote Edwin O. Reischauer, a former U.S. ambassador to Japan.[13]

Japan imports more oil, coal, iron ore, cotton, wool and lumber than any other nation. The Japanese Ministry of International Trade and Industry reports that in 1979, the last year for which complete statistics are available, Japan imported 87 percent of all its energy sources. The United States, in contrast, imported 21 percent *(see box, p. 71)*.

In the past, the world's colonial powers milked their colonies of raw materials to feed their own industrial machines. But today the world's leading industrial nation — the United States — supplies billions of dollars worth of raw materials to Japan, which in 1981 passed the Soviet Union to become the second-richest nation in the world as measured by annual GNP. Eleven of the top 15 U.S. exports to Japan last year were raw materials *(see box, p. 72)*.

This disparity — Japan, the manufacturer vs. America, the raw materials supplier — is one reason for current U.S.-Japanese frictions, according to Daniel Yergin. "Americans have some difficulty in seeing themselves mainly as a nation that supplies raw materials . . . ," he said. "It defies America's industrial machismo."

Attempts to Restrict Automobile Exports

In 1981 Japan sold $9.5 billion worth of automobiles to the United States and over $2 billion worth of trucks. This influx of

---

[12] See "News From Japan," a newsletter published by Washington-International Communications, a division of the Embassy of Japan, Feb. 26, 1982.
[13] Edwin O. Reischauer, *The Japanese* (1977), p. 25. Japan has a population of 117 million. Its land area of 143,000 square miles is about the size of Montana, but only about 20 percent of Japan's land is arable.

Japanese and U.S. Imports of Raw Materials
(1979 figures)

	Percentage Imported	
	Japan	United States
All Energy Sources	87.0%	20.6%
Coal	79.2	−9.6
Oil	99.8	42.3
Natural gas	88.7	5.8
Iron ore	98.6	29.7
Copper	95.6	33.5
Lead	82.4	59.9
Zinc	68.7	70.6
Tin	97.7	100.0
Aluminum	100.0	63.6
Nickel	100.0	93.0
Lumber	69.2	3.8
Wool	100.0	23.2
Cotton	100.0	−84.4
Soybeans	95.4	−51.2
Corn	100.0	−42.9
Wheat	93.0	−147.1

Source: Japanese Ministry of International Trade and Industry

Japanese imports came in a year when American automobile makers were forced to lay off tens of thousands of workers, close numerous plants and cope with multimillion-dollar corporate losses. Even with the "voluntary" auto-import restrictions *(see p. 66)*, 1.9 million Japanese cars and 443,500 Japanese trucks were sold in the United States in 1981, compared to 6.9 million American cars and 1.8 million American trucks.[14]

The flood of Japanese auto imports, in combination with the sagging U.S. auto industry, has given rise to calls for the government to cut back further on Japanese imports. Speaker of the House Thomas P. O'Neill Jr., D-Mass., told an auto workers' group in March that if he were president he would put an embargo on Japanese autos. Charles Peters, editor of *The Washington Monthly,* also has called for an embargo on Japanese cars. "I know all my liberal friends will scream and say, 'Don't you believe in free trade?'" Peters wrote recently. "My answer is: not when it's killing us."[15]

Others believe Japanese cars have sold well in this country because American automakers have not given consumers what

---

[14] Figures provided by the U.S. Motor Vehicle Manufacturers Association. Toyota was the leading Japanese exporter with 576,491 cars and 137,529 trucks sold in the United States in 1981. Datsun followed with 464,806 cars and 119,684 trucks; Honda sold 370,705 cars in the United States. Japan became the world's leading manufacturer of automobiles in 1980 when that nation's automakers built 10 million cars.
[15] Writing in *The Washington Monthly,* March 1982, p. 9.

U.S.-Japan Trade at a Glance, 1981

U.S. Exports to Japan	Value (in millions)
Total	$21,823
Corn	1,792
Bituminous coal	1,472
Soybeans	1,139
Logs/lumber	1,021
Aircraft	815
Computers and equipment	747
Organic chemicals	686
Wheat	615
Fish	553
Paper-based products	544
Inorganic chemicals	529
Raw cotton	504
Nonferrous ores and scrap	503
Meat	502
Pharmaceuticals	449

U.S. Imports from Japan	
Total	$37,612
Cars	9,497
Steel mill products	3,801
Trucks	2,014
Business machines	1,780
Audio and video recorders	1,762
Auto parts	1,437
Motorcycles and parts	1,297

Source: U.S. Department of Commerce

they want — reliability and economy. When asked if the Japanese are to blame for Detroit's troubles, Trade Representative Brock told Editorial Research Reports: "I don't think you've ever heard anybody in this administration blame the Japanese for our domestic automobile problems. That is just not a valid point of criticism."

One sign that Detroit may be learning from Japan's success is the recent meeting in New York between Roger B. Smith, chairman of General Motors Corp., and Eiji Toyoda, president and founder of Toyota Motor Co., to discuss joint production of a line of small cars. The automakers reportedly are considering two types of joint production: a G.M.-Toyota venture in one of G.M.'s idle American plants and the licensing of a Toyota subcompact to G.M. for production in the United States. A decision on the cooperative venture could come by June.

One reason G.M. would be receptive to joint production is that its J-car — a $5 billion investment — has been a big disappointment. "G.M. has not been so successful yet with its small lines like the J-car," said Yukio Kobayashi, an analyst for Nomura Securities Co. "If G.M. had full confidence in its ability to develop small cars by itself, it would not talk to Toyota." [16]

From Toyota's perspective, the use of a General Motors plant would be a chance to start American production without making a heavy investment in equipment. Moreover, cooperation with a U.S. automaker could cool some of the growing anti-Japanese sentiment in the United States. The possible G.M. deal marks the second time Toyota has tested the waters in the United States. Two years ago preliminary joint production talks were held with the Ford Motor Co., but no agreement was reached.

Productivity, Unemployment and Deficits

In the last two years exports have assumed even greater importance to Japan's economy. The nation's growth rate slipped from 4.2 percent in 1980 to 4.1 percent in 1981, and economists predict that it will be 3.5 percent in 1982. The only reason there has been any growth at all is the nation's strong export trade. "If exports were restrained, Japan could easily topple into recession," said *Business Week* Editor-in-Chief Lewis H. Young.[17]

In spite of the sluggish growth rate, Japan does not have high unemployment or inflation. The nation's unemployment rate today is 2.2 percent, one of the lowest in the industrialized world. A decade ago, when Japan's economy was growing 10 percent annually, unemployment was only 1.1 percent. The primary reason for Japan's low unemployment is the widespread practice of "permanent employment," in which an employee goes to work for a firm after leaving school and stays through retirement. "The firm is committed to the employee and provides a sense of belonging, personal support, welfare and retirement benefits, and increases in salary and rank with age," Ezra Vogel wrote. "Barring serious long-term depression, the employee expects that he will never be laid off, and even if the company were to disband or be absorbed by another company, he expects that a new job elsewhere will be arranged." [18]

Along with the near guarantee of lifetime employment come other benefits, which can include inexpensive company housing, low-cost company vacation resorts and company-sponsored sports teams and social events. "The permanent work force of a factory or office become for the individual workers a lasting group to which they are proud to belong," said Edwin

---

[16] Quoted in *The New York Times*, March 9, 1982.
[17] Issue of March 15, 1981, p. 18D.
[18] Ezra F. Vogel, *Japan as Number One* (1979), p. 137.

GATT's The Answer

The United States is not the only nation in disagreement with Japan on trade practices. The Western European countries also are unhappy with Japan's refusal to open its domestic market to manufactured goods and processed foods. In late March the foreign ministers of the European Common Market filed a complaint against Japan with the General Agreement on Tariffs and Trade (GATT), the 86-nation international trading agency. Under GATT's Article 23, member nations can ask the group to examine another nation's trading practices. If the Common Market-Japanese disagreement cannot be worked out on a bilateral level, an international GATT panel will be set up to examine the problem. The full GATT council would be the final arbiter in case of appeal.

GATT was set up in 1948 to draw up international trading rules. GATT members have worked together to reduce tariffs and non-tariff barriers to trade and discriminatory treatment in international commerce. GATT members also meet regularly to consider international trade issues, and nearly all important tariff negotiations today are carried out under GATT rules and auspices.

Reischauer. "Their loyalty to the company assures it of an enthusiastic labor force which takes pride and satisfaction in its work. Both blue and white collar workers ... are all diligent ... and can be counted on to police the quality of their own work. The lack of the need for outside inspectors stands in sharp contrast to the situation in western factories." [19]

This attitude also helps explain why Japanese productivity is so high. From 1950 to 1980, productivity in Japanese manufacturing rose an average of 9.1 percent per year. At the same time, American productivity rose only 2.4 percent annually. Productivity actually declined in the United States in 1978, 1979 and 1980. Last year U.S. productivity rose 1.1 percent. Japanese productivity grew 6.2 percent in 1980, the last year for which complete statistics are available.[20]

Unemployment may be low, exports growing and inflation under control,[21] but the Japanese government has had trouble balancing its budget in recent years. Japan's cumulative budget deficit is about $400 billion. This is due mainly to the rapid rise of energy prices in the 1970s. This situation forced the Suzuki government to draw up an austere budget for fiscal year 1982, which began April 1. The $226 billion budget is 6.2 percent higher than 1981, the lowest budgetary growth rate in 26 years.

[19] Reischauer, *op. cit.*, p. 184.
[20] Data from the U.S. Bureau of Labor Statistics.
[21] The inflation rate in Japan is currently 4-5 percent a year.

The new budget freezes spending on public works and provides only small increases for social welfare and education programs. This tight fiscal policy, analysts say, is designed to stimulate Japan's domestic economy.

Western government officials and bankers claim that Japan is trying to stimulate its economy in another way — by keeping the value of the yen at artificially low levels. A weakened yen spurs Japanese exports because the prices of Japanese goods sold abroad are less expensive. Conversely, imports are more expensive for Japanese consumers. The value of the yen has been between 228-245 per dollar this year; Western analysts think the level should be 190-200, or even lower.

The Japanese blame high interest rates in the United States and the resulting overvalued dollar for the yen's weakness. Nevertheless, the Bank of Japan has pledged to strengthen the yen. "We've got to have a stronger yen," said the bank's governor, Haruo Maekawa. "A weaker yen would tend to encourage exports, and trade frictions could increase. Therefore, we don't have any intention of keeping the yen weak." [22]

The Debate Over Defense

TRADE is not the only area of disagreement between the United States and Japan. The question of how much Japan should spend on defense has also been a source of tension between the two countries. "Differences over the appropriate burden each country should carry to help protect their mutual security interests have created serious strains in U.S.-Japanese relations," Rep. Stephen J. Solarz, D-N.Y., chairman of the House Foreign Affairs Subcommittee on Pacific and Asian Affairs, said in his opening remarks before a March 17 hearing on Japan-U.S. defense issues.

The relatively small amount Japan spends on defense *(see p. 77)* is related to its burgeoning economy and large trade imbalance with the United States. "You simply cannot ignore the fact that the two are intertwined," Trade Representative Brock said in an interview. "If they spend less money on defense, they have far more opportunity for investing in support of selected industries, R&D support, lower interest rates and the like that make them more competitive economically." Secretary of Defense Caspar W. Weinberger, who recently spent three days in Japan

---

[22] Quoted in *Business Week*, March 8, 1982, p. 89.

lobbying that nation's leaders to step up defense spending, took a different position. In a March 26 speech at the Japan National Press Club in Tokyo, Weinberger said: "We do not believe that action on trade problems resolves our concerns with defense — or vice-versa."

Japan has maintained a philosophy of pacifism since its defeat in World War II. Article IX of Japan's 1947 Constitution states in part: "The Japanese people forever renounce war as a sovereign right of the nation and the threat or use of force as a means of settling international disputes.... Land, sea and air forces ... will never be maintained." Even though Japan rearmed with American support and encouragement after the start of the Korean War, the Japanese military is designed primarily for defense. The Japanese Self-Defense Force contains about 250,000 troops, and includes an army with 13 divisions, a 400-plane air force and a navy equipped with 50 destroyers.

Under the 1960 U.S.-Japan Treaty of Mutual Cooperation and Security — which also puts Japan under the U.S. nuclear umbrella — the United States has about 46,000 troops stationed in Japan. The U.S. Seventh Fleet often patrols the nation's coastal waters and a division of Marines and an Air Force division are based on nearby Okinawa. It costs the United States about $2.4 billion a year to operate its bases in Japan. The Japanese contribute an additional $800 million annually. William H. Ginn Jr., a retired Air Force general who commanded American forces in Japan until August 1981, said recently that Japan's contribution to the U.S. military there has "grown significantly" in recent years. According to Gen. Ginn, Japan is "building us permanent housing and facilities, contributing to our labor costs, and subsidizing our presence in a variety of other ways." [23]

U.S. Reaction to Suzuki's Defense Policy

The main reason the United States is putting pressure on Japan to increase defense spending is the massive buildup of Soviet forces in Central Asia and the Far East in the past 10 years. "The Soviet force in Asia is so complex that it may be possible for the U.S.S.R. to reach out with its nuclear might and destroy all the modernized sectors of China ... within a matter of hours...," said Robert J. Pranger of the American Enterprise Institute. "The sheer fall-out from such an attack, of course, could possibly bring havoc to Japan as well." [24]

---

[23] Testifying March 17, 1982, before the House Foreign Affairs Subcommittee on Asian and Pacific Affairs.

[24] Testifying March 24, 1982, before the House Foreign Affairs Subcommittee on Asian and Pacific Affairs. The American Enterprise Institute for Public Policy Research is a non-profit research and educational organization based in Washington, D.C.

Tensions in U.S.-Japanese Relations

Although the Japanese are less concerned about the Russian threat than the Americans are, Japanese Prime Minister Suzuki  increased defense spending for fiscal year 1982 by 7.75 percent to about $11 billion. This made Japan's defense budget the eighth largest among non-communist nations. "We must ... try to improve the quality of our defense capability so that we will be able to defend ourselves," the prime minister said last year. "And we shall continue with this endeavor. We shall also continue to contribute to a smooth and effective operation of the Japanese-U.S. security arrangement." [25]

**Prime Minister
Zenko Suzuki**

Since the late 1960s Japan has spent less than 1 percent of its gross national product (GNP) each year on defense. The United States, in contrast, has spent between 5 and 10 percent of GNP on defense — today the U.S. figure is 5.2 percent. Sen. Carl Levin, D-Mich., a member of the Senate Armed Services Committee, and Rep. Clement J. Zablocki, D-Wis., chairman of the House Foreign Affairs Committee, introduced a concurrent resolution in Congress late last year calling on Japan to increase its defense expenditures to at least 1 percent of GNP. "Despite their strong economy," Levin said Nov. 9 on the Senate floor, "the Japanese have shirked some of their defense responsibilities to themselves and to the United States."

Some foreign policy analysts believe that focusing on the 1 percent GNP figure is not the best way to influence Japan to take on a greater share of its defense. "The U.S.-Japanese relationship is essential to both nations and should not be reduced to percentage terms or be threatened by dire consequences should one or both nations not always meet the other's expectations," said Rep. Paul Findley, R-Ill.[26] Findley and others say the best way to influence Japan is to continue the process of high-level negotiations that focus on specific issues and to encourage the administration to consult with Japan before making foreign policy decisions that affect that nation.

Several times in the 1970s the United States did not consult with Japan on key international issues, causing the Japanese government and public to question the reliability of its key ally.

---

[25] Interview published in the American Enterprise Institute publication "U.S.-Japanese Relations: What Should the Future Hold?" July 1981, p. 3.
[26] Testifying March 24, before the House Foreign Affairs Subcommittee on Asian and Pacific Affairs.

President Nixon's surprise 1971 announcement of his intention to visit China, for example, led to speculation that the United States was abandoning Japan in favor of China. Japan's response was to open full diplomatic relations with the Chinese in 1972. Later in 1971, and again in 1973, Nixon introduced economic controls on imports and exports without consulting the Japanese. More recent shocks to Japan were the U.S. defeat in Vietnam and President Carter's January 1977 decision to withdraw U.S. ground troops from South Korea, and Carter's reversal of that decision a year later. "The consequences of those shocks has been to reduce the confidence of the Japanese public in the credibility of U.S. security guarantees to Japan," said Michael Nacht, associate director of Harvard's Center for Science and International Affairs.[27]

Public Opinion in Japan Sharply Divided

The Japanese public is by no means united behind its government's decision to increase military spending. "At present, 40 percent of the Japanese public do not share the government's views on defense," said Jiro Tokuyama, executive director and dean of the Nomura School of Advanced Management in Tokyo.[28] Michael Nacht has divided the Japanese into four groups: minimalists, who react mainly to American pressure; gradualists, who support a more assertive Japanese defense picture; neutralists, who want to sever the U.S. defense connection in favor of unarmed neutrality; and Gaullists, who want Japan to build a strong navy and adopt an independent military posture.

Nacht told the House Foreign Affairs Subcommittee on Asian and Pacific Affairs that the majority of Japanese today could be classified as minimalists. Support for the gradualist position comes mainly from members of the ruling Liberal Democratic Party and officials in the Japanese Defense Agency. The neutralists, whose ranks are made up primarily of members of the Japanese Socialist Party, have been receiving "declining public support," and "are unlikely to reverse direction in the near term," Nacht said. The Gaullists, who want to model Japan's defense forces along the lines chosen by French President Charles de Gaulle in the late 1950s, seem to be gaining small but growing support, he said.

Many observers believe Japan ultimately will adopt the minimalist position of spending just enough on defense to satisfy American demands. Lewis H. Young of *Business Week* wrote recently from Tokyo that it is a "widely held view" in

---

[27] Testifying, March 17, 1982, before the House Foreign Affairs Subcommittee on Asian and Pacific Affairs.
[28] Quoted in *Japan Economic Survey*, March 1982, p. 7.

The Language Barrier

One barrier Americans face when trying to do business with Japan is the immensely complicated Japanese language. While many Japanese businessmen are conversant in English, relatively few Americans speak Japanese. Nearly all Japanese study English in junior and senior high schools. English also is a popular course in Japanese universities. "The Japanese government in its Foreign Office and other ministries has sufficient officers with adequate foreign language skills to conduct Japan's official business with the outside world in a satisfactory manner," Edwin O. Reischauer wrote in *The Japanese* (1977). "The Japanese business community has developed adequate language skills to conduct its huge international economic activities."

Japan that the nation "suffered a defense binge in the '30s and now, like the alcoholic, cannot stand the sight of another drink. In the decades of the '20s and '30s Japan's military establishment operated as a government on its own. Nobody wants to go back to those days." [29]

The Japanese government's primary international goal is to maintain the uninterrupted flow of world commerce. Japan sees "maintaining good relations with other countries to guarantee the flow of natural resources as more important for national security than military weaponry," said Ezra Vogel of Harvard.[30] That view is shared by a former Japanese ambassador to the United States, Nobuhiko Ushiba, now an adviser to the Japanese minister for foreign affairs. Ushiba said that since Japan cannot build a navy to patrol the world's sea lanes, it is trying to use diplomacy to safeguard its overseas interests, particularly in the Persian Gulf area.

"We have increased our assistance to Pakistan, to Turkey and to Thailand. Now we are also trying to help smaller nations around the Persian Gulf," Ushiba said in an interview last year. "Japan's contribution to world peace and stability will be more in the economic field than in the defense field. In the economic field, we have been trying to increase our cooperation with the developing countries, although the amount is not yet very large. In the next five years, we hope to double what we have spent in the past five years. . . . Although there are many other things that could be improved in our foreign aid program, economic assistance is the area in which we can contribute most effectively to world peace." [31]

---

[29] *Business Week*, March 15, 1982, p. 18D.
[30] Vogel, *op. cit.*, p. 68.
[31] Interview published by American Enterprise Institute in "U.S.-Japanese Relations: What Should the Future Hold?" July 1981, pp. 14-15.

New Sources of Tension

J APAN is banking on high technology — specifically the semiconductors, or chips, used in computers and consumer electronics — to be the key to its long-term exporting future. This plan puts Japan once again on a collision course with the United States since this country has dominated the microelectronics industry since it began. Indeed, American entrepreneurs invented the semiconductor, and American businesses taught Japanese firms the mechanics of semiconductor manufacturing.

Japan has made little secret of its future plans in the computer technology arena. A report by the U.S. House Ways and Means Committee underscores what that challenge means: ". . . [I]n the high technology products that count — the products which will dominate the world trade and economy for the rest of the century — the Japanese are second to none . . . the trend lines indicate that they will surpass the United States and that the gap will widen dramatically, UNLESS the United States responds." [32]

Until recently, American companies — including Texas Instruments, National Semiconductor and Intel — built and sold about 70 percent of the world's semiconductors, the "brains" of computers. Japan is in second place in worldwide semiconductor sales. But the Japanese producers — especially Nipon Electronic, Hitachi and Fujitsu — with the help of hundreds of millions of dollars in government research money, have cut deeply into the American-controlled market. This comes at a time when American semiconductor firms are being hurt by rising research and equipment costs, which in combination with intense domestic competition, have forced U.S. companies to sell their products at very low profit margins.

Japanese firms now are selling in the U.S. market at prices that are below the lowest American prices. The Japanese make up the difference by selling at higher prices in their domestic market. Moreover, Japanese non-tariff barriers have prevented American microprocessor firms from selling significant amounts of chips in Japan. This has led to charges that the Japanese are "dumping" semiconductors on the U.S. market — selling them for less than cost — to gain control of the industry.

"A number of firms in the industry believe that Japanese sales are occurring below the cost of production, at predatory levels, with the results that American companies cannot get an

[32] House Ways and Means Subcommittee on Trade, "Report on Trade Mission to the Far East," Dec. 21, 1981, p. 12. See also "The Computer Age," E.R.R., 1981 Vol. I, pp. 105-128.

Japan's Success with Video Recorders

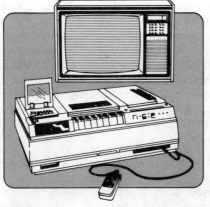

Japan is the world's largest manufacturer of consumer electronics equipment. The newest and brightest star in that field is the videocasette recorder (VCR). Last year Japan sold nearly $1.8 billion worth of audio and video recorders in the United States — a phenomenal 69.9 percent increase over 1980 sales. Japan dominates the booming U.S. market because no American electronics firms manufacture VCRs; all of those they sell are built by the Japanese.

American inventors developed the original idea and technology for videocasette recorders. But the first two U.S. ventures into the home VCR market, by CBS and Ampex, were costly failures. In the early 1970s, after the Americans had given up on the idea, Sony and Victor Co. of Japan (JVC, a division of Matsushita Electric Industrial) came out with successful home VCRs.

Worldwide, Japan shipped more than 7.4 million VCRs in 1981, more than doubling 1980's total. For the first time last year Japanese VCR exports surpassed those of color televisions. Matsushita, Japan's leading electronics firm, had its best year ever in 1981 with nearly $13 billion in sales. Matsushita's sales of VCRs — marketed under the brand names Quasar, Panasonic and National — rose 80 percent over 1980; total overseas sales jumped 36 percent.

adequate return and are forced out of the market," said Alan W. Wolff, Washington counsel to the Semiconductor Industry Association.[33] The Reagan administration is looking into the "dumping" allegations. This could lead eventually to some form of import controls.

One example of Japan's success in the field involves the 64K RAM, a random access memory chip that can store 64,000 bits of digital computer data. It is the main memory bank used in most of today's computers. The Japanese now control 70 percent of the world market in 64K RAMs. Only two American companies — Motorola and Texas Instruments — are manufacturing 64K RAM chips, which were developed in late 1980. Most of the other U.S. semiconductor firms are selling the nearly obsolete 16K RAM chip.

[33] Quoted in *The New York Times*, March 4, 1982.

"The biggest mistake most of the domestic merchants made was that they thought the 16K memory chips would run longer and at higher prices than they eventually did," said John Veiga, purchasing supervisor for components at Apple Computer Inc. "Once prices bombed, they made the mistake of trying to ride a little longer with the 16K than they should have." [34] Hitachi has begun work on a 256K RAM chip, with mass production set for early 1983. Another Japanese firm, Toshiba Corp. of Tokyo, is planning to build an $86 million facility to manufacture the first 1 megabit unit — a chip capable of containing one million bits of data.

Most of the leading U.S. semiconductor manufacturers are relatively small, independent firms. But most Japanese manufacturers are part of larger electronics companies, and this gives them a big advantage. "These [parent] companies are ready to provide the big sums needed for developing new microchips — and not just to earn profits from sales," *The Economist* of London noted. "They also believe that the future of other products depends heavily on developing good components. Japanese companies can back this hunch by borrowing at low rates unheard of in America for a decade or more." [35]

Some U.S. semiconductor firms have been trying to sell and manufacture their products in Japan. Texas Instruments, for example, has been making semiconductors in Japan since 1968. Fairchild Camera and Instrument Corp. in February announced plans to build a $25 million integrated-circuit plant in Nagasaki. Motorola, which two years ago bought a half interest in a Japanese electronics firm near Tokyo, may soon begin operating its own manufacturing plant to turn out 64K RAM and other larger chips in Kyushu. Intel Corp. and Advanced Micro Devices also are investigating the Japanese market.

Japan also dominates another sector of the high technology arena, robotics. Helped by government subsidies, Japanese industry has made wide use of these labor-saving devices in factories, where workers — with the guarantee of lifetime employment — welcome robots. Japanese companies now operate about 100,000 robots, including more than 20,000 "advanced" models, versus an estimated 5,000 advanced models in use in the United States. The Japan Industrial Robot Association reports that there are 140 robot manufacturers in Japan, but only about 40 in the United States.[36]

---

[34] Quoted in *Industry Week*, Feb. 22, 1982, p. 17. The price of 16K RAM chips dropped 90 percent last year. As for the 64K RAM chips, they sold for about $100 each when they were introduced in 1980; now they cost from $5 to $10.
[35] "Silicon Valley has a Big Chip about Japan," *The Economist*, March 20, 1982, p. 70.
[36] *Journal of Japanese Trade and Industry*, January 1982, pp. 6-9.

The one bright spot for the future of U.S.-Japanese trade — from the American point of view — is the strong U.S. showing in the services sector. The United States is the world leader in service exports, which include accounting, advertising, banking, construction, engineering, insurance, tourism and transportation. Trade analysts say that U.S. exports of goods and services exceeded imports by some $12 billion in 1981.

Protecting U.S. Lead in Services Sector

The main problem on the horizon for U.S. service exports is the same one facing merchandise exports: non-tariff barriers to trade. "For the moment the U.S. is the number one exporter of services in the world," said Joan E. Spero, vice president of corporate strategic planning for American Express Co. "However, our position is being challenged. Increasingly, we are encountering trade barriers which other countries have erected and continue to expand." [37] These non-tariff barriers include personnel restrictions, national cartels and monopolies, discriminatory licensing practices and procedures and discriminatory foreign exchange restrictions. All of these, Spero said, "reduce the ability of U.S. firms to compete abroad."

GATT regulations do not apply to services. U.S. Trade Representative Brock and Commerce Secretary Malcolm Baldrige support provisions in the reciprocity bills that would strengthen the administration's authority to negotiate reductions of non-tariff barriers on services. Brock told the Senate Finance Subcommittee on Trade March 24 that it is "timely to clarify the president's authority to negotiate international agreements for services." Brock said that the United States will ask the GATT signatories to study the issue of international trade in services and the growing number of non-tariff barriers in that area at the ministerial meeting of member countries to be held Nov. 23-26 in Geneva. The hope is that GATT eventually will adapt regulations on services similar to those in effect on goods.

It is clear that Japan will continue to maintain its booming export economy in the near future. It is also clear that Japan and the United States agree on Japan's need to open its markets further to foreign goods and to spend more money on defense. But it will take at least several years before U.S.-Japan trade is evened out. "Even if [the Japanese] do everything we've asked them to do — and that's a lot — it will take us several years for American business people to get over there, establish a market presence and really begin to seize the opportunity," Brock said. Until that time, the U.S. trade deficit with Japan is going to continue to be an irritant in U.S.-Japanese relations.

---

[37] Testifying, Nov. 9, 1981, before the U.S. Senate Banking, Housing and Urban Affairs Subcommittee on International Finance and Monetary Policy.

Selected Bibliography

Books

Baldwin, Robert E., *Nontariff Distortions of International Trade,* Brookings Institution, 1970.

Caves, Richard E., and Ronald W. Jones, *World Trade and Payments: An Introduction,* 3rd ed., Little, Brown, 1981.

Gibney, Frank, *Japan: The Fragile Superpower,* Norton, 1975.

Kahn, Herman and Thomas Pepper, *The Japanese Challenge: The Success or Failure of Economic Success,* Crowell, 1979.

Pascale, Richard Tanner and Anthony G. Athos, *The Art of Japanese Management: Applications for American Executives,* Simon and Schuster, 1981.

Reischauer, Edwin O., *The Japanese,* Harvard University Press, 1977.

Vogel, Ezra F., *Japan as Number One: Lessons for America,* Harvard University Press, 1979.

Articles

Abegglen, James C. and Thomas M. Hout, "Facing up to the Trade Gap with Japan," *Foreign Affairs,* fall 1978.

Benjamin, Gerald, "Japan in the World of the 1980s," *Current History,* April 1982.

Business Week, selected issues.

Japan Economic Survey, published by Japan Economic Institute of America, selected issues.

Kirkland, Richard I. Jr., "Washington's Trade War of Words," *Fortune,* April 5, 1982.

Reports and Studies

American Enterprise Institute, "U.S.-Japanese Relations: What Should the Future Hold?" July 1981.

Editorial Research Reports: "Job Protection and Free Trade," 1977 Vol. II, p. 953; "Japanese Elections," 1977 Vol. II, p. 497; "International Trade Negotiations," 1976 Vol. I, p. 343.

Heritage Foundation, "The Defense of Japan: An Alternative View From Tokyo," Aug. 7, 1981.

Japan Economic Institute of America, "Yearbook of U.S.-Japan Economic Relations in 1980," June 1981; "Japan's Import Barriers: An Analysis of Divergent Bilateral Views," 1982.

Kaplan, Eugene J., "Japan's Tariff and Nontariff Barriers: The Perception Gap," United States-Japan Trade Council, May 1979.

U.S. General Accounting Office, "U.S. Military Coproduction Programs Assist Japan in Developing Its Civil Aircraft Industry," March 18, 1982.

U.S. House of Representatives, Committee on Ways and Means, Subcommittee on Trade, "Report on Trade Mission to the Far East," Dec. 21, 1981.

SOVIET ECONOMIC DILEMMAS

by

Mary Costello

**Feb. 19
1 9 8 2**

Editor's Note: Brezhnev's death in November 1982 brought in a successor, Yuri V. Andropov, who said his "highest priority" would be to revive the stagnant Soviet economy. On Nov. 22, 10 days after he was chosen head of the Soviet Communist Party, Andropov told Central Committee members there was need for increased productivity, realistic planning targets, greater discipline, more independence for farms and factories, and the appointment of "politically mature, competent and resourceful people" as economic supervisors.

Andropov seemed to offer some "capitalist incentives" for Russian workers. Some Soviet-affairs analysts believe he will opt for some type of economic decentralization, similar to those undertaken by Hungary, the most prosperous of all Eastern bloc nations.

However, there were later indications that he planned to use a stick as well as a carrot. By early in 1983 Soviet publications were mentioning "Operation Trawl" in which truant or laggard workers would be hauled in for questioning. Western observers have suggested that intimidation would come naturally to Andropov, who was head of the Russian secret police apparatus — the KGB — from 1967 until 1982.

SOVIET ECONOMIC DILEMMAS

R ECENT EVENTS, including the crisis in Poland, a succession of poor harvests in the U.S.S.R., and the shakiness and interdependence of world financial institutions, have focused attention on the Soviet economy. It is widely acknowledged, even by Russian leaders, that the performance of that economy leaves much to be desired. How bad the Soviet economy really is and what measures the Russians might take to improve it, or adversaries might impose to punish the Kremlin, are subjects of controversy.

What is certain is that the situation in Poland has compounded Soviet economic woes. To keep its Eastern European satellite afloat, Moscow has poured billions of dollars into Poland in the past year. Exactly how much the Russians have expended in subsidies, loans, grants and repayment of Poland's huge debt is difficult to ascertain. The sanctions President Reagan imposed on Poland and the Soviet Union after the Dec. 13, 1981, declaration of martial law in Poland and the silencing of the Polish trade union Solidarity are, to date, largely symbolic.[1] "The Soviet Union," Reagan declared when he imposed those sanctions on Dec. 29, "bears a heavy and direct responsibility for the repression in Poland."

Other than a recent agreement among NATO countries not to reschedule payments of Poland's debt to Western governments and banks this year, the allies, except for Britain, have issued only verbal criticism or condemnation of Soviet complicity in Poland.[2] But if the situation in Poland deteriorates or, less likely, the Russians invade, sanctions against the Soviet Union might cost Moscow dearly. President Reagan would be pressured to reimpose the grain embargo decreed by President Carter after the Soviet invasion of Afghanistan in December 1979 and lifted by Reagan in April 1981. Western Europe, which

---

[1] Reagan cut off U.S. government aid to the military regime in Poland. Sanctions against the U.S.S.R. included postponement of negotiations for a new grain treaty to replace the one that expires Sept. 30, 1982; suspension of talks on the export of electronic equipment and other high technology items and on a new maritime accord; barring of new licenses for oil and gas equipment; closure of the Soviet Purchasing Commission in New York; and refusal to renew a number of exchange agreements.

[2] In early February, Britain announced that movements of Polish and Soviet diplomats in the country would be restricted, new credits to Poland would not be granted, information exchanges with Moscow would be reduced and shipping and fishing agreements would be renegotiated.

has far more trade with the Soviet bloc *(see box, p. 95)*, might be less likely to sell what Washington has embargoed and might curtail sales of high-technology items, particularly equipment for the natural gas pipeline from Siberia to Western Europe *(see p. 91)*. Most serious of all, Western banks and governments could declare Poland in default on its more than $20 billion debt to the West and perhaps force the Soviet Union to assume responsibility for it.[3]

The Polish crisis comes at a time when Moscow is faced with serious economic problems of its own. Military spending continues to devour 12-14 percent of the Soviet GNP and, in light of the U.S. defense buildup, may be increased. Shortages of food and consumer goods and the need for technology to develop the country's vast oil and gas fields have forced the nation to rely on costly imports and to use its petroleum and gold to pay for these necessities. This has resulted in a deterioration in the Soviet balance of payments and foreign reserves. A glance at the most recent five-year plan illustrates the U.S.S.R.'s economic problems.

The official Five-Year Plan for 1981-85 called for the lowest overall growth in the country's history. Despite the plan's very modest goals, the Russians announced in December that the original targets were being further reduced. On Jan. 23, 1982, the government newspaper *Izvestia* published figures showing that national income in 1981 had increased by 3.2 percent against a target of 3.4 percent; industrial production rose by 3.4 percent, down from a 4.1 percent target and agricultural production and labor productivity on the farm each fell 2 percent from 1980. Soviet party leader Leonid I. Brezhnev and other officials have called for higher productivity and better management.

That the Soviet economy, like most others, is not functioning well is undisputed. There has been some debate, however, about how serious the problems are, even among U.S. intelligence agencies. A Central Intelligence Agency (CIA) study noted that "shoddy goods and services, queues and shortages have become characteristic features of everyday life, along with endemic black markets and corruption.... In the 1980s, overall economic growth probably will slow markedly under the impact of sharply declining increments to the labor force, energy shortages and sluggish productivity advance. As a result, the Soviet leadership faces a painful dilemma. A boost in consumption will be needed

---

[3] Figures are difficult to verify. Various publications cited a Polish debt of $27 billion or more at the end of 1981. But Wharton Econometric Forecasting Associates, a private economic analysis and consulting firm, concluded in a Dec. 17, 1981, study, "Size of Polish Debt to the West," that "the highest reasonable figure representing the Polish debt to the West at the end of 1981 that can be claimed is $22 billion." See also "Third World Debts," *E.R.R.*, 1980 Vol. II, pp. 541-560.

to meet expectations of gradual improvements in living standards and to maintain work incentives. At the same time, more investment will be required to raise productivity and spur economic growth." [4]

Maj. Gen. Richard X. Larkin, deputy director of the Defense Intelligence Agency, painted a rosier picture in testimony to the Congressional Joint Economic Committee on July 8, 1981. CIA studies had forecast a decline in Soviet oil production within a few years. Larkin argued that "the outlook for Soviet energy, from the perspective of the Soviet leadership, is highly favorable. Prospects for full satisfaction of domestic needs, planned energy exports to Eastern European Communist countries and negotiated quantities for customers in Western Europe appear to meet Soviet expectations through the 1980s and beyond. In addition to providing solid economic benefits to the U.S.S.R., Soviet energy self-sufficiency is also likely to result in greater political influence by the Soviet Union over certain decisions of its Western European customers and, perhaps to a lesser extent, of Japan."

Cost of Assistance to Friendly Countries

One problem in assessing Soviet economic difficulties is the lack of reliable, unclassified information. It is widely assumed, for example, that Soviet figures for defense spending are grossly underreported and ignore expenditures that are hidden in other categories. Similarly, the extent of Russian aid to its friends and allies is almost impossible to determine since assistance is given in a variety of ways: grants, subsidized prices, low-interest loans and, on occasion, gifts with no financial strings attached.

Wharton Econometric Forecasting Associates noted that "the fact that the Soviet Union has granted only relatively small *formal* loans to Eastern Europe over the past decade — an equivalent of about $4.5 billion on a net basis in terms of 1980 dollars — compared to the approximately $50 billion the West has loaned to Eastern Europe leads some to conclude that the West has been the chief financier and aid-giver to Eastern Europe, while the Soviet Union has provided minimal economic support." But according to the private economic analysis firm, "this conclusion is incorrect. The Soviet Union has been assisting Eastern Europe economically on a massive scale. This aid has been overlooked by many because it has not been given in the traditional form of official loans, but rather through 'implicit' trade subsidization. The Soviet Union sells its energy and non-food raw materials at prices below prevailing world market prices and buys machinery and consumer goods from Eastern

---

[4] The study, "Consumption in the USSR: An International Comparison," was published by the Congressional Joint Economic Committee, Aug. 17, 1981.

Europe at prices above world market prices. By offering Eastern Europe preferential terms of trade compared to those available to Eastern Europe in Western markets, the Soviet Union has transferred resources equivalent to almost $80 billion in 1980 dollars during the decade 1971-80." [5]

If Western banks and governments declare Poland in default, the Soviet Union would be faced with either paying Poland's huge debts or losing its own and the rest of Eastern Europe's credit-worthiness in international financial markets. Ironically, the Reagan administration decided in late January to repay $71 million in interest that Poland owed American banks in 1981, rather than require the banks to declare Poland in default. Those favoring the decision argued that declaring a default would damage Western banks and governments far more than Poland or the U.S.S.R., worsen relations with U.S. allies, push Poland even closer to the Kremlin and even precipitate similar defaults in other debtor nations.

Moscow's credit and hard-currency problems are believed responsible for the rise in its oil and raw material prices in late 1981 and the doubling of its gold sales last year. In its foreign trade, the Soviet Union relies primarily on the export of raw materials, particularly oil and natural gas, about half of which goes to Eastern Europe. Sales of gold, energy and military equipment have provided the U.S.S.R. with hard currency to pay its ever-growing import debts, its huge defense expenditures, its estimated $3 billion annual subsidy to Cuba, its aid to Vietnam and other friendly governments and the 110,000 troops it maintains in Afghanistan.

Russian and Eastern-bloc hard-currency debt to the West grew enormously between 1970 and 1980 and is expected to increase far more by 1985 *(see box, p. 105)*. If the hard-currency debt grows to this extent, it will become increasingly difficult for Moscow and its satellites to borrow money to pay for needed food and technology. "According to figures recently published by the Bank of England, Soviet currency reserves in major Western countries totaled $3.6 billion at the end of June, compared with $5.5 billion just three months earlier. As recently as 1980, the total touched $9 billion. . . . The decline . . . resulted from a marked deterioration in the Soviet balance of payments, which was thought to be as much as $8 billion in deficit in 1981, compared with a modest surplus in 1980."[6]

One bright spot on the Soviet economic horizon is the projected earnings on a more than 3,000-mile pipeline that, when

---

[5] Wharton Econometric Forecasting Associates, "East European Debts to the Soviet Union and the West," Jan. 20, 1981, p. 1.
[6] Steven Rattner, writing in *The New York Times*, Jan. 5, 1982.

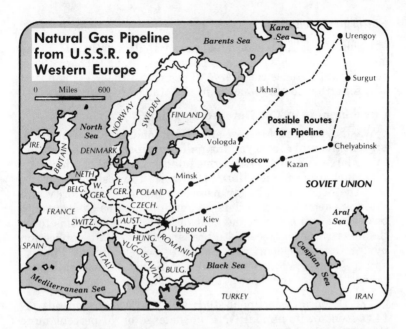

Natural Gas Pipeline from U.S.S.R. to Western Europe

0 Miles 600

North Sea

IRE

BRITAIN

NORWAY

SWEDEN

FINLAND

DENMARK

NETH.

BELG. W. GER. E. GER. POLAND

CZECH.

FRANCE

SWITZ. AUST.

HUNG. ROMANIA

YUGOSLAVIA

SPAIN

ITALY

BULG.

Mediterranean Sea

Barents Sea

Kara Sea

Urengoy

Surgut

Ukhta

Vologda

Chelyabinsk

Possible Routes for Pipeline

Moscow

Kazan

Minsk

SOVIET UNION

Kiev

Uzhgorod

Aral Sea

Caspian Sea

Black Sea

TURKEY

IRAN

completed, will deliver natural gas from Siberia to Western Europe *(see map, above)*. Western analysts estimate that gas sales from the pipeline would bring the Soviet Union about $10 billion annually. The project, which will be built with Western credits and technology, is strongly opposed by many in the Reagan administration. In retaliation for alleged Soviet complicity in Poland, the administration suspended a $175 million contract that General Electric had to supply components for the compressors that will be used on the pipeline. U.S. efforts to convince European governments and multinational corporations to stop supplying material and technology for the pipeline have been unsuccessful to date. A group of French banks announced Feb. 10 that they were lending the Soviet Union an additional $140 million to help finance purchases of French-built pipeline equipment. The new loan will enable the U.S.S.R. to avoid spending its own cash for the purchases.

Washington argues that the pipeline will make Western Europe dangerously dependent on the Kremlin, will relieve economic pressures on Moscow and will be used to continue or accelerate the Russian military buildup. Assistant Secretary of Commerce Lawrence J. Brady, in a speech in San Francisco on Jan. 13, 1982, warned that the U.S.S.R. was buying high-technology equipment for "the Soviet military machine." Vladimir Lenin, he went on to say, "prophesied that the capitalists would gladly sell the rope with which they would be hung. The Siberian pipeline represents such a rope." The theme that American technology is being used to advance the Soviet military buildup is being heard with increasing frequency from administration officials. "Western technology finds its way into a very large number of Soviet weapons systems," said Richard Perle, an assistant defense secretary. "The cost to the West is out of all proportion to the benefits in the trade." [7]

Unwillingness to Cut Defense Spending

Washington and Moscow are understandably determined to prevent the other from gaining military superiority. In addition to the large U.S. and Soviet arms buildups, each is conducting a vehement propaganda effort to convince the rest of the world that the other side already has clear military superiority and that the enemy's current defense buildup must be challenged to protect its own security and that of its allies. This seems to be the message of two recent studies, an October 1981 publication by the Defense Department entitled "Soviet Military Power," and a January 1982 rebuttal by the Soviet Defense Ministry called "Whence the Threat to Peace?"

The Defense Department study said that Moscow spends 12-14 percent of its annual GNP on defense or 70 percent more than the United States did in 1979. "There are no signs of a de-emphasis on military programs" although "the Soviets' own economy is in difficulty and facing competing priorities for scarce resources," the study stated. Moscow's "research and development priorities and continued expansion of military industrial production capabilities are keyed to supporting continuing military growth and modernization. In turn, the combined capabilities of the Soviet Ground Forces, Strategic Rocket Forces, Air Forces, Air Defense Forces and Navy are keyed to assisting the projection of Soviet power abroad and the spreading and solidifying of the Soviet Union's political, economic and military influence around the world. This is the challenge we face." [8]

The Soviet rebuttal to the Defense Department was widely viewed as an effort to convince other governments, notably those in Western Europe, that the Reagan administration represented the primary threat to world peace. The Soviet study claimed that the United States was completing the "development of a so-called first strike potential in the 1980s." The American military buildup has nothing to do with redressing the military balance because "the balance is there...," the study said.

That the Soviet Union would like to reduce its defense budget seems evident from recent statements from Moscow about the

---

[7] Quoted in *The Wall Street Journal*, Feb. 11, 1982.
[8] Critics of the Defense Department study said that claims the Soviets devoted about twice as much of their GNP to defense were misleading since America's GNP was twice as large and therefore spending by both sides was about equal.

Soviet and American Military Sales

Figures on American and particularly Soviet arms sales are either difficult to obtain or tend to be contradictory. What is known is that most superpower military sales are now made to 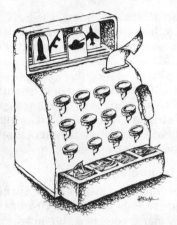 Third World governments or organizations. The Department of Defense's October 1981 study, "Soviet Military Power," states: "In recent years, in addition to being the world's largest producer, the U.S.S.R. has become the world's largest exporter of major items of military equipment to the Third World." Moscow's answer to that study, a January 1982 report by the Defense Ministry entitled "Whence the Threat to Peace?" claims that the United States, with 45 percent of world military sales, is the world's primary arms salesman. Western Europe, the Soviet study stated, provides 20 percent of world arms sales.

Andrew J. Pierre, a senior fellow at the Council on Foreign Relations in New York, concluded in his book *The Global Politics of Arms Sales* (1982) that U.S. military sales had increased from $1 billion in 1970 to $16 billion in 1980. Soviet arms sales had also soared during the last decade and "it is not impossible that Moscow will achieve the dubious distinction of becoming 'Number One' during the 1980s." For the Russians, Pierre continued, weapons sales have become an important source of needed hard currency. Nevertheless, the U.S.S.R. is still willing to provide arms to friendly governments or groups at a financial loss if that suits Moscow's political goals.

stalled arms reduction negotiations. Russian leaders have denounced what they claim is U.S. insistence on linking progress on the Strategic Arms Reduction Talks (START) with the situation in Poland. Brezhnev, in remarks to members of the Socialist International on Feb. 3, 1982, reportedly said that "diplomacy calls for the unraveling, not the linking of issues. . . . The only way is to engage in patient, constructive talks, talks insuring a real reduction and destruction of armaments."

At that meeting, Brezhnev called for a two-thirds reduction in U.S. and Soviet medium-range nuclear weapons in Europe by 1990. Washington rejects this and similar proposals because the Kremlin has more of these missiles and equal reductions by both sides would preserve the current imbalance. Since President Reagan proposed the "zero option" for reducing missiles in

Europe on Nov. 18, 1981,[9] there have been a host of arms reduction proposals by both sides. Each has been rejected by the other for allegedly giving unfair advantage to the side that proposed it.

If the U.S. continues to increase defense spending, the Soviet Union will likely boost its own military expenditures, despite the problems that a sizable increase would have on the country's stagnant economy. Soviet Prime Minister Nikolai A. Tikhanov noted in a speech on Jan. 20, 1982, that his country "does not seek confrontation" and wants to "direct the course of events into constructive dialogue." But "those who prefer the language of threats and demonstrations of strength to a peaceful dialogue should understand that we will take all the necessary measures to ensure our security and the security of our allies."

Need for Imported Grain and Technology

One change in Soviet pronouncements in recent years is the admission that the economy is in serious difficulty. Brezhnev has alluded to these problems on many occasions, blaming not only American or "imperialist" policies, but bad weather, low productivity and corruption. The study prepared for the Joint Economic Committee by the CIA noted that "about 20 years ago, the Communist Party of the Soviet Union unveiled a grandiose program designed to provide the Soviet people with 'the highest living standard in the world by 1980.' Events have turned out quite differently."

> Real per capita consumption in the U.S.S.R. currently is less than a third of that in the United States [the study said]. Long-continued investment priorities favoring heavy industry and defense, coupled with a rigid and cumbersome system of economic organization, have combined to produce a consumer sector that not only lags badly behind both West and Eastern Europe, but also is in many respects primitive, grossly unbalanced and in massive disequilibrium.

Recent speeches by Soviet leaders urging greater worker productivity, condemning corruption and instituting a few free-market reforms indicate that the party elite is well aware of the growing problems confronting the country. Yet the propensity of many Westerners to dwell on the hardships facing the Russians ignores the considerable improvement in their standard of living in the last two decades *(see box, p. 91)*. There has been a substantial equalization of income distribution, the prices of food, housing, transportation and leisure are subsidized by the state, while medical care and education are free.

While the price of basic foods may be relatively low, shortages

---

[9] That offer called for the destruction of Soviet SS4, SS5 and SS20 missiles targeted on Europe in exchange for U.S. agreement not to deploy a new generation of missiles there.

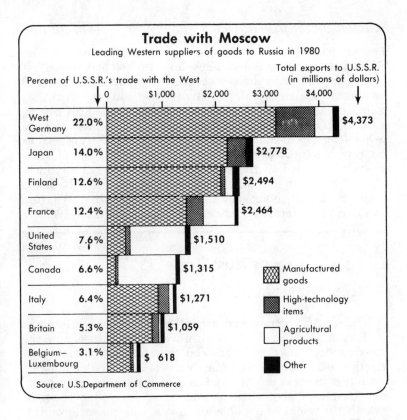

Trade with Moscow
Leading Western suppliers of goods to Russia in 1980

Percent of U.S.S.R.'s trade with the West

Total exports to U.S.S.R.
(in millions of dollars)

	0	$1,000	$2,000	$3,000	$4,000	
West Germany	22.0%					$4,373
Japan	14.0%					$2,778
Finland	12.6%					$2,494
France	12.4%					$2,464
United States	7.6%					$1,510
Canada	6.6%					$1,315
Italy	6.4%					$1,271
Britain	5.3%					$1,059
Belgium—Luxembourg	3.1%					$ 618

Manufactured goods

High-technology items

Agricultural products

Other

Source: U.S. Department of Commerce

are chronic. Responding to growing shortages, the Soviet Union is currently devoting about 27 percent of the country's capital formation or net investment to farms each year, compared to 20 percent from 1976-80. Large amounts of technology have been imported from Western Europe, Japan and the United States to bolster agricultural productivity. Despite these expenditures, the amount spent on imports of grain, meat, flour, wheat, butter and other products has skyrocketed. Hard-currency outlays for food imports rose from $5 billion in 1979 to $8.5 billion in 1980 to an estimated $12 billion in 1981.

The Soviet Union has been plagued by three disastrous grain harvests in a row and the country, which was a net exporter of grain two decades ago, is expected to purchase almost 50 million tons this year at an estimated cost of over $6 billion. Most of this grain will come from Argentina, Australia, Canada and the United States. If President Reagan reimposes the grain embargo he lifted on April 24, 1981, the price could be considerably higher. Grain shortages result not only in less bread but in less feed for livestock and reduced beef and poultry supplies.

Soviet agriculture has five times as many farmers as the United States, but productivity is less than one-third as high as the American. The Soviet food situation has three causes, *The Economist* of London noted. These are: "(a) bad luck — the last three harvests have been exceptionally poor; (b) the bureaucratic inefficiency of collectivized agriculture, which has slowed up the growth of productivity; and (c) foolish pricing policies." [10] In farming, as in virtually every other sector of the Soviet economy, technology imported from the West is seen as the key to improved production. Unless technology sales are severely restricted in the next few years, they will doubtless account for a large and growing share of the $30 billion-$35 billion Soviet hard-currency debt to the West that Wharton Econometric Forecasting Associates has projected for 1985.

Priorities Since 1917

THE YEARS before and after the communist takeover in Russia on Nov. 7, 1917, disproved Marx's theory of the "inevitability" of communism and the economic nirvana that Marxism would bring. Karl Marx expected the first communist revolution to break out in an advanced capitalist country, probably Germany, and when he was asked by young Russians "whether it would be possible for Russia, with its ancient peasant communes, to pass straight to a socialist economy without transversing all the stages of large-scale capitalist exploitation, he had ... expressed himself as very doubtful." [11] The czarist government, which had made considerable economic progress before the outbreak of World War I, might have survived if Russia had managed to stay out of that conflict.

The Bolsheviks, later communists, inherited an economic machine run down by years of war and civil conflict. In an effort to put communist theories into practice, the new regime decreed worker control of industry on Nov. 27, 1917. The results were disastrous. The government, after mid-1918, tried to counteract the anarchy that worker control had brought by instituting a host of "capitalist" measures in management, discipline and efficiency. At this time, the new rulers were also faced with a civil war and the subsequent intervention of anti-Bolshevik European and American troops. By the time the civil war ended in 1920, the country was devastated and its leader, Vladimir I. Lenin, seemed to realize that the victory of socialism in Eu-

---

[10] "Eastern Europe's Food Crisis," *The Economist*, Dec. 26, 1981, p. 14. Soviet food prices are low because of large subsidies provided by the state. These subsidies grew from 3 percent of the country's budget in 1970 to 10 percent in 1980. Subsidies for farm equipment more than doubled between 1970 and 1980.
[11] Edmund Wilson, *To the Finland Station* (1940), p. 140.

rope's leading industrial nations was not imminent. His primary aim thus became the consolidation of "state capitalism" and the retention of power by the communists.

That policy, Leonard Schapiro noted, was "catastrophic." Food shortages "produced near starvation in the towns. . . . The drain of industrial workers to the villages in search of food halved the industrial proletariat by 1920 as compared with 1917. By 1921, overall production had fallen to between a quarter and a third of the figure for 1913 and production per individual worker to about the same. Hunger, lack of incentives and government policy of trying to put down as 'speculation' the attempts by workers to obtain food in the villages, while at the same time failing to provide it by official means, had . . . brought the temper of the proletariat to the breaking point." [12]

As a result of the economic collapse and of a revolt by naval forces at Kronstadt in March 1921, Lenin reversed his program and instituted the New Economic Policy which brought wide-ranging concessions to the peasants and private enterprise. The changes included legalization of private trade and industrial production, substitution of economic and market incentives for coercion and efforts to induce foreign capitalists to invest in the country. Lenin was careful, however, to maintain party control of the economy's most important elements: heavy industry, transportation, foreign trade and banks. The new policy, which was opposed by the more doctrinaire communists, made possible a partial economic recovery.

Joseph Stalin, who took power after Lenin's death in 1924, continued the New Economic Policy until 1928. By the late 1920s, it was realized that Russia would remain the only communist country for some time. This meant that the government had to develop the nation economically without much foreign aid, to direct economic growth to make the U.S.S.R. immune to blockade or military aggression, to improve living standards and to ensure the regime's survival. In late 1927, therefore, Stalin and his colleagues decided to develop the economy according to long-term industrial and agricultural plans.

Stalin's Iron Fist; Khrushchev's Failures

That strategy was implemented by revolutionizing industry and agriculture simultaneously. The first Five-Year Plan, launched in 1928, provided for the rapid development of heavy industry. At the same time, an agrarian reform law called for the collectivization of agriculture. Large collective farms, it was reasoned, would produce more food and require less labor and farmers who were no longer needed could migrate to the cities to

---

[12] Leonard Schapiro, *The Communist Party of the Soviet Union* (1960), p. 192.

work in heavy industry. The first Five-Year Plan was completed in four years but the collectivization drive was calamitous. Soviet agricultural production suffered: between 1928 and 1932, the number of cattle dropped from 70 million to 40 million, the number of pigs from 26 million to 11 million and the number of sheep and goats from 146 million to 52 million.

In the process of industrializing the country, Stalin used threats and brutality to extract the required sacrifices. The German invasion in June 1941 halted whatever hopes he had for rapid industrial or agricultural growth. The fighting that followed laid waste to great stretches of the Soviet Union west of the Urals. Once the most fertile and industrialized part of the country, it was a devastated region at the end of the war. Some 20 million Russians were killed in World War II and, in March 1947, Soviet Foreign Minister Molotov estimated that the destruction amounted to $128 billion, including 32,000 industries.

With the division of Europe and the start of the Cold War, negotiations over Soviet demands for $200 billion in reparations from Germany broke down. But Red Army control of Eastern Europe contributed to the rebuilding of Russian industry. Net Soviet gains from Eastern Europe from 1945 to 1956, including reparations, have been put at $20 billion.[13] Disregarding his country's ravaged condition, Stalin insisted on a policy of rapid industrialization in the early postwar years. The flaws in that policy, including the immeasurable human costs, were many. But the results were impressive. The failures, notably in agriculture, were equally remarkable. Between 1949 and 1953, annual grain production averaged only 10 percent above the 1909-13 output. Nevertheless, by the time Stalin died on March 5, 1953, his iron-fisted policy had transformed the Soviet Union from a backward nation to the world's second most powerful country, politically and economically.

The collective leadership that took power after Stalin's death took steps to alleviate the harshness of certain aspects of Stalin's economic policy. There were reductions in the prices of food and consumer goods and repeated promises of great improvements in living standards. Despite the promotion and cancellation of innumerable new economic programs and continuing agricultural problems, Nikita S. Khrushchev, who had emerged as party leader, told the 21st Party Congress in January 1959 that by 1970 the Soviet Union would outproduce the United States in both total output and on a per capital basis. The early 1960s dashed such hopes. Increased grain output from 1955 to 1958 was not sustained and the industrial

---

[13] Zbigniew Brzezinski, *The Soviet Bloc: Unity and Conflict* (1960), p. 284, fn.

growth rate slowed. On Oct. 15, 1964, it was announced that Khrushchev had been removed from his leadership posts.

The Khrushchev era, despite the unkept promises, did witness an improvement in living standards. The gap between the annual rates of growth for heavy industry and consumer goods narrowed and, by the late 1960s, budgetary increases for consumer goods were, for the first time, larger than those for heavy industry. But as the Soviet economy became stronger and more complex, the system of central controls became more cumbersome and less able to meet the nation's needs. The rapid growth rate attained in the post-World War II years slowed from 6 percent in 1956-60 to 4 percent in 1961-65.

Suggestions for Economic Decentralization

The decline sparked support for changes in the system of centralized economic controls. Under that system, the government promulgated output goals for various sectors of the economy, usually for five-year periods. Government ministries established production goals for each mine, factory and store within a sector and for each type of product. They also fixed the number of workers at each enterprise, determined the suppliers or markets and set prices for the products. More than 30 indexes were established for the local manager; the principal index was the gross value of production, which included the cost of raw materials.

A number of abuses developed within the system. Planners often knew little about the problems and needs of individual enterprises, unrealistic goals were set and scant attention was paid to competing goals between sectors. Bonuses were paid for overfulfilling quotas and, as a result, managers lobbied for low quotas or falsified reports of actual output. Because the major index was the gross value of the product, costly materials were employed wastefully. Consumer desires were ignored since the goal was output rather than sales.

The need to reform the system had been discussed in Soviet economic circles since the late 1940s when Yevsei Liberman, an obscure university professor, proposed using profits instead of the gross value of production as a gauge of industrial efficiency. Liberman's ideas went unnoticed at the time. But as the economic growth rate began declining and as the supply of food and consumer goods became unsatisfactory, his suggestions about economic reform received wide attention when they appeared in *Pravda* in late 1960.

After publication of Liberman's proposals, complaints about the system's inadequacies mounted. Khrushchev suggested that the plan be studied sympathetically; critics charged that the proposal was a form of "creeping capitalism," since it stressed profits and conservation of capital. Liberman and his supporters denied the accusation, arguing that the state still owned all means of production. In mid-1964, the Soviet leadership instituted an experiment in "Libermanism." [14]

The success of this and subsequent experiments paved the way for a reorganization of the economy announced by Premier Aleksei N. Kosygin on Sept. 27, 1965. Kosygin emphasized the need to improve methods of management and outlined two reforms: (1) institution of a percentage charge on invested capital to be paid by enterprises and (2) changes in the type and number of obligatory production targets to be set by the central planning apparatus. An important change was the substitution of indexes based on profit, sales value and output of major commodities for the gross value of output. In addition, a larger share of the profits could be used by local managers for technical improvements or bonus incentives.

These reforms, however, met strong resistance from the more conservative and ideological party leaders who feared the economic and particularly the political consequences of a loss of centralized control. Two days after Kosygin's death on Dec. 18, 1980, *The Washington Post* editorialized: "Mr. Brezhnev, standing for party primary, won and Mr. Kosygin, standing for a modicum of economic sense, lost. They could agree, later, only to try to limit the damage by importing as much Western capital and technology as possible."

Growing Trade With West in Brezhnev Era

The enormous amount of East-West trade that developed during the 1970s seemed beneficial to both sides at the time. The Soviet Union and its satellites needed the food, particularly grain, and technology that they were unable to produce. To some extent, trade with the West made improvements in Soviet living standards possible *(see box, p. 91)*. Despite the slowing down in the rate of growth in the 1960s and particularly in the late 1970s, the gross national product has continued to increase. In 1955, the Soviet GNP was 40 percent of the American; by 1980, it had risen to 60 percent.

In the 1970s, many of the industrialized nations on whom the Soviets depended for imports were experiencing trade deficits and balance of payments problems and the Russians paid promptly for what they bought. Some Americans believed that trade links with Moscow would force the Soviet Union to act with restraint in troubled areas or risk losing the goods and services it so desperately needed. One of the principal architects

---

[14] For details, see "Soviet Economy: Incentives Under Communism, *E.R.R.*, 1966 Vol. II, p. 686.

Indicators of Soviet Living Standards

Indicator	1965	1978
Monthly wage	96.5 rubles	159.9 rubles
Number of doctors	554,000	929,000
Families with TV sets	24 percent	82 percent
Families with refrigerators	11 percent	78 percent
Living space per person, urban areas	10 sq. meters	12.7 sq. meters
Consumption of meat and meat products per person	41 kilograms	57 kilograms
Consumption of vegetables per person	72 kilograms	90 kilograms
Consumption of potatoes per person	142 kilograms	120 kilograms
Consumption of bread and grain per person	156 kilograms	140 kilograms

Source: *Narodnoe Khoziaistvo SSSR v 1978 g., Statisticheskii ezhegodnik* (Moscow: Statistika, 1979).

of linkage and détente, former Secretary of State Henry A. Kissinger, recently described his disillusionment with the way the policy he had once espoused had worked out.

"A decade or so ago, when East-West trade, technology transfer and financial relations began to develop, many believed that economic ties could become an instrument — among others — for moderating Soviet behavior. In a crisis, we thought, the fear of losing markets or access to raw materials, Western technical innovations or bank credits would produce Soviet caution. But this assumption presupposed a Western willingness to use its economic strength in the service of overall strategy. This clearly has not happened. On the contrary, so many Western nations have let themselves become dependent on Soviet trade that a trade cutoff is more likely to turn into a Soviet weapon against the West.[15]

About half of Soviet foreign trade is currently with Eastern Europe and roughly 35 percent with the West. Prices for Soviet goods sold to Eastern Europe are highly subsidized and generally are not paid for in hard currency. Estimates compiled by the Bank for International Settlements found that Moscow borrowed more than $15 billion in 1981, largely to pay for the grain and technology it imported from the West. For the Soviet Union and Eastern Europe, the debt was well over $70 billion.

Moscow's hard-currency problems might have been much worse. Zygmunt Nagorski recently revealed that in 1976 "Soviet leaders convinced their Polish counterparts that it would be in their mutual interest to transact trade in a specially created

---

[15] Writing in *The New York Times*, Jan. 16, 1982.

accounting system and that the Russians should be permitted, even encouraged, to purchase from Poland finished and semi-finished products in exchange for raw materials." This agreement "allowed the Soviet Union to bypass the problem of hard-currency. Using hard-currency received in loans from the West, Poland would purchase licenses, some raw materials, semi-finished products and food from Western suppliers. Poland was then asked to sell a wide range of finished products to the Soviet Union." As a result, the Soviet Union was able to obtain many of the products it needed and would otherwise have been forced to buy with hard currency.[16]

Prospects For Reform

E CONOMIC SANCTIONS against the U.S.S.R. that are both severe and coordinated seem unlikely at this time. U.S. allies defend their refusal to impose a trade and credit freeze by citing their own economic problems and noting that President Reagan has not reimposed an American grain embargo. A Russian seer, however, might conclude that dramatic trade sanctions would be the greatest gift the West could give the Soviet Union. Such action might convince Russian leaders to make the reforms that scores of economists have said are necessary to the well-being or even the survival of the country.

As both industrial and particularly agricultural productivity have declined in recent years, several reforms have been approved. Brezhnev has praised the country's private farms, which with under 3 percent of the agricultural land produce 25 percent of farm output, and taken measures to encourage them. The leadership has improved incentive payments and bonuses to state farms and streamlined the vast agricultural bureaucracy.

There has been considerable debate in recent years about whether the passing of Brezhnev and the ruling gerontocracy will witness a continuation or an intensification of the reforms instituted so far.[17] A new generation, it is argued, will be better educated and more willing to decentralize the stagnant economic system. On the other hand, a marked decentralization and reliance on market forces might tend to lessen the primacy of the Communist Party and the political power and control of the new leaders.

One problem in predicting imminent changes in Soviet eco-

---

[16] Writing in *The Wall Street Journal*, Jan. 8, 1982. Nagorski is the director of executive seminars at the Aspen Institute for Humanistic Studies.
[17] See "Russia After Détente," *E.R.R.*, 1981 Vol. I, pp. 81-104, and "Soviet Leadership Transition," *E.R.R.*, 1979 Vol. II, pp. 603-620.

nomic policy is that there is only speculation about who the new leaders might be or what policies they are likely to adopt. Brezhnev has not designated a successor and may survive many of the Politburo septuagenarians frequently mentioned as his replacement. One school of thought is that whoever replaces Brezhnev will probably serve as an interim leader, dependent on consensus. If so, there is likely to be little radical innovation in domestic policy. But in a society as secretive as the Soviet Union, predictions are, at best, educated guesswork.

Predictions, nonetheless, abound. At one extreme are those like Soviet dissident Andrei Amalrik who, more than a decade ago, forecast that the Soviet Union as a highly centralized state would not survive beyond 1984. In his book "Will the Soviet Union Survive Until 1984?" (1970), Amalrik wrote that "economic hardships, particularly related to food supplies . . . popular dissatisfactions . . . [and] the nationalist tendencies of the non-Russian people" would intensify after the outbreak of a war with China.

William G. Hyland, a senior associate at the Carnegie Endowment, discussed the possible connections between economic problems and foreign policy. "If Soviet leaders are determined to avoid economic reform and experimentation in order to overcome the looming crisis of slow growth and declining productivity, then they will be increasingly under pressure to turn to Europe, the United States and Japan for economic support, credit, trade and technology," Hyland wrote. "This suggests a more conciliatory foreign policy. And if this is unacceptable, then a new leadership will have to contemplate the consequences of a period of economic stringencies that might even weaken the Soviet defense effort. Foreseeing this Soviet crisis, some observers fear that Soviet leaders will be tempted to embark on a foreign adventure." [18]

Philip Hanson presented a more optimistic forecast. He believes that the U.S.S.R. can avoid a dangerous "radical decentralization" by achieving "three elements" of a "minimum satisfactory performance. First, the avoidance of internal discontent about living standards. This might well require, as a minimum, that per capita household consumption should not fall. Secondly, the maintenance of a military effort such that the balance of forces with the West is at least maintained. Thirdly, an economic growth rate such that the ratio of Soviet to American output does not fall. . . . The sorts of growth rates projected by Western analysts for the Soviet economy in the 1980s are not obviously too low to meet our hypothetical minimum demands

---

[18] William G. Hyland, "The Soviet Union and the United States," *Current History,* October 1981, p. 345.

— unless Western economic growth resumes a steady upward movement of well over 3 percent a year." [19]

Worsening Conditions in Eastern Europe

The political and economic crisis in Poland has focused attention on what is often said to be a precarious situation throughout Eastern Europe.[20] While figures vary, some place the combined debt of all Soviet bloc countries to the West at almost $90 billion. But as Wharton Econometric Forecasting Associates pointed out, not all Soviet bloc countries face the same crisis situation that Poland does: "At the end of 1981, our qualitative assessment of the external payments and debt situation is as follows: Bulgaria — satisfactory; Czechoslovakia — satisfactory; East Germany — fair, but should be watched closely; Poland — crisis situation; Romania — critical, but probably manageable; U.S.S.R. — good; Yugoslovia — fair, but should be watched closely." [21]

There have been some efforts to reform the Soviet and East European economies. In addition to a host of consumer price increases for its own people, Moscow has raised the costs of its raw materials and reduced the amount it makes available to most of Eastern Europe. On Feb. 1, Poland's military government instituted price increases of up to 400 percent on food, energy and consumer goods. Economic reform has been carried further in Hungary than in any other Soviet bloc country. Some 55 percent of its trade is currently with the West and managers and workers have considerable autonomy.

Hungary's "goulash communism" has helped make it the Eastern bloc's most prosperous member, but its decentralization is strictly limited to economic matters. Hungarian leaders have been careful not to provoke the Soviet Union by granting political concessions. Censorship is strictly enforced and criticism of the Communist Party is suppressed. The Hungarian case seems to indicate that Moscow will tolerate a certain amount of "capitalist" innovation as long as it is divorced from political concessions. The separation, however, is difficult to maintain. What began as economic discontent and soon developed into political revolt spurred either overt or covert Soviet intervention in East Germany in 1953, Hungary in 1956, Czechoslovakia in 1968 and Poland in 1981.

It has become almost a truism to assert that Eastern Europe

---

[19] "Economic Constraints on Soviet Policy in the 1980s," *International Affairs*, winter 1980-81, pp. 33, 30. Hanson is a Reader in Soviet Economics at the Center for East European Studies, University of Birmingham, U.K.
[20] For background on the situation in Poland, see "Agriculture: Key to Poland's Future," *E.R.R.*, 1981 Vol. II, pp. 837-856.
[21] Wharton Econometric Forecasting Associates, "East European and Soviet Hard Currency Trade and Debt in 1981," Jan. 7, 1982.

Eastern Europe's Net Hard-Currency Debt to the West**

(in billion current U.S. dollars)

	1970	1975	1980	1981*	1985*
Bulgaria	0.7	2.1	2.7	2.6	4.0-5.0
Czechoslovakia	0.6	1.2	3.4	3.5	5.0-6.0
Hungary	0.6	2.3	7.0	7.7	10.0-11.0
Poland	1.1	7.7	21.9	22.0	31.0-35.0
Romania	1.6	3.1	9.0	10.8	19.0-21.0
East Germany	1.4	4.8	11.8	13.0	18.0-20.0
USSR	1.0	7.8	9.6	14.0	30.0-35.0
CMEA banks***	0.3	2.2	4.1	3.9	6.0-7.0
Yugoslavia	1.9	5.7	16.8	18.0	25.0-28.0
Eastern Europe and USSR total	9.2	36.9	86.3	95.5	148.0-168.0

* Forecast
** Net hard-currency debt to the West is defined as gross hard-currency debt to Western banks (including most of the debt owed to Middle Eastern and LDC banks whenever data are available), Western governments, and international financial organizations (IMF and the World Bank, in the case of Romania) minus CMEA deposits in Western banks.
*** Two multinational banks owned by the Council for Mutual Economic Assistance, which includes Russia and all Eastern European countries except Yugoslavia.

Source: Centrally Planned Economies Service, Wharton Econometric Forecasting Associates.

represents an increasing economic liability to the Soviet Union. But Peter Summerscale argues that, for Moscow, the economic costs must be balanced by the political benefits. "It would be misleading to suggest that, overall, Eastern Europe has necessarily become a liability to the Soviet Union," he wrote. "The continuing strategic benefit represented by the area would alone cast doubt on so sweeping a conclusion. However, it can certainly be postulated that the benefits are now much less clearcut than 10 or 15 years ago. In the military field, recent events have raised new question marks about the security of Soviet supply lines and the reliability of Warsaw Pact forces. In the economic sphere, despite a degree of natural complementarity, benefits are balanced by increasing costs to the Soviet Union." [22]

Perhaps the most important question facing the Soviet leadership is whether to insist on control over Eastern Europe, despite the growing economic, military and propagandistic costs, or to allow a kind of Finlandization or limited neutralization of the area. Brezhnev and other Soviet leaders have insisted that they intend to maintain the present borders, even if it

[22] Peter Summerscale, "Is Eastern Europe a Liability to the Soviet Union?" *International Affairs*, autumn 1981, p. 579. Summerscale is a Counselor in Great Britain's Diplomatic Service.

means a world war. But one expert maintains that Moscow's control over Eastern Europe is already in danger. "For the first time, legitimate communist governments willing to seek autonomy from the Kremlin might take power through an orderly political process," Dimitri K. Simes wrote last year.[23]

Accusations of U.S. Revival of Cold War

The Russians have responded to American furor over Poland and to President Reagan's determination to increase U.S. defense spending in predictable fashion. The Soviet news agency Tass declared on Dec. 30 that the sanctions imposed after the declaration of martial law in Poland were an attempt "to haul the world back to the dark times of the cold war." The Kremlin accused the United States of violating the 1945 Yalta Agreement, which gave the Soviet Union certain rights in Eastern Europe, and the 1975 Helsinki Accords, which accepted the division of Europe. These accusations fail to mention that the Russians never allowed the holding of free elections that were promised for Eastern Europe at Yalta or that the Final Act at Helsinki pledged the 35 signatories not only to accept the division of Europe but to respect and promote human rights and fundamental freedoms.

Soviet motives for the current propaganda barrage are obvious. One is certainly to prepare the Russian people for more sacrifice and greater scarcity that increased defense spending will entail. By painting the United States as intent upon destroying the country, the leaders are able to play upon the deep psychological fears of the Russian people. Another reason is to portray the United States as the villain in destroying détente and delaying arms control negotiations.[24] To many Europeans and a few Americans, the Reagan administration's insistence on huge defense increases to counter the perceived Soviet threat is both simplistic and counterproductive. Any large-scale American buildup, they insist, has been and always will be matched by the Kremlin, no matter what sacrifices must be made.

In view of the serious domestic economic problems facing the U.S.S.R. and the growing cost of countering reform in Eastern Europe, threats from a China that may move closer to the

---

[23] Dimitri K. Simes, "Disciplining Soviet Power," *Foreign Policy*, summer 1981, pp. 45-46. Simes is executive director of the Soviet and Eastern European Research Program at the School of Advanced International Studies, Johns Hopkins University.

[24] In a column in *The Washington Post* on Feb. 5, 1982, Stephen S. Rosenfeld argued that "notwithstanding Afghanistan, notwithstanding Poland, notwithstanding the Caribbean, economic détente generally is on track. Europe insists on buying Soviet gas. The United States keeps shipping Moscow grain. The West's bankers want to keep the ties that may eventually save their East-bloc loans. American scientists pine for exchanges. The Soviets find an American to give a ballet prize to. Evidence of the hardiness of détente is embarrassingly pervasive and strong."

United States and foreign involvements elsewhere, there have been proposals for economic measures to contain the Kremlin. An editorial in *The New York Times* on Feb. 2, 1982, discussed the possibility of declaring the Soviet bloc in default on its colossal debt to the West: "In the back of every banker's mind has been the thought that the Kremlin was good for the entire $70 billion lent to communist countries in recent years. If America now insists that the most brutal Soviet methods will not be condoned in the service of this debt, then it has to employ the only significant leverage at hand: make the Russians pay for the luxury of their tyranny." The problem is that the United States cannot do it alone and Washington's allies have shown little inclination to go along with such a move.

It can be argued that economic pressure, like military pressure, can be sustained and that the Soviet Union will suffer the necessary sanctions rather than back down. It can also be argued that if economic or military pressures become unbearable, Moscow could well strike out with the only means at its disposal: military and nuclear might. History has many examples of how weakened or severely challenged nations choose war or foreign adventure to divert their people's attention or to obtain what they could not procure otherwise.

Selected Bibliography

Books

Bialer, Seweryn, *Stalin's Successors: Leadership, Stability and Change in the Soviet Union*, Cambridge University Press, 1980.

Bornstein, Morris, Zvi Gitelman and William Zimmerman (eds.), *East-West Relations and the Future of Eastern Europe*, Allen & Unwin, 1981.

Goldman, Marshall I., *The Enigma of Soviet Petroleum*, Allen & Unwin, 1980.

Hanson, Philip, *Trade and Technology in Soviet-Western Relations*, Columbia University Press, 1981.

Hough, Jerry F. and Merle Fainsod, *How the Soviet Union is Governed*, Harvard University Press, 1980.

Katsenelinboigen, Aron, *Soviet Economic Thought and Political Power in the USSR*, Pergamon, 1980.

Millar, James R., *The ABCs of Soviet Socialism: The Soviet Economic Experiment*, University of Illinois Press, 1980.

Moore, John (ed.), *The Soviet Union*, Congressional Quarterly, forthcoming.

Pierre, Andrew J., *The Global Politics of Arms Sales*, Princeton University Press, 1982.

Spulber, Nicholas, *Organizational Alternatives in Soviet-Type Economics*, Cambridge University Press, 1979.

Articles

Foreign Affairs, selected issues.

Foreign Policy, selected issues.

Hanson, Philip, "Economic Constraints on Soviet Policies in the 1980s," *International Affairs*, winter 1980-81.

Hough, Jerry F., "Soviet Perspectives," *The Brookings Bulletin*, winter 1981.

"The Soviet Union, 1981," *Current History*, October 1981.

Summerscale, Peter, "Is Eastern Europe a Liability to the Soviet Union," *International Affairs*, autumn 1981.

Reports and Studies

Department of Defense, "Annual Report, Fiscal Year 1983," Feb. 8, 1982; "Soviet Military Power," October 1981.

Department of State, "Soviet and Soviet-Proxy Involvement in Poland," January 1982.

Editorial Research Reports: "Agriculture: Key to Poland's Future," 1981 Vol. II, p. 839; "MX Missile Decision," 1981 Vol. I, p. 411; "Russia After Détente," 1981 Vol. I, p. 83; "Soviet Economy: Incentives Under Communism," 1966 Vol. II, p. 863; "Soviet Leadership Transition," 1979 Vol. II, p. 603; "Trading With Communist Nations," 1972 Vol. I, p. 197.

International Monetary Fund, "World Economic Outlook," June 1981.

Joint Economic Committee, "Consumption in the USSR: An International Comparison," Aug. 17, 1981.

Wharton Econometric Forecasting Associates, selected studies.

Cover by Staff Artist Robert Redding;
illustrations on p. 93 and p. 107 by George Rebh.

European
WELFARE STATES
UNDER ATTACK

by

**David Fouquet
and Hoyt Gimlin**

**April 17
1 9 8 1**

Editor's Note: Since this Report was written, France has elected a Socialist government and West Germany a conservative government. But the basic economic conditions described in the Report still prevail in both countries and through Western Europe generally, causing further squeezes on social welfare programs.

In West Germany, for instance, the great postwar prosperity has continued to slip away and is credited with influencing the political decision to turn Chancellor Helmut Schmidt out of office last fall and give his successor, Helmut Kohl, a national election victory March 8.

At the time of the election, the unemployment rate was running as high as America's and inflation was twice as high. In neighboring Holland, another model of postwar prosperity until recent years, the jobless rate was almost 15 percent. In France, where the Socialist government of President François Mitterrand took office in the spring of 1981, voter discontent has remained unchecked. The country's continued economic slippage was at least a sizable factor in his party's losses, March 1983 in municipal elections.

In Britain, Prime Minister Margaret Thatcher's austerity policies remain essentially in tact. And though they have not returned prosperity to the country, her popularity has risen — in recognition of her leadership in the country's victorious conflict with Argentina over the Falkland Islands. Britain, which had pegged much of its future revenue to North Sea oil, is expected to suffer with other oil-exporting countries by the decline in world oil prices.

EUROPEAN WELFARE STATES
UNDER ATTACK

WITH economies stagnating and unemployment at postwar highs, most of the Western European governments are facing hard and frequently unpopular decisions about austerity — extending even to the dismantling of some parts of their once-sacrosanct social-welfare programs. Virtually all of these countries are calling into question social-welfare standards that took decades to develop and that have successfully defused social discontent in the past.

Faced with rising bills for such programs as unemployment aid, family services and old-age pensions, the governments are looking for ways to limit the traditional patterns of growth in public services. In Europe these programs are far more advanced than in the United States, where President Reagan is engaged in a similar exercise of cutting social-welfare budgets. How well, or badly, Europe manages to reduce public spending without tearing the fabric of society may hold significant lessons for the United States. Reagan's economic course of action has already been compared, in its general thrust, to that which Prime Minister Margaret Thatcher instituted in Britain nearly two years ago.

Experts from the 24 major Western, mostly European, industrial nations belonging to the Organization for Economic Cooperation and Development (OECD) met in Paris last October to examine the strains that a faltering world economy had placed on their welfare states. An official report on the meeting noted that social-welfare spending in those countries averaged 25 percent of the gross national product — the sum of all spending on goods and services — and 60 percent of total public spending. "It is tempting in these circumstances to call for a moratorium on social development and indeed governments appear to be trying to limit the growth of public expenditure on a case-by-case basis," the report said. "There can be little doubt that OECD countries are in a welfare crunch."[1]

---

[1] Report published in the organization's publication, *OECD Observer*, November 1980. The OECD was established by an international treaty signed in Paris in 1960 "to promote . . . economic growth and employment and a rising standard of living in member countries . . . and contribute to the development of the world economy." Member countries are Autralia, Austria, Belgium, Britain, Canada, Denmark, Finland, France, West Germany, Greece, Icelnd, Ireland, Italy, Japan, Luxembourg, the Netherlands, New Zealand, Norway, Portugal, Spain, Sweden, Switzerland, Turkey and the United States.

This crunch began in the years following the first international oil crisis in 1973-74. As oil prices rose fourfold, oil-dependent Europe was especially hard hit. The "economic miracle" of the 1950s and 1960s began to evaporate. Inflation and unemployment burst upon the scene, pricking the bubble of prosperity and social progress that had been taken almost for granted in Europe for nearly two decades. Feeling the pinch, governments began to nibble away at some of the ingredients of their elaborate welfare systems.

Cutbacks, Tax Revolts on the Continent

One of the first to become unmanageable was the system of cost-of-living indexation, which automatically linked wages and benefits to rising consumer costs in various countries. An early example of this type of rollback occurred in Belgium. A drought in the mid-1970s shot up the price of potatoes, a daily staple in the Belgian diet. The lowly spud was one of the main components of the national cost-of-living index on which nearly all salaries and benefits were based. Finally the government stepped in to lessen the weight of potato prices in the index calculations. A similar event took place in Denmark when the socialist-led government in Copenhagen was forced to remove inexorably rising energy costs from the consumer index to keep wages and other index-linked expenses under control.

In addition, European governments have been shelving plans for new and innovative social benefits. Two noteworthy victims during the late 1970s were national profit-sharing systems being planned for workers in the Netherlands and Denmark. Already hotly contested by employers and political conservatives, those proposals were expediently dropped by their government sponsors — although the Danish government has hesitantly begun toying with the idea again in recent months. Except in West Germany, a similar fate awaited plans for extending existing rules that require worker participation in the decision-making of some industrial companies. "Co-determination," as it is called, is legally mandated in Austria, Denmark, Luxembourg, the Netherlands, Norway and West Germany, its birthplace. Germany, unlike the other countries, expanded co-determination last year.[2]

Political shifts in some European countries have produced what has been called, perhaps prematurely, "the demise of the welfare state." A mini-revolt among Danish taxpayers in 1973 shook the established political and social system there *(see p. 122)*. Upheavals also took place in two of the other main testing

[2] For background, see "Collective Bargaining and Employee Participation in Western Europe, North America and Japan," a report by the Trilateral Commission, 345 E. 46th St., New York, N.Y. 10017. The report was based on a meeting of experts under Trilateral Commission auspices, in Washington, D.C., June 11-13, 1978.

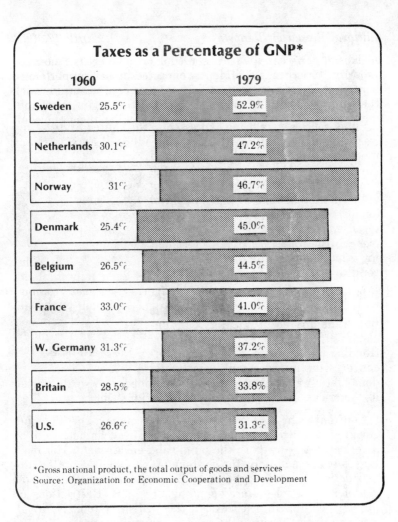

Taxes as a Percentage of GNP*

	1960	1979
Sweden	25.5%	52.9%
Netherlands	30.1%	47.2%
Norway	31%	46.7%
Denmark	25.4%	45.0%
Belgium	26.5%	44.5%
France	33.0%	41.0%
W. Germany	31.3%	37.2%
Britain	28.5%	33.8%
U.S.	26.6%	31.3%

*Gross national product, the total output of goods and services
Source: Organization for Economic Cooperation and Development

grounds for the welfare state, in Sweden in 1976 and in the Netherlands in 1972-73 and again in 1977. In both countries, socialist governments were toppled by conservative-minded voters; in the case of Sweden, the upset came after 44 years of uninterrupted socialist rule *(see p. 122)*. In country after country, election results reflected a discernible change of mood toward more fiscal restraint and reduced welfare spending.

'Thatcherism': Britain's Ideological Shift

The ideological shift was arguably the most pronounced in Britain. The Conservative Party victory at the polls in May 1979 ousted the Labor government of Prime Minister James Callaghan and put Margaret Thatcher in office. "Just as the British Labor Party in 1945 was watched throughout the Western world as the first full-blooded practitioner of democratic socialism," *The Economist* observed shortly before the election, "so Mrs. Thatcher is confidently expected by her supporters to become the first Tory prime minister to succeed in turning back that process begun in 1945. . . ."

Similar views were being expressed in the United States. Only weeks after the election, the managing editor of *Foreign Policy* magazine wrote: "Already pundits and partisans in America are citing the Conservatives' victory as a turning point in the history of the industrial democracies, a sign that noble Western (even American) ideals have prevailed over hostile forces, setting a precedent for other nations in a similarly woeful condition."[3]

Ben J. Wattenberg, co-editor of *Public Opinion* magazine, said that "for the first time in recent memory, an unashamed, unapologetic, non-center-trending party of the ideological right-center won an election in a social

Margaret Thatcher

democratic welfare state." It was, he added, "no small matter; its American and international implications will be great."[4]

Confronted by a steadily worsening economy, the Thatcher government introduced a host of remedies characterized by severe austerity for both the public and government. Her main targets were not only the system of nationalized, often unproductive, industries erected by Labor governments, but also a complex of social-welfare spending programs. Restrictions on public spending ripped through the British system. Nationalized companies began to be sold to private investors; subsidies and other financial assistance to businesses and individuals were significantly cut back.

Local governments received far less money to provide council (public) housing, run the schools, underwrite free-milk programs and finance a large number of similar services. Despite some relief to the British economy from North Sea oil discoveries, the government was convinced that it could not continue to fund many programs at their traditional levels and at the same time help sustain 2.5 million unemployed workers.

Americans have been asking for nearly two years if "Thatcherism" represents the wave of the future in their own

³ Sanford J. Ungar, "Dateline Britain: Thatcherism," *Foreign Policy*, summer 1979, p. 181.
⁴ Ben J. Wattenberg, "Uncle Jim and the Iron Lady," *Public Opinion*, June-July 1979, p. 47. Wattenberg is a senior fellow at the American Enterprise Institute in Washington, D.C.

country. The question became especially pertinent with Ronald Reagan's election victory last November, for Mrs. Thatcher's campaign promises in 1978-79 resembled his in 1979-80 — to eliminate waste, reduce welfare rolls, trim the bureaucracy, cut public spending and restore national confidence. However, well before Reagan came into office it had become apparent that Thatcher's cures for the ailing British economy had not begun to work. In the 18 months between her election and Reagan's, both inflation and unemployment rose in Britain, creating the deepest recession and the highest level of joblessness since the 1930s.[5] With apparent understatement, economist Herbert Stein, a political conservative who was chief economic adviser to Presidents Nixon and Ford, pronounced her efforts a "disappointment."[6]

Although Reagan greeted the British prime minister warmly when she paid an official visit to Washington in February, administration officials went to some lengths to try to divorce his economic program from hers in the public mind. News reporters were reminded of the great differences between the two countries and their economies. Nevertheless, political columnist David Broder observed, "her presence is a reminder to President Reagan and the nation that good intentions do not always produce desired results." Rep. James R. Jones, D-Okla., chairman of the House Budget Committee, suggested that the president and prime minister should have met in London, for there "the president would see the future and judge whether it indeed works."[7]

Germany's Vanishing 'Economic Miracle'

For at least two decades, economists have looked to West Germany — and Japan — to see how the future was working. With this in mind, *Fortune* writer David B. Tinnin commented recently: "For Americans who have long regarded the West German economy as a model of efficiency, it will come as a distinct shock to learn that the land of the economic miracle has suddenly and unexpectedly tumbled into serious difficulties." Unemployment reached 1.3 million this year, nearly 6 percent of the work force, the highest level since 1954. And for the first time since its founding in 1949, "the country faces the prospect of prolonged negative growth and declining real personal incomes."[8]

---

[5] The inflation rate was 10.1 percent and the unemployment rate 5.5 percent when she entered office; in November 1980, inflation was up to 15 percent and unemployment 8.5 percent. Since then inflation has declined to about 13 percent but joblessness remains at about the same level.

[6] Writing in *The Wall Street Journal*, Feb. 25, 1981.

[7] Jones and Broder were writing, separately, in *The Washington Post*, Feb. 25, 1981.

[8] David B. Tinnin, "The Miracle Economy Hits the Skids," *Fortune*, April 20, 1981, p. 137.

Though the reasons for the economic decline are admittedly "complex," the magazine left no doubt that a basic cause was an expansion of social benefits under the Social Democratic rule of Chancellor Willy Brandt (1969-74), Helmut Schmidt's predecessor. "Brandt eagerly began to expand the welfare state," Tinnin wrote. "The catch was that he did it when Germany was at the zenith of its economic success. So the social safety net, as Brandt liked to call it, was woven with scant regard for the staggering future cost of well-intentioned largess."

Willy Brandt

More than one-third of the federal budget now goes for social programs. The entire 1981 budget of $106 billion is twice as high as a decade earlier, and only a small part of the increase can be attributed to inflation. Germany, still remembering the horror of a runaway inflation after World War I, has done a better job of keeping it under control than any other Western industrial nation.[9]

In the Netherlands, whose welfare system is older than West Germany's and comparable to those of Scandinavian countries, welfare outlays account for 30 percent of this year's $150 billion national budget. Efforts to reduce the level of welfare spending have been blocked in the States General (parliament). "Everyone agrees to the welfare state, but not on how to pay for it," said Wim Kok, head of the Dutch Labor Federation. "We are in the middle of a choice on how to divide a pie that is no longer getting bigger."[10]

The Belgian government collapsed at the beginning of April over the same kind of economic problems besetting all Western European countries. Belgium's aging industries, hard hit by recession, were pushing unemployment toward 10 percent and adding to the cost of maintaining generous jobless benefits and other social services. Industrial wages in Belgium are among the highest in the world. The federal budget has been running a deficit since 1978 and this year is expected to reach $5.8 billion, more than double last year's $2.6 billion. Wilfried Martens resigned after two years as prime minister when socialists and

---

[9] The West German cost-of-living early this year was running at nearly 6 percent above the comparable 1980 period — high by German standards. Chancellor Schmidt's Christian Democratic government — returned to office in a resounding election victory last May 11 — seeks to reduce inflation to 4 percent for the year. But a new round of bargaining with German trade unions is in the offing and the trend-setting Metal Workers' Union is demanding 8 percent. For a study of German inflation in the 1920s, see *The Penniless Billionaires* (1981) by Max Shapiro.

[10] Quoted in *Time*, Jan. 12, 1981, p. 32.

labor unions blocked his package of austerity measures. King Baudouin asked Finance Minister Marc Eyskens, of Martens' Flemish Social Christian Party, to form a new government.

Even in France, where the government contributes less to the welfare system than in some neighboring countries, rising costs — especially for medical benefits — are contributing to an expected deficit of $5.3 billion in the national budget this year. The cost of providing French social services rose fourfold in the past decade, to $124 billion last year. While most of these services are paid by employers and employees, the expense threatens to undermine the welfare system. It has become an issue in the French presidential election, scheduled for April 26, and May 10 if a runoff is necessary. The rises have occurred despite the efforts of President Valéry Giscard d'Estaing's austerity-minded premier, Raymond Barre. Giscard is opposed in the election by Socialist leader François Mitterand and several minor candidates.

The Scandinavian Laboratory

ALTHOUGH its roots reach back to medieval times, the modern concept of the welfare state celebrated its 100th anniversary this year. Its birth is placed by most social historians, incongruously enough, in the autocratic Germany of Bismarck, who visualized it as a way of ensuring social stability. "One who can look forward to an old-age pension," the Iron Chancellor observed, "is far more contented and much easier to manage."[11] This was one of his preoccupations since he had just outlawed the Socialist Party and had to give something in return.

Initially, the system was aimed at protecting industrial workers against loss of income resulting from accidents and old age. Health insurance was added to the list of benefits in 1881, and by 1889 the complete structure of Bismarckian social insurance was in place. It established a pattern which was, in time, to be emulated to some degree by every modern industrial society, especially in Western Europe.

While state-supported social welfare was originally conceived by a political conservative as a calculated instrument in mass control rather than as a social reform, it was seized upon, adopted, enlarged and closely identified with socialist or popu-

---

[11] Quotation cited by Anthony King, professor of government at the University of Essex, writing in *The Times* of London, Feb. 23, 1981.

list reform governments. But whether instituted by regimes of the left or right, such welfare programs have become effective means of improving living and working conditions, and also of limiting unrest.

The welfare state has become a catchall term for all types of social services linked to "cradle to grave" state benefits. These were first granted by Scandinavian countries beginning in the 1930s. Since World War II, nearly all Western European countries have embraced most, if not all, of the various benefits pioneered by their northern neighbors — Sweden, Denmark and Norway, and also by the Netherlands.

Scandinavia's Pioneering Welfare States

The "point of departure" in a historical examination of the welfare state, writes American political scientist John Logue, "is the Scandinavian experience, for Denmark, Norway and Sweden are welfare states par excellence." Since American journalist Marquis Childs popularized the Swedish experiment in 1936 with his book *Sweden: The Middle Way,* that country in particular has been regarded as a laboratory of social change. The "middle way" is a fusion of capitalism and socialism which rejects the extremes of both. Logue contends that since the Scandinavian countries have not been plagued by separatist movements, urban terrorists, racial divisions, or ethnic and linguistic strife, "their politics have been able to focus on the central issues of the welfare state — economic production, distribution, and security."[12]

While the welfare state drew support from a variety of sources, its main strength was the Social Democratic labor movement. This movement departed from the orthodox socialist view that the abolition of poverty had to be accompanied by a redistribution of property from the wealthy few to the masses. Preaching that capitalism and welfare for the working people were not hopelessly incompatible, Social Democrats succeeded in taking power in Denmark in 1929, Sweden in 1932 and Norway in 1935, and in holding it — although failing to do so elsewhere in Europe.[13]

In several other countries, including Britain and the United States, the economic trials of the Depression Thirties were straining the social fabric and preparing the political climate for welfare measures to come. The U.S. Congress in 1935 enacted the nation's original Social Security law at President Roo-

[12] John Logue, "The Welfare State: Victim of Its Success," *Daedalus* (journal of the American Academy of Arts and Sciences), fall 1979, p. 69. Logue is assistant professor of political science at Kent State University.
[13] An important exception was Vienna, where Austrian Social Democrats in the 1930s constructed a model welfare system when they were denied power nationally.

sevelt's urging — in response, it has been suggested, to far more radical "share-the-wealth" notions being advanced by Sen. Huey Long, D-La., and Francis Everett Townsend's old folks' clubs in California.[14] The British welfare state was born at the end of World War II and resembled others arising in Europe, while in the United States programs grew piecemeal under the New Deal, New Frontier and Great Society but fell short of European-style "womb to tomb" security.

Development of the Swedish 'Middle Way'

The two great architects of the Swedish welfare state were Per Albin Hansson and Ernst Wigforss, an odd couple in every way except their mutual commitment to the "middle way." Childs described Hansson as sturdy and plainspoken, "in every appearance a typical working-class Swede," who in his years as prime minister rode a streetcar to work. Wigforss, an intellectual and ideologue from the University of Lund faculty, became finance minister in Hansson's Cabinet and held the post from 1932 to 1949, the years in which the Swedish welfare state was fashioned and came into full flower.

Wigforss was an early believer in Keynesian economics, a brand expounded by the English theorist John Maynard Keynes (1883-1946), which called for public spending and government intervention to stimulate the Depression-ridden economies of nations throughout the world. The Swedish Social Democrats' goal of full employment fit Keynesian theory, as did welfare-related measures for reviving consumer demand. Wigforss also drew on the thinking of Gunnar Myrdal, the distinguished Swede who years later (1977) received the Nobel Prize for economics and is perhaps best known in the United States for his classic study of American race relations in the 1940s.[15]

Childs, who returned to Sweden for a new look at the "middle way," charted its post-1930s path in a sequel to his first book, tellingly titled *Sweden: The Middle Way on Trial* (1980). The added words "on trial" are descriptive of the book's thesis but they pertain to a relatively recent situation, one that has gained world attention only since the mid-1970s. In tracing the Swedish welfare state from its infancy to postwar maturity, Childs observed — as others had — how dependent it had become on continuous economic prosperity.

---

[14] Townsend, a physician and social reformer, developed the "Townsendites" into a formidable political pressure group. His "Townsend Plan," repeatedly proposed but blocked in Congress, envisioned a $200 a month pension for everyone over age 60. One condition was that the entire amount had to be spent within the month.

[15] Gunnar Myrdal, *An American Dilemma: The Negro Problem and Democracy*, a two-volume study for the Carnegie Corporation, published in 1944.

The Uruguayan Example

The premier welfare state is not in Europe but in South America. It is tiny Uruguay (pop. 2.9 million; area 68,548 square miles). Endowed with rich farmland, nearly universal literacy and a stable democracy, Uruguay was once known as the "Switzerland of South America." Since the mid-1950s, however, the country has been ravaged by mounting deficits, inflation, unemployment and political instability.

The plethora of social-welfare programs cannot be held entirely responsible for Uruguay's current plight. A weak central government, disastrous economic planning and a protectionist trade stance did their part. But there is little doubt about the ruinous effects of the extensive social programs and a bloated bureaucracy.

Uruguay's "cradle-to-grave" security started in the second presidential term of José Batlle y Ordóñez (1911-15). Batlle, often called the father of modern Uruguay, established a comprehensive social security system, including paid retirement, health care, housing loans and state-subsidized institutions. The state took charge of utility services, transportation and moved into such private-sector areas as banking and even meatpacking and hotel management.

Over the years, the Uruguayan system grew out of control. Including employment at state corporations, one-third of the work force was on the public payroll. At one time, Pluna, the state-owned airline, had 3,000 employees and only three airplanes. Three-fourths of the chronically deficit-ridden national budget went to paying salaries and rescuing social-welfare funds from bankruptcy.

For the past eight years, under military rule, the government has restored some — but not enough — fiscal health to the country. Bureaucratic corruption is still endemic and the country's foreign deficits are still high.

—Richard C. Schroeder

Immediately after World War II, he said, the Social Democratic left wing as directed by Wigforss and Myrdal formulated a 27-point program that, while not following orthodox Marxist tenets, went a considerable way in the direction of the nationalization of basic industries and credit institutions such as banks and insurance companies. This touched off an intense debate crossing party lines, but was rendered academic by a swift rise in prosperity. Unlike its European neighbors, Sweden came out of World War II with its neutrality and its industry intact, giving the country a distinct advantage in international trade. Its high technology, iron ore and forest products were all in demand as the rest of Europe recovered.

"There seemed no reason prosperity would not continue into the indefinite future," Childs wrote. "It was perhaps with the illusion that this prosperity would be sustained that the Social Democratic government, with little or no opposition from the right-of-center parties, adopted a series of welfare measures that, together with rising taxes, sharply increased the cost of industrial production and put a heavy burden on taxpayers in the middle-income brackets."[16]

Sweden's Benefits and the Taxpayers' Price

State-supplied security includes a general family allowance for children under age 16, who each year receive $400 not subject to taxation. They also receive dental and medical care regardless of family income. Working parents pay for nursery care on the basis of their earnings. As for education, tuition is free, even in college and postgraduate studies. Students receive free meals in school from kindergarten through high school, and at age 16 become eligible for a $30 a month allowance. Marriage and maternity benefits include home-furnishing loans and free advice on contraception and abortion at maternity centers. Beginning 60 days before the birth of a child and for 210 days afterward, one parent — either one — draws a cash benefit.

There are also state rent allowances for families, with and without children, and for single persons. In addition, aid services for the aged and handicapped are free for those who cannot pay and are adjusted to income for others. An official guide to the comprehensive national health insurance benefits fills 23 pages; a national pension plan offers generous benefits to the retired and disabled.

The Riksdag (parliament) in 1978 enacted a law guaranteeing a minimum of five weeks of paid vacation. By this time the Swede was the highest paid worker in Europe, perhaps in the world.[17] Through the 1973-74 oil crisis, profits continued to increase for Swedish industry, which remained temporarily immune to the gathering global recession. So sizable wage increases followed.

But as oil imports cut harder into the national budget, complaints about taxes grew louder. Many people in the middle-income brackets were paying over half of their earnings in taxes. In the spring of 1975 the major political parties jointly held a conference on taxation and spoke of the possibility that a self-employed professional person earning $40,000 or more a year might have to pay the entire amount in taxes. This turned out to be a mistake, it subsequently developed in parliamentary

---

[16] *The Middle Way on Trial*, p. 44.
[17] The average hourly pay for an adult male in Sweden was $8.50 in 1975, according to OECD statistics. U.S. hourly pay, by contrast, was $7. The Swedes, along with the Belgians and West Germans, still have the highest pay scales in Europe.

debate, but — as Childs observed — "the damage had been done."

Swedish taxes drew even wider attention in another incident at about the same time. Ingmar Bergman, the film director, was hauled off a rehearsal stage by tax police and taken into a court of inquiry on charges of tax evasion. Swedish authorities dropped the charges a few months later, but the publicity set off an emotional debate in the press and in Parliament. Bergman subsequently left his native land vowing never to return.

Political Shiftings in Sweden and Denmark

By now, 1976, the economy was showing signs of distress and national elections were approaching. Sweden had suddenly developed nagging doubts about the welfare-state philosophies it had lived under for four decades. The voters were also troubled and divided by the government's espousal of nuclear power as a way of overcoming the country's lack of oil fields. The voting that September left the Social Democrats without enough seats in Parliament to run the government. Bowing out after 44 years, they were replaced by a coalition of parties headed by Thorbjorn Falldin, a sheep farmer who fiercely opposed nuclear development.

A similar tax protest had occurred three years earlier in Denmark. Danish voters in December 1973 swept out a Social Democratic government, disrupting a long and stable pattern of Danish party politics. In that election, every fourth voter cast a ballot for one of two new anti-tax parties. The larger of the two (the Progress Party) was led by a maverick tax lawyer, Morgan Glistrup, who became a celebrity by declaring on television that he had paid no income taxes. Nor, he suggested, should any other reasonably intelligent Dane. The defection from traditional parties gave several political groupings, such as Glipstrup's, representation in the Folketing (parliament) for the first time.

In this new situation, no political alignment was able to retain control of the government for long. National elections followed in January 1975, February 1977 and October 1979. Each time a minority government fell there was lack of agreement on how to impose austerity measures. Norway, like Denmark, has gone through successive changes of government — five in the past decade — but unlike Denmark and Sweden, its economy has been cushioned by the discovery of oil in the North Sea. While Norway's income from oil and gas production has made it one of the world's most affluent nations and at least postponed a welfare-state crisis, it has not spared Norway a high rate of inflation and related economic problems.

Britain's Postwar Experience

WHEN the history of the second half of the 20th century is written, the fact that OECD countries achieved full employment and the Welfare State in the 1950s and 1960s will certainly be hailed as evidence of a successful combination of economic and social policies." With that preface, OECD Secretary-General Emile van Lennep made clear that he, in common with most Europeans, considered the welfare state one of mankind's blessings. It has been observed that only in the United States does the phrase "welfare state" have a bad odor.

But van Lennep acknowledged that setbacks to economic growth in the 1970s brought social and economic policies into conflict. "In the 1980s," he went on to say, "it is essential for our political and economic systems to re-establish our conviction that economic and social progress are part of the same process in liberal societies."[18]

According to John Logue, the welfare state is a victim of its successes, not its failures. "It has succeeded in banishing the specter of material deprivation through illness, loss of employment, disability, and old age that haunted past generations," he wrote. "But abolition of the threat has also abolished the fear it engendered. . . . For the present generation, the welfare system is the status quo, not a monument to the courage, ingenuity, luck, compromises, and (perhaps) brilliance of its pioneers."[19]

In Europe, aside from Scandinavia, it was World War II that gave the welfare state its great impetus because, Logue wrote, "wartime sacrifices demanded recompense." Roosevelt and Churchill enshrined freedom from want in the pantheon of Allied values,[20] and the British government's Committee on Social Insurance and Allied Services, under the chairmanship of William Beveridge, turned the welfare state into a war goal. Its report,[21] proclaiming at the height of the war that "the object of government . . . is the happiness of the common man," became the blueprint for the basic social welfare system that a new Labor government put into effect immediately after the war.

So eager were the British for their promised benefits that in

---

[18] Emile van Lennep, "From the Welfare State to the Welfare Society," *OECD Observer*, November 1980, p. 19.

[19] Logue, *op. cit.*, p. 85.

[20] In proposing lend-lease legislation to Congress, Jan. 6, 1941, President Roosevelt said Four Freedoms should prevail everywhere: freedom of speech and expression; of worship; and from want and fear. These were included in the Atlantic Charter of postwar peace aims which Roosevelt and Prime Minister Winston Churchill adopted the following August.

[21] *Social Insurance and Allied Services* (the Beveridge Report), 1943. Beveridge was a former head of the London School of Economics and later a Liberal peer.

July 1945, only three months after the fighting ended in Europe, the voters turned out their wartime leader, Winston Churchill, by rejecting the Conservative Party. Clement Attlee, the new prime minister, and his Labor colleague, Ernest Bevin, set about installing the basic structure of the British welfare system. The Labor government, the first since 1931, promptly made pensions, unemployment benefits and social security universally available. They established the National Health Service,[22] put substantial resources into housing programs, and nationalized most of Britain's basic industries. Electricity, coal, gas, steel and the railways came under the ownership of large public corporations.

Nor did Churchill slow the tide toward the welfare state significantly when the Conservatives were returned to power in 1951. "The Conservatives preserved the welfare legislation," wrote S. E. Finer, professor of government and public administration at All Souls College, Oxford. The Labor Party, in its turn after again defeating the Tories, "accepted in office much that it had found unpalatable or even immoral in opposition," he added.[23] British journalist Geoffrey Smith and American political scientist Nelson W. Polsby came to a similar conclusion in their new book, *British Government and Its Discontents.* "The structures and assumptions of the Attlee government have been adjusted and modified by succeeding administrations — but not seriously challenged until recently," they wrote.

Thatcher's 'British Model'; U.S. Analogy

"Until recently," of course, refers to Margaret Thatcher's coming to power. But it can be argued, as does *The Times* of London political analyst Roger Berthoud, that it was never her aim to dismantle the welfare system. Nor, he adds, did Britons vote for that course of action when they went to the polls in May 1979. It has been argued elsewhere — Berthoud does not make the analogy — that just as the Republican Party has long since ceased trying to repeal Social Security in the United States, the British Conservative Party has accepted the reality of a welfare state.

What Thatcher wants, Berthoud maintains, is to reform the welfare state by providing incentives through tax revisions and other measures for Britons to work harder, earn more and prosper.[24] She has told her countrymen they will enjoy German prosperity when they work like Germans. "I never promised you a rose garden," she told them in defense of a still-ailing economy.

---

[22] See "Health Care in Britain and America," *E.R.R.*, 1973 Vol. I, pp. 437-456.
[23] S. E. Finer, *The Changing British Party System, 1945-1979* (1980), p. 193.
[24] Roger Berthoud, "Britain's Conservatives and the Welfare State: Reflections on the 1979 Election," *The Journal* (of the Institute of Socioeconomic Studies, White Plains, N.Y.), autumn 1980, pp. 32-46.

The Tory party speaks of "caring Conservatism," but it readily acknowledges inherent tensions in its efforts to maintain a welfare state and at the same time try to live within the nation's means. "We are totally committed to improving standards in the public services," said Sir Geoffry Howe, the chancellor of the exchequer, in his initial budget message to Parliament. "But that can be achieved only if the economy is strong.... Finance must determine expenditure, not expenditure finance...." He went on to say that "reductions in public expenditures must not be done in a way that bears unfairly on the most vulnerable members of society." His remark seems the equivalent of President Reagan's promise, in an economic message to Congress on Feb. 18, to protect the "truly needy" while slashing federal welfare programs.

Whether the "vulnerable" and "truly needy" can be protected adequately in an era of retrenchment is a subject of debate on both sides of the Atlantic. Nevertheless, economists and government officials on the European continent talk of following the conservative "British model" rather than the former "Swedish model" of government involvement and expansion. That kind of talk must seem quite strange to the British, who for decades have heard their economy — even their national will — scorned as an awful example among industrial nations.

Defenders and Detractors of Britain's Role

The picture is not unrelievedly bad. The Brookings Institution in 1968 published a study, entitled *Britain's Economic Prospects,* in which the authors noted that as of 1967 "Britain's economic performance since World War II outstrips any earlier period in the past half century." Thus, measured by Britain's own economic history, the first dozen postwar years were successes, not failures. But compared to other Western industrial countries, British economic growth was slow. In the 1957-67 period, Britain's annual economic growth was only 70 percent as high as the average of all OECD countries. Compared to West Germany and France, it was only about 50 percent.

Brookings last year published a follow-up study, with a slight change of title, *Britain's Economic Performance.* The story was essentially the same, although the gap had widened. In 1967-78, the British economic growth rate declined to 60 percent of the OECD average. For the final five years of that period it was down to 45 percent.

Smith and Polsby observed that "it has become fashionable over the last twenty years to regard Britain not just as a country with problems but as a problem country."

Bathrooms: Index of Affluence

Economists on both sides of the Atlantic long have eyed bathrooms with special fascination: they see indoor plumbing as a basic index of affluence. The following figures on dwellings with bath or shower, based on OECD and United Nations' statistics, chart a sharp rise in European family prosperity between 1950 and 1975:

Country	1950	1960	1970	1975
Austria	11%	30%	53%	66%
Britain	63	77	91	95
Denmark	38	60	73	81
France	10	29	48	70
W. Germany	20	48	82	91
Netherlands	27	—	81	93
United States	66	86	94	97

What is the reason [they ask] for this pervasive sense of failure? At one level Britain's record since the Second World War may be seen as a success story. Over the past thirty-five years Britain has become a more prosperous country.

The British people have more money in their pockets, enjoy better housing, have more modern appliances in their homes, run more cars, work a shorter day, week and year, take more holidays at home and abroad, and have improved health care — most of it free at the point of delivery.

Pensions are higher, and sickness and unemployment insurance covered by the state are virtually comprehensive for the working population. So material security in and out of work is much enhanced for most individuals in Britain compared with their condition in 1945 — and even more so compared with the years before the war.

Throughout the postwar years, they added, "Britain has been a country in which it has been exceedingly comfortable to live. In the face of great social change — the loss of empire, the liquidation of investments abroad, the establishment of a welfare state — a sense of fundamental decency has, on the whole, been preserved in British society."

That the British have been prepared to pay this price, the sacrifice of economic success for social advantages, has been applauded by some foreigners, notably Bernard Nossiter, the former London correspondent of *The Washington Post,* in his book *Britain: A Future That Works* (1978). But — to return to Smith and Polsby's theme — the British people have been beset by discontent over the greater economic progress made by their neighbors abroad. More than that "they have not been prepared to pay for their leisure, at least not on a pay-as-you-go basis. . . . Britain presents the paradox of an unambitious society that is not content with the fruits of its relaxation."[25]

Competitive Spirit vs. the 'Good Life'

This raises questions that are more philosophical than economic or political: Can a society simultaneously enjoy its leisure, "the good life," and still maintain a competitive spirit? At some point, does too much of the first overwhelm the second? Can the two somehow be held in proper balance, achieving the Greek ideal of everything in moderation, nothing in excess? Such questions are asked almost daily, in one form or another, of the British, the Swedes, and now the West Germans and, yes, Americans.

The European experience with the welfare state, especially the current British attempt to halt its growth, seems to have influenced American thinking in recent years. An underlying if generally unstated theme of the Reagan economic doctrine is that Washington must act to prevent the British economic "future" from reaching American shores in full force. At the same time it can be asked in Britain and America — indeed in many industrial countries — if the price of economic recovery must be the neglect of many of its citizens whose needs are genuine. The European experience so far has not been encouraging in terms of economic recovery.

In a book that captured considerable attention when it appeared last year, economist Lester C. Thurow wrote about "the zero-sum society."[26] Explaining that the mathematics phrase "zero-sum" means that for every winner there is a loser, Thurow maintained that this described the current condition of the U.S. economy. When the economy no longer expands significantly, something cannot be given to one group without taking it from another. While European welfare systems do not fall within Thurow's overview, his principle seems to apply — and to explain — the core problem that confronts society today in Europe and America.

---

[25] *British Government and Its Discontents* (1981), pp. 8-9. Previous passages quoted from pp. 3-4. For a view in contrast to Nossiter's, see *The Future That Doesn't Work: Social Democracy's Failure in Britain* (1977) by R. Emmett Tyrrell Jr. and others.

[26] It is his book's title. Thurow is professor of economics and public administration at Massachusetts Institute of Technology.

Selected Bibliography

Books

Caves, E. Richard and Lawrence B. Krause, eds., *Britain's Economic Performance,* The Brookings Institution, 1980.

Cerny, Karl H., ed., *Scandinavia at the Polls,* American Enterprise Institute for Public Policy Research, 1977.

Childs, Marquis W., *Sweden: The Middle Way,* Yale University Press, 1936.

——*Sweden: The Middle Way on Trial,* Yale University Press, 1980.

Finer, S. E., *The Changing British Party System,* American Enterprise Institute for Public Policy Research, 1980.

Smith, Geoffrey and Nelson W. Polsby, *British Government and Its Discontents,* Basic Books Inc., 1981.

Thurow, Lester C., *The Zero-Sum Society,* Basic Books Inc., 1980.

Articles

Berthoud, Roger, "Britain's Conservatives and the Welfare State: Reflections on the 1979 Election," *The Journal* (of the Institute of Socioeconomic Studies), autumn 1980.

The Economist, selected issues.

Holden, Anthony, "Muddling Through," *The New Republic,* Jan 24, 1981.

Logue, John, "The Welfare State: Victim of Its Success," *Daedalus* (journal of the American Academy of Arts and Sciences), fall 1979.

Painton, Frederick, "Reassessing the Welfare State," *Time,* Jan. 12, 1981.

Tinnin, David B., "The Miracle Economy Hits the Skids," *Fortune,* issue dated April 20, 1981.

Ungar, Sanford T., "Dateline Britain: Thatcherism," *Foreign Policy,* summer 1979.

Van Lennep, Emile, "From the Welfare State to the Welfare Society," *OECD Observer* (publication of the Organization for Economic Cooperation and Development, Paris), November 1980.

Zanker, Alfred, "If You Think Taxes Are High in the U.S.—" *U.S. News & World Report,* March 2, 1981.

Reports and Studies

Editorial Research Reports: "Reagan's 'New Federalism,' " 1981 Vol. I, p. 249; "Britain: Debtor Nation," 1977 Vol. I, p. 245; "Welfare in America and Europe," 1977 Vol. II, p. 933; "Scandinavia and Socialism," 1968 Vol. II, p. 625.

The Heritage Foundation, "Britain After the Elections: Thatcher's Conservative Government," June 11, 1979.

The Trilateral Commission, "Collective Bargaining and Employee Participation in Western Europe, North America and Japan," 1979.

U.S. Department of Labor, Bureau of International Labor Affairs, "Country Labor Profiles," various dates for individual countries.

TELECOMMUNICATIONS IN THE EIGHTIES

by

Richard C. Schroeder

Feb. 4
1 9 8 3

TELECOMMUNICATIONS
IN THE EIGHTIES

THE CHINESE name their years for animals. In Peking, this is the Year of the Boar. The United Nations uses a different system: it picks out issues of international concern and devotes a full year to their consideration. For example, 1974 was World Population Year, 1975 was International Women's Year, and 1981 was the Year of the Child.

In the U.N.'s scheme of things, 1983 is World Communications Year. The United Nations and its related agencies, ranging from the International Telecommunication Union to the Food and Agriculture Organization, UNESCO and the World Health Organization,[1] will undertake a series of projects this year to promote the establishment and improvement of communications systems around the world. "In recent years," said a U.N. press release, "decision-makers, planners and implementers at all levels have become increasingly aware that the biggest bottleneck for economic and social progress is inadequate communications."

The U.N.'s World Communications Year comes at a time of rapid transition in global communications systems. The convergence of emerging telecommunications technologies and computers is transforming business operations and human interactions in such fundamental ways that social scientists speak confidently of the dawn of a new era — the "information age" *(see p. 135).* "We are rapidly developing into an information society in which computer technologies, networking, and other enhanced forms of interpersonal and institutional communications are a major force," Kenneth W. Hunter told the delegates to the fourth general assembly of the World Future Society last July. "The technological and social changes affect us in our personal and professional lives. Understanding the nature of the changes and the alternatives available to the individual and society is crucial at this watershed in history."[2]

---

[1] The International Telecommunication Union (ITU) is a specialized agency of the United Nations, established in 1932 as an amalgamation of the International Telegraph Union and the International Radiotelegraph Union. It allocates radio frequencies among countries and regulates international telegraph, telephone and radio communications. UNESCO stands for United Nations Educational, Scientific and Cultural Organization.
[2] The theme of the conference, which was held July 18-22, 1982, in Washington, D.C., was "Communications and the Future." The address of the World Future Society is 4916 St. Elmo Ave., Bethesda, Md. 20814.

Recent Breakup of Bell System Network

In the United States, the richest and most technologically advanced member of the United Nations, 1983 promises to be a year of uncertainty about the future of the nation's telecommunications industry.[3] The world's largest and most efficient telecommunications network, the "Bell System" of the American Telephone & Telegraph Co. (AT&T), is being broken up into seven regional operating companies, under terms of a consent agreement reached on Jan. 8, 1982, ending an eight-year-old antitrust suit against AT&T by the U.S. Department of Justice.[4]

The agreement required divestiture of AT&T's 22 wholly and partly owned local operating companies, but it permitted AT&T to retain its long-distance phone operations, as well as its research subsidiary, Bell Laboratories, and its manufacturing division, Western Electric. In addition, for the first time, AT&T will be able to produce and sell computers, computer components and telecommunications equipment in competition with such firms as RCA, General Telephone & Electronics (GTE), International Business Machines (IBM) and International Telephone and Telegraph (ITT). The latter firms will, in turn, be free to sell equipment to the newly independent regional telephone companies, as well as to individual customers.[5]

Final details of the breakup of the Bell System will remain unclear until March, when U.S. District Judge Harold Green, who is overseeing the divestiture, is scheduled to rule on a 471-page divestiture plan submitted to him by AT&T in December. As it now stands, the divestiture is scheduled to be completed by Jan. 1, 1984. By that date, the 22 local subsidiaries will be spun off and consolidated into seven wholly independent firms, each with assets of from $16 billion to $22 billion. It is unquestionably the largest corporate breakup in American history. Just one of the new regionals, the Mid-Atlantic Co., will have assets of $17.2 billion and over 108,000 employees. AT&T will transfer up to three-quarters of its total assets to the regional operating

---

[3] Telecommunications is defined in *Webster's New Collegiate Dictionary* (1975) as "communications at a distance," *tele* being a Greek word meaning "far off." In practice, however, the term is usually applied to the transmission of information by telephone, telegraph, radio, television or other electromagnetic means.

[4] See "Business Mergers and Antitrust," *E.R.R.*, 1982 Vol. I, pp. 21-44. For background information on other antitrust cases, see "Oil Antitrust Action," *E.R.R.*, 1978 Vol. I, pp. 101-120 and "Antitrust Action," *E.R.R.*, 1975 Vol. I, pp. 61-80.

[5] As of Jan. 1, 1981, the United States had 191.6 million telephones, or 83.7 phones per 100 persons. Japan had the second-largest number of telephones, 58 million, but its per capita phone density was only 49.5 per 100 people. Sweden ranked second on a per capita basis, with 79.5 per 100 people, but its total number of phones was only 6.6 million. The Soviet Union had 23.7 million telephones and a density of only 8.8 per 100 persons. Washington, D.C., had more phones per capita than any other city in the world, 172.7 per 100 people. Source: "The World's Telephones: A Statistical Compilation as of January 1981," AT&T Long Lines, Overseas Administration, July 1982.

companies, a spin-off variously estimated at $80 billion to $110 billion.[6] About 60 percent of AT&T's employees will move to the regional operating companies; AT&T says 80 percent of those transferred will remain in their current work places. Under the plan submitted by AT&T to Judge Green, AT&T's 3.2 million stockholders will become owners of the new regionals, receiving shares proportional to their holdings in AT&T.

In the meantime, AT&T has created a new marketing subsidiary, American Bell — already nicknamed "Baby Bell" — to sell the wide range of communications and computing devices developed at Bell Lab and manufactured by Western Electric. Like the regional operating companies, American Bell emerged on Jan. 3, 1983, as a full-blown corporation with a life of its own. It got $1 billion in start-up capital from its parent company, with $4.7 million more to be given by AT&T between 1983 and 1985, at which point American Bell is expected to begin showing a profit, perhaps as high as $2 billion a year.[7]

American Bell has already leased 8.5 million square feet of office and commercial space at 555 locations in every state of the Union to house its 28,000 employees. As evidence of its relative independence from AT&T, Robert McNulty, a vice president of American Bell, reported that when the company ordered telephones, "We had no credit references, and one telephone company turned us down and asked for a deposit." [8] For overseas operations, AT&T created a subsidiary, AT&T International, in August 1980, and transferred the foreign marketing activities of Western Electric to it.

Impact of AT&T Divestiture on Consumers

For consumers, the most immediate and visible impact of the changes taking place in the Bell System will be a shift in the patterns of ownership and servicing of telephones. Phone users have been authorized for the past several years to buy and install their own equipment, including phones made by manufacturers other than Western Electric. Nonetheless, about 80 percent of the telephones in use in this country — 142.4 million according to AT&T's 1981 Annual Report — are currently owned by the phone company and leased to users for a monthly rental fee.

Beginning the first of this year, local AT&T subsidiaries started to phase out of the equipment leasing business. The companies have stopped restocking telephone inventories. They will lease or sell phone equipment only until current inventories

[6] The lower figure was published in AT&T's 1981 Annual Report, p. 5. The higher figure was reported by *Newsweek*, Dec. 27, 1982, p. 55.
[7] See "American Bell: Bathroom Brawl," *The Economist*, Dec. 18, 1982, p. 76.
[8] Quoted by Merrill Brown in *The Washington Post*, Dec. 26, 1982.

run out, probably before the end of this year. Customers currently leasing phones will have the option to continue to do so, but will be offered discounts to purchase phones already installed, thereby saving the monthly equipment rental fee. When the phase-out period is ended, new telephones may be obtained from retail stores operated by American Bell or from its numerous competitors.

For consumers, there is good and bad news in the new system. The good news is that competition among equipment manufacturers has already spurred the development of a new generation of telephones, such as cordless instruments that can be carried around the house or yard and phones that automatically dial preselected numbers at the touch of a single button.[9] There are also decorator phones bearing the imprint of famous designers such as Oscar de la Renta, Bill Blass, Givenchy and Oleg Cassini. The price of decorator phones generally runs from $60 to $200, but one Gucci model in silver carries a $1,500 tag. Experts believe the annual market for new phones may be as high as $300 million. Alfred Franks, a vice president of American Bell, expects 30 million new phones to be sold or leased during 1983.

The bad news is that consumers will be responsible for repair and maintenance of their telephones at their own expense. This could be more of a problem than might be expected. Western Electric has traditionally manufactured telephones for the rental market, designing them to last for 30 years. Newer telephones produced for sale, not lease, are expected to be cheaper but less durable.

Another piece of bad news is that divestiture will boost charges for local telephone calls. Over the years, local service has been subsidized partly by long-distance tolls. With the breakup of the Bell System, about $10.5 billion in fixed and operating costs previously borne by AT&T long lines will have to be sustained by the seven regional independent companies. Access charges for local service are expected to rise by about $2 a month in 1984, and will be $8.50 higher by 1991, under a plan

---

[9] See "The Telephone War: Dialing for Dollars," *Time*, Dec. 20, 1983, pp. 72-75.

approved by the Federal Communications Commission late last year.

Long-distance service, on the other hand, will be deregulated and increased competition in that area is expected to cut long-distance rates by 30 to 35 percent in the next few years. Even before the consent agreement was signed, the Bell System was beginning to feel competitive pressure from firms using microwave or satellite connections to offer cheaper long-distance rates. AT&T's principal long-distance competitors are ITT Longer Lines, MCI Communications, Satellite Business Systems Skyline, Southern Pacific Communications Sprint and Western Union Metrofone.

These competing firms depend on the local Bell System companies for access from their customers' locations to transmitting facilities. At least two court cases were filed charging AT&T with impeding such access. In November 1982, Federal Judge Charles R. Richey in Washington, D.C., ruled against one such complaint entered by Southern Pacific Communications Co. The following month, a federal appeals court in Chicago overturned a $1.8 billion judgment previously awarded to MCI on the ground that AT&T had engaged in "predatory pricing" in 1973, when MCI was just entering the business. The appeals court sustained eight of 22 charges of alleged "illegal actions" by AT&T, but said that "the predatory pricing allegations play such a significant part in MCI's case" that their dismissal requires re-evaluation of the entire damage claim.

New Communications Era

THE BREAKUP of the Bell System seems certain to change the way telecommunications equipment and services are marketed and used in the United States. But as revolutionary as the coming divestiture may be, it is matched and even exceeded by another kind of revolution — this one technological — which has overtaken the communications industry in recent years. In a real sense, the technological revolution underlies the change in the operating ground rules of the industry. So rapid have been the advances in telecommunications technology in recent years that all the players, the Bell System and its competitors, and makers of computers, office machines, television and other electronic devices, have come to recognize the need not only for restructuring, but for rethinking marketing and utilization strategies.

Telecommunications technology now available and new technologies emerging from the laboratory will affect nearly every aspect of society: where people live and work; the way they live and the work they do; how they are educated and how they spend their leisure time; even the condition of the environment and the patterns of exploitation of natural resources. For example, a recent Bell System advertisement noted:

> At this very moment, some homeowners are using the telephone network to dial up news and weather maps on their home video screens. They can shop from department-store catalogs. And even compare supermarket specials.
>
> With their ordinary home telephone lines providing transmission to a video screen, they can dial up information on seats on airlines or in local restaurants. They can even bank at home.
>
> Soon, local utilities will be able to use telephone lines to take remote readings of your gas and electric meters. And you'll be able to use those same telephone lines to monitor and remotely control home energy usage. . . .[10]

In Great Britain, the national post office publishes an "electronic newspaper." By tying a computer to a television set and linking the two to a central memory bank, the post office is able to print news — on demand — on home TV screens. In France, the telephone company is installing television sets with built-in computer terminals in the homes of all its subscribers — at no charge. When the system is fully in place, the telephone company will stop printing the "Yellow Pages" and other directories. Subscribers will use their home screen to scan advertisements and find telephone numbers and addresses.

In the United States, a number of companies, including CBS, NBC, AT&T, Knight-Ridder Newspapers, Dow Jones and Field Enterprises, have tested computer-TV systems that permit consumers to receive weather reports and stock market news on demand, and even to shop at home from "electronic catalogs." Some systems, called teletext, permit one-way transmission of graphics and text — airline schedules, for example — while others called videotex, or viewdata, permit two-way communication by phone lines or cable.[11]

On the business side, a service called "video teleconferencing" is being tried out by an increasing number of firms. The service provides two-way audio-visual contact among businessmen in distant cities, along with computer processing facilities and instantaneous electronic exchange of documents. Teleconfer-

---

[10] The advertisement appeared in *Newsweek*, Nov. 8, 1982, p. 1.
[11] See Kenneth Edwards, "Broadcast Teletext," *The Futurist*, October 1982, pp. 21-24, and John Tydeman, "Videotex: Ushering in the Electronic Household," *The Futurist*, February 1982, pp. 54-61.

The basis of today's telecommunications revolution was the marriage of communications technologies and data-processing technologies.

encing is already a $3 billion business in the United States, but that figure is minuscule compared to the cost of business travel, which, by one estimate, is nearly $300 billion a year.[12]

Telematics: Basis of the Information Age

Telecommunications technology is less than 150 years old. The first public demonstration of Samuel F. B. Morse's telegraph took place between Baltimore, Md., and Washington, D.C., on May 24, 1844. Seventeen years later, in October 1861, coast-to-coast telegraph service was initiated in the United States. Alexander Graham Bell received the first patent on the telephone on March 7, 1876. The world's first two-way "long-distance" telephone call was made on October 9th of that year, between Boston and Cambridgeport, Mass., a distance of only a few miles.[13]

The basis of today's telecommunications revolution was the marriage of communications technologies and data-processing technologies. Two French scientists, Simon Nora and Alain Minc, in a report to the president of France a few years ago, called the merging of telecommunications with computers and television *télématique,* which was translated into English as telematics. Harvard University Professor Anthony Oettinger coined a slightly more cumbersome term, compunication.

---

[12] *Video Teleconferencing,* Satellite Business Systems, (undated), p. 3.
[13] American Telephone & Telegraph Co., *Events in Telecommunications History,* May 1979.

Telematics appears to have gained a somewhat wider acceptance, especially since the publication of James Martin's book, *Telematic Society: Challenge for Tomorrow* (1981). Martin is considered one of the leading writers in the field.[14]

Telematics has ushered in a new era alternatively called "the communications age," "the information age," or "the information society." It is, by consensus, qualitatively different from all previous eras. Dean Gillette, executive director of corporate studies at Bell Labs, described the change this way:

> Society had wagons for thousands of years, and in the late 18th century, it had access to steam engines that sat on the ground and could pull things around or turn mills. The really important change that occurred was when the steam engine was made small enough to be put on a wagon and then you had a railroad train. That was just plain different! To me, the combination of computing and communications which we have now ... is really a qualitative change. It's just plain different from either of them separately. That's the revolution in communicatons....[15]

A Stanford University professor, Edward Steinmuller, has said: "If the airlines had progressed as rapidly as this technology, the Concorde would be carrying half a million passengers at 20 million miles an hour for less than a penny apiece."[16]

Despite such enthusiastic assessments, most experts believe the telecommunications revolution has not yet peaked. According to Solomon J. Buchsbaum, an executive vice president of Bell Labs: "I define the Information Age, for our business, as that time when a large fraction — say 50 percent or more — of the more than 10 million businesses in this country and 20 percent of all households will find it necessary, desirable, and even pleasurable to have at least one terminal connected to a switched network of terminals and data bases. It will be years before this happens...."[17]

The technological explosion of recent years has produced thousands of discoveries, inventions and patents in the telecommunications and computer fields. Bell Laboratories, the leader in industry research, has turned out more than 19,000 patents, a rate of one each working day since the labs opened in 1925. Research done by Bell Labs was, in fact, a deciding factor in AT&T's acquiescence to demands for the breakup of the Bell System. Before divestiture, AT&T had been enjoined from sell-

---

[14] See also Daniel Bell, "Communications Technology," *Economic Impact*, No. 34, reprinted from the *Harvard Business Review. Economic Impact* is a quarterly review of world economics published by the U.S. Information Agency.
[15] Interview, June 11, 1982.
[16] Quoted by Edward Cornish in "The Coming of an Information Society," *The Futurist*, April 1981, p. 17.
[17] Quoted in the *Bell Laboratories 1981 Annual Report*, p. 18.

ing its advanced computer technology on the open market, and "some of the best and fastest silicon ware wound up hidden in the switching systems of the Bell System." [18]

Bell, although an acknowledged leader in telecommunications technology, is not alone in advanced research and applications. In the United States, such companies as General Electric, GTE, RCA, ITT and Western Union Telegraph maintain expensive research establishments, as do such overseas competitors as Phillips of the Netherlands, Siemens of West Germany, and several Japanese companies.

Supporting Technologies

FOUR DEVELOPMENTS underlie the communications revolution: solid-state microelectronics; digital transmission; photonics, or light-wave transmission; and software, or computer input and programming. There is a fifth category that utilizes these four technologies together with a bundle of non-communications technologies: satellite communications, a development that has made transmission of information from distant points virtually instantaneous, reliable and cheap. Perhaps the most important technology in the communications revolution has been solid-state microelectronics. The core of modern computers and electronic switching systems are microprocessors, thousands of transistors, diodes, capacitors, and connecting circuits embedded in thin, small slices of silicon or other substances. These small, so-called "chips," generally smaller than a thumbnail, constitute the memory of computers, and also the devices to perform the logical calculating functions of the machine.[19]

Before the advent of the transistor, the integrated circuit and the silicon chip, computers consisted of a vast array of vacuum tubes hooked together. The first electronic computer, ENIAC, built 37 years ago at the University of Pennsylvania, filled a large room, had 18,000 vacuum tubes, and required 140,000 watts of electricity. Today, a computer with ENIAC's capacity — and with much greater reliability — costs less than $100, fits into a pants pocket and runs on flashlight batteries. Whirlwind I, another pioneering computer of the 1950s, cost about $5

---

[18] "Ma Bell's Dream Factory," *Newsweek*, Jan. 25, 1982, pp. 68-69.
[19] See "The Age of Computers," *E.R.R.*, 1981 Vol. I, pp. 105-128.

million. Today, a hand-held machine of comparable capability sells for less than $20.

Larger main-frame computers used in industry today have far greater capacity than was imagined possible a few decades ago. For example, the Bible can be encoded in a digital memory bank of about 25 million bits (a bit is the smallest unit of information in the digital system).[20] Computers systems now in use in business and industry store 100,000 times that amount of information. Assuming the average hard-bound book occupies two inches of library shelf space, a modern computer system contains the equivalent of more than 16,000 feet of library shelves.

To call what is happening in microelectronics "miniaturization" is to vastly understate the case. Microprocessors are getting very small very fast. Each year for the past decade, the number of elements that can be implanted on a chip has doubled. No more than five years ago, one such chip containing 16,000 bits of information was the talk of the industry. Today, the same chip, called the 16K RAM, is sold at retail radio and electronics stores for $3.95. Chips containing more than half a million components (the 256K RAM) are now being introduced by Western Electric. Other high-capacity chips are marketed by companies such as ITT and GTE. Toshiba, a Japanese firm, has introduced a chip made up of gallium and arsenic, instead of the conventional silicon wafer, which can carry out calculations at a speed of 80 picoseconds (one picosecond equals 1,000 billionth of a second).[21]

Link Provided by Digital Transmission

The binary or *digital* language of microprocessors and computers provides the link between telecommunications transmission and computer functioning. The telephone was invented as an *analog* transmitting and receiving system. In analog transmissions, sound is converted into an electrical signal that is a replica (analog) of the sound itself. The electrical signal changes in frequency and amplitude in direct relation to changes in the voice speaking into the telephone. The analog electric signal is converted back into sound at the receiving end.

In *digital* transmission, sound is measured at frequent intervals and the measurement, rather than an analog of the sound is transmitted. Computer devices on the receiving end are able to reconstruct the sound from the information transmitted to it. The information is sent as a discontinuous series of pulses of electricity, encoded in binary fashion — that is, each pulse can

---

[20] James Martin, *Telematic Society* (1981), p. 27.
[21] Reported in the *Wall Street Journal*, Aug. 25, 1982.

contain only one of two possible pieces of information, negative or positive, on or off.

Analog transmission requires a band width, or carrying capacity, of roughly 3,000 to 4,000 cycles per second. But in digital transmission, the standard human voice requires 64,000 pulses, or bits of information, per second. Other types of information may require much larger band widths. A digital-encoded signal for color television, for example, even when sophisticated compression techniques are used, requires up to 45 million pulses a second. Since most telephone trunk lines are designed to carry only 1.544 million bits per second, television signals must be sent by other means — coaxial cables, microwave relay stations, or by fiber-optic techniques *(see below)*.

Most industrialized countries have introduced digital, or "pulse code modulated" signaling. Less developed countries are just beginning to install such equipment. By the mid-1970s, Japan alone had 500,000 digital circuits. New developments, such as time division multiplexing (sandwiching different signals between each other), permit greatly increased transmission capacity.

Photonics: Transmission by Light Waves

Photonics, the transmission of sound or other information by light wave, is the newest of the technologies of the communications revolution. Most communications companies are developing light wave equipment, based mainly on the use of fiber-optic technology. Optic systems convert voice, television or data signals into extremely brief pulses of light that are sent through strands of ultra-pure glass, thinner than a human hair. The light pulses are generated by solid-state devices, either lasers or light-emitting diodes, about the size of a grain of sand. Lasers now in use generate pulses at the rate of 45 million per second — conveniently, the frequency needed to transmit color television signals. Lasers now being developed in the laboratory function at speeds 44,000 times faster.

The light pulses remain within the glass fiber, no matter how much the fiber twists or bends. They travel considerable distances without needing to be reinforced, and are received at the other end of the system by photo-diodes which convert them back into sound, television signals or data messages.

Fiber-optic technology has numerous advantages over other transmission systems. One is the enormous potential capacity of the hair-thin glass fibers. The most efficient fiber systems in use today consist of 72 pairs of glass fibers bundled together in a cable no thicker than a finger. Such cables can handle 300,000 simultaneous two-way telephone calls. In theory, fiber-optic capacity is still greater: one pair of fibers can transmit 10,000 simultaneous telephone calls by using multiplexing techniques — intermingling the signals of three different light frequencies. Optical fibers also provide dependable, noise-free telephone circuits because the light is free from electrical interference from nearby power lines, lightning, and "cross-talk" from other channels. They are also corrosion proof and highly resistant to electronic eavesdropping techniques.

The first experimental light-wave systems were installed only six years ago, but their use is expanding rapidly. Thousands of miles of glass fibers are now in use in North America, Europe and Japan, and the installation rate is multiplying almost geometrically each year. MCI recently signed a $32 million agreement with the CSX Corp., a railroad company, that will allow MCI to lay fiber-optic cables along the railway's 4,000 miles of right of way. AT&T is building a fiber-optic line between Richmond, Va. and Boston.[22]

Importance of Programming and Software

Microelectronics provides the "muscle" of the communications system; software is the "brain" that tells the muscle what to do. Software is so important that in Bell Labs alone, 40 percent of the technical personnel work on its development.[23] A glance at the want ads of any metropolitan newspaper confirms the importance of software —and the programmers who produce it — to the business world. Programming is the act of writing instructions to be stored in the memory cells of computers, enabling them to perform certain functions, such as moving a bit of information from one location to another.

As computers grow more powerful and more sophisticated, the limit of what they can do increasingly lies in the creativity of the programmer. One computer program may utilize the overall capacity of a computer more efficiently than another program. Similarly, the instructions built into microprocessors are critical factors in determining whether the entire unit functions as intended.

Development of Satellite Communications

Satellites are, in the words of Dean Gillette, "very high microwave towers" that receive signals from a ground station and retransmit them over a very broad area. The era of satellite communications began more than 20 years ago, when AT&T launched Telstar, the first working communications satellite to orbit the earth, on July 20, 1962. Largely experimental, Telstar

---

[22] Reported in *The Washington Post*, Dec. 23, 1982.
[23] *Bell Laboratories Annual Report, 1981*, p. 38.

transmitted telephone calls and even some television signals across the Atlantic until it was disabled by radiation in February 1963. Shortly before Telstar was crippled, however, Relay, a communications satellite developed by the National Aeronautics and Space Agency (NASA) for RCA, went into operation.

The Communications Satellite Corp. (COMSAT), a private company, was organized in 1963 and authorized by the government to act as the U.S. representative in international satellite affairs. The following year, INTELSAT, the international telecommunications satellite consortium, was set up. All countries but the United States are represented in INTELSAT by government agencies; the United States is represented by COMSAT. Two-thirds of the world's international transoceanic communications now go via INTELSAT satellites.[24] The European Space Agency (ESA) has its own communications satellites covering the continent, and is planning a large-capacity satellite capable of handling television signals.[25] In the United States, several communications companies employ satellites for domestic communications purposes. A new entry into the field is Satellite Business Systems (SBS), a joint venture of COMSAT, IBM and the Aetna Life and Casualty Insurance Co. SBS went into operation in 1981 using its own satellites to provide direct service to earth stations.[26]

Satellite capacity is currently in short supply, but this is likely to be a short-lived situation. Projections are that available facilities will double in the next few years. Satellite communication is inherently a very high-capacity and high-speed operation, matched only by fiber-optic transmission. INTELSAT V, the current generation of INTELSAT satellites, has a capacity of 12,000 simultaneous two-way telephone circuits and two television channels, using advanced time division multiplexing systems. INTELSAT V-A, scheduled for launch next year, will accommodate 15,000 two-way telephone circuits and two television channels, while INTELSAT VI, still on the drawing boards, is being designed to accommodate 40,000 simultaneous telephone circuits.

[24] *INTELSAT Is...*, undated publication of INTELSAT.
[25] *Europe's Place in Space*, publication of the European Space Agency, January 1981.
[26] Satellite Business Systems, *1981 Annual Report*.

Prospects for the Future

THE INTERNATIONAL telecommunications network has over 500 million telephones and well over a million telex terminals, interconnected by a maze of transmission channels and switching devices. The entire system is expanding rapidly — and changing profoundly — as computers, data banks, television sets and word processors are hooked into the international grid. "Networking," establishing telecommunications links between all these disparate elements, is a basic aspect of the telecommunications revolution.

One of the prime functions of computers is to store vast amounts of information and to produce such information on command, either as a display on a television screen or in printed form. Specialized information collections, equivalent to the contents of an entire library, are encoded and stored in the memory cells of a computer. In this form, the information is known as a data bank and, through networking, is available to other computers. The contents of such data banks vary widely and can include academic topics, daily newspapers, newsletters, business and economic news, encyclopedias and abstracts of articles.

"Cellular Radio" is a name that will be heard increasingly in the near future. This technological development will multiply by several hundred times the number of mobile telephones that can operate in a given area. It involves the construction of several transmitting towers in a local calling area, each serving a "cell," within its range. As a car with a telephone moves about the city, electronic switching devices pass the car from the transmitting tower in one cell to the next. Bidding for licenses to run cellular radio operations was opened last June and dozens of companies are currently competing for the right to serve the 30 largest cities in the United States.

There are new technological developments ahead for home television, too. During the past decade, pay-as-you-see television networks experienced rapid growth in the United States. Most bring their signals into homes by cables dedicated to that use. In contrast to commercial stations and networks which broadcast their signals free for all to receive, cable television companies charge a monthly fee for the service. Now, a number of companies have applied to the Federal Trade Commission for permission to begin pay-television service by direct broadcast from satellites. The satellite signals would be scrambled to prevent their interception by non-subscribers; subscribers would receive the signals through a small dish antenna, which would then be processed by a decoder attached to the television set. A COMSAT subsidiary, Satellite Broadcasting Corporation (SBC), recently received the first FCC license for direct satellite broadcasting and says it is prepared to invest up to $400 million in the venture.[27]

Some Long-Range Problems and Prospects

The full implications of the changes occurring in computer and telecommunications technology are yet to be realized. The United States — and most of the rest of the world — stand poised on the threshold of a new era whose characteristics remain undefined. Vast changes lie ahead, but the substance of the change cannot be foreseen.

Of immediate concern to some analysts is what effect the breakup of the national Bell System will have on the efficiency of telecommunications in the United States. John F. Dealy, a fellow at the Brookings Institution in Washington, D.C., and a professor at the Georgetown University School of Business Administration, put the problem this way:

> One potential threat to the growth and practical impact of tele-communications in the eighties is a side effect of the new competition, deregulation, and technological advancements themselves. That is the breakdown of the old system of technical standards set and maintained domestically by the Bell System. Moreover, the marriage of computers and communications in modern integrated networks, using transmission links as diverse as synchronous satellites and fiber optics, compounds the standards problem with issues of computer protocol compatibility across the end-to-end system. A complex political and technical challenge during the next decade will be to evolve a domestic, and international, set of technical transmission standards and interface protocols that manufacturers and common carriers will honor.[28]

A second concern is whether the enormous capital requirements of new telecommunications technology can be satisfied, particularly in a world economy where austerity and retrenchment are the watchwords. It is clear that the United States must be "rewired" to accommodate the wide-band requirements of the information age *(see p. 141)*. The old narrow-band telephone lines are in a state of obsolescence. Microwave relay stations, satellite systems, and, particularly, fiber-optic cables seem to be the wave of the future. AT&T spokesmen, for example, talk optimistically of laying a transoceanic fiber-optic cable, not only to replace existing conventional under-sea cables, but to compete with satellite transmission systems.

---

[27] See "Cable TV's Future," *E.R.R.*, 1982 Vol. II, pp. 717-736.
[28] John F. Dealy, "Telecommunications: Policy Issues and Options for 1980s," *The Brookings Review*, winter 1982, pp. 30-33.

Telephones by World Regions*

World Regions	Total in Service	Percent of World	Per 100 Pop.
Africa	5,028,177	1.0	2.5
Asia	74,905,484	14.7	7.1
Europe	189,896,985	37.4	24.6
Middle America	6,236,897	1.2	6.9
North America	208,479,406	41.0	81.4
Oceania	10,182,879	2.0	14.7
South America	13,556,038	2.7	6.3
World (Total)	508,285,866	100.0	19.1

*As of Jan. 1, 1981.

Source: AT&T Long Lines, "The World's Telephones: A Statistical Compilation as of January 1981," July 1982.

There is also growing uneasiness that the looser regulatory climate in the United States will attract increasing competition from high-tech industries overseas. According to John F. Dealy, "Foreign telecommunications manufacturers view the U.S. deregulation trend as a major business opportunity and are flooding the United States with their products and services." [29] Many of the foreign companies benefit from government subsidies and other aid, while their own domestic markets are insulated from significant foreign competition by tariff and nontariff barriers. Telecommunications is, in large part, a service industry — software, for example, falls into that category. The United States has been trying for some time to initiate international negotiations under the General Agreement on Tariffs and Trade (GATT)[30] on rules for world trade in services. The best the United States could obtain at last November's GATT ministerial meeting was a promise by the governments of Europe and Japan to look into the matter on a national level.

Beyond the marketing implications is the growing realization that the revolution in telecommunications and computer technology will affect the composition of the American work force. According to Sen. Gary Hart, "As many as 45 million existing jobs could be affected by factory and office automation, and much of that impact will occur in the next 20 years." Even using more conservative forecasts, Hart said, "We can still expect to

[29] *Ibid.*, p. 31.

[30] In 1947, as part of an effort to ease critical economic conditions abroad after World War II, the United States helped establish GATT with 22 of its trading partners. GATT represented a break from the previous mode of negotiating with one country at a time. It enabled all of the participating countries to bargain with all of the others simultaneously. Concessions agreed upon by individual negotiating teams had to be extended to all, an agreement that is known as the "most favored nation" principle.

lose between five and seven million manufacturing jobs. That is job loss at a rate 20 times higher than the auto industry is experiencing today. No wonder American workers worry that their only future is as 'computer fodder' in the information revolution."

Many people believe that a massive retraining effort is needed to prepare workers for jobs in the information society. "The theory that displaced workers could leave one industry and move to another as the economy grew and changed hit a roadblock. And that roadblock was skills," said Dina Beaumont, executive assistant to the president of the Communications Workers of America. "The day has passed when a single education or skill will be enough to last for a lifetime of employment. Our union is promoting the concept of employment security rather than job security." [31]

Finally, there is the question of the impact of the communications revolution on the relationship between the industrialized world and the less developed countries. Sociologist Daniel Bell has observed that the advent of the information age has transformed the industrialized countries into "post-industrial" societies, where the essential economic activities are concentrated in the service sector, rather than in the production of goods, and where the most prized skills are scientific, technical and professional. Right now, the Third World, and especially the middle level, the so-called "newly industrialized countries" such as Brazil, Mexico and Argentina, are caught in the grip of the worst foreign debt problem in history.[32] The crunch came just when it seemed these countries were approaching a stage of relative competitiveness in world markets — not only for basic commodities, but also for industrial goods with a fairly high level of technological content. Experts wonder whether these countries can emerge unscathed from the current debt crisis and continue their progress into the world of modern technology.

There are no easy answers to such questions. Clearly, the revolution in telecommunications brings potential threats, as well as benefits, to society. But the process of scientific advance is irreversible. The information age is upon us, and we must somehow learn to cope with the vast changes that lie ahead.

---

[31] Hart and Beaumont spoke at a session on "Transformation of the Economy to the Communication and Information Era," at the fourth general assembly of the World Future Society *(see p. 131)*.

[32] See "World Debt Crisis," *E.R.R.*, 1983 Vol. I, pp. 45-64.

Selected Bibliography

Books

Ganley, Oswald Harold, *To Inform or to Control?* McGraw-Hill, 1982.
Leinwoll, Stanley, *From Spark to Satellite,* Scribner, 1979.
Martin, James, *Telematic Society,* Prentice-Hall, 1981.
Nora, Simon and Alain Minc, *The Computerization of Society,* MIT Press, 1980.
Pierce, John R., *Signals: The Telephone and Beyond,* W. H. Freemand & Co., 1981.

Articles

"A Budding Market for Data Bases," *Business Week,* Jan. 17, 1983.
"A New World Dawns," *Time,* Jan. 3, 1983.
Bell Telephone Magazine, selected issues.
Brown, Arnold, "Equipping Ourselves for the Computer Age," *The Futurist,* August 1981.
"Computers for the Masses: The Revolution is Just Beginning," *U.S. News & World Report,* Jan. 3, 1983.
Comsat (Communications Satellite Corp. magazine), selected issues.
Cornish, Edward, "The Coming of an Information Society," *The Futurist,* April 1981.
Dealy, John F., "Telecommunications: Policy Issues and Options for the 1980s," *The Brookings Review,* winter 1982.
"Ma Bell's Dream Factory," *Newsweek,* Jan. 25, 1982.
"The Telephone War: Dialing for Dollars," *Newsweek,* Dec. 20, 1982.

Reports and Studies

American Telephone & Telegraph, "1981 Annual Report."
_____ "Events in Telecommunications History," New York, N.Y., 1979.
AT&T Long Lines, Overseas Administration, "The World's Telephones: A Statistical Compilation as of January 1981," Morris Plains, N.J., July 1982.
Bell Laboratories, "Impact: A Compilation of Bell System Innovations in Science and Engineering," 1981.
Communications Satellite Corp., "COMSAT at 15," 1978.
Editorial Research Reports: "Cable TV's Future," 1982 Vol. II, p. 717; "The Robot Revolution," 1982 Vol. I, p. 345; "The Age of Computers," 1981 Vol. I, p. 105; "America's Information Boom," 1978 Vol. II, p. 801.
European Space Agency, "Europe in Space," January 1981.
Satellite Business Systems, "Video Teleconferencing," undated.

AMERICAN OPTIONS IN SPACE

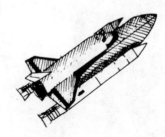

by

Katrina Farrell-Gisse
and Hoyt Gimlin

**Feb. 18
1 9 8 3**

Editor's Note: In its thrust to "commercialize space," the Reagan administration in March said it planned to sell its weather satellites to private industry. The government, as the main user of weather information collected by the satellites, would guarantee to pay the new owner for the information. The Communications Satellite Corp. (Comsat) appeared to be the leading potential purchaser. It was reported that Comsat wanted to purchase the satellite system for about $300 million. However, opposition to the plan soon surfaced in Congress and it was uncertain whether the "privatization" of weather data would be permitted.

The first flight of the new shuttle Challenger *(p. 151)* was further postponed to April 4 because of a recurring problem with the fuel tank.

AMERICAN OPTIONS IN SPACE

I T HAS been a quarter-century since America put its first satellite into space and a decade since the last lunar expedition closed the era of flag-bearing astronauts *(see Space Events, p. 154)*. These exploits captured the public's imagination and ensured financial support for the U.S. space program through the 1960s. During the following decade, the National Aeronautics and Space Administration (NASA) scored remarkable successes with its unmanned probes of other planets, and it mapped plans for space travel in the 1980s as difficult and perhaps as exciting as the Man-on-the-Moon program that President Kennedy set in motion in 1961.

Motivated by the high cost of space travel, NASA searched for more efficient ways to exploit space and its resources. This fostered the idea of a Space Transportation System, or STS, for carrying cargoes ("payloads") into orbit and returning to Earth aboard a fleet of reusable space shuttles *(see illustrations, p. 153)*. Now after five successful flights of the space shuttle *Columbia*, the first flight of the new shuttle *Challenger* from the Kennedy Space Flight Center in Florida is scheduled for sometime in middle or late March — barring further delay that postponed the original launch date from Jan. 27 because of a fuel tank flaw. Though a setback, which is likely to postpone the launching of other flights this year, it does not dampen optimism in the space agency that the United States is on the verge of a commercial, scientific and military renaissance in space.

However, this view is not universally shared. The science community is complaining that space sciences are taking a back seat to the military applications of space. And as for America's attempt to push ahead with the commercialization of space, it is encountering competition from Russia, Europe and Japan. In recent years, all three have been developing inexpensive means of launching satellites, and at least Europe and Japan are trying to attract some of the international business — including American business — that NASA was counting on to support the commercial aspect of the Space Transportation System.

There is an ambitious schedule of shuttle flights, nevertheless. Sixty-three are planned through 1987. This September the

Columbia is due to carry aloft a $1 billion Spacelab developed by the European Space Agency[1] for NASA, enabling scientists to work in a "shirt-sleeve environment" — without bulky spacesuits and carry out experiments for research institutes, commercial customers and government agencies.

Then in March 1984, if the timetable holds firm, the new shuttle *Discovery* will make its first flight. It will carry a communications satellite and a facility for experimenting with the separation of chemical compounds that can best be performed where gravity is weak or virtually absent. This kind of "materials processing" will be studied further in April 1985 when the shuttle *Atlantis* is sent into orbit. This will be done in a Spacelab mission jointly sponsored by NASA and the West German goverment.

About one-third of the *Atlantis* payload capacity will be leased to private, commerical interests — unless opposition that has been reported in the White House materializes to block the plan. The trade magazine *Aviation Week & Space Technology* has reported that David A. Stockman, director of the presidential Office of Management and Budget, does not want federally funded space transportation to haul private cargoes unless the government realizes a profit from that activity.[2]

Selling Industry the Shuttle's Services

NASA is moving ahead despite any official misgivings, promoting its "Getaway Special." For fees up to $10,000, individuals and corporations can lease up to five cubic feet of space aboard a future shuttle flight, and place up to 200 pounds on board. So far about 500 customers have signed up to have their cargoes, usually involving scientific experiments, taken into orbit. The agency is also developing plans to take passengers into space late in this decade.

Business involvement in the U.S. space program is not new, of course. Since its inception, NASA has contracted with large companies for a variety of services and products. Private industry has supplied parts and developed entire systems for space projects. The prime contractor for the space shuttle orbiter, for instance, is Rockwell International's Space Division at Downey, Calif. Hundreds of other private companies are subcontractors. Now that the space shuttle is operational, the private sector of the economy is looking at it with wider interest.

---

[1] The agency is an adjunct of the European Economic Community composed of Belgium, Britain, Denmark, France, West Germany, Greece, Ireland, Italy, Luxembourg and the Netherlands.
[2] *Aviation Week & Space Technology*, Oct. 25, 1982, p. 11.

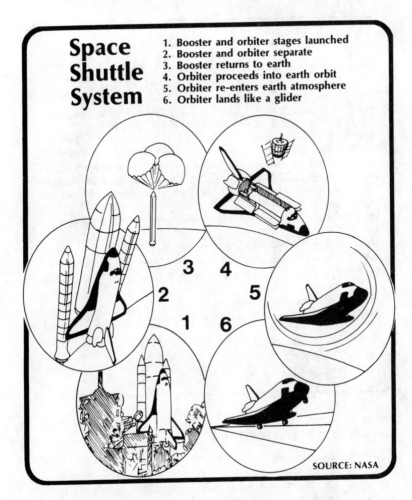

Space Shuttle System

1. Booster and orbiter stages launched
2. Booster and orbiter separate
3. Booster returns to earth
4. Orbiter proceeds into earth orbit
5. Orbiter re-enters earth atmosphere
6. Orbiter lands like a glider

SOURCE: NASA

Communications satellites were the shuttle's first commercial payload. Last November the *Columbia* carried into space and launched two $30 million satellites for Telsat Systems of Canada and Satellite Business Systems of McLean, Va. Each paid NASA $9 million for performing this service, enabling Telsat to beam television signals to rooftop antennas in Canada and SBS to operate a long-distance telephone system.

More than three years before that event, a NASA planner, Jesco von Puttakamer, predicted that communication satellites would constitute the shuttle's main payloads throughout the 1980s. "[U]sing the shuttle," he explained, it will be practical "to assemble much larger antennas and reflector structures than those we now have in orbit." [3] Even then, in 1979, commercial investments in satellites had exceeded $1 billion, von Putta-

[3] Jesco von Puttakamer, "The Industrialization of Space: Transcending the Limits of Growth," *The Futurist* (magazine of the World Future Society), June 1979, p. 184.

Space Events, 1957-82

1957. Russia launches first satellite Sputnik on Oct. 4.

1958. U.S. sends up its first satellite, Explorer, Jan. 31.

1960. Echo 1, first TV communications satellite in orbit.

1961. Cosmonaut Yuri A. Gagarin becomes first human in orbit, April 12. President Kennedy calls May 26 for moon landing.

1962. John Glenn becomes first American to orbit the Earth, Feb. 20. First successful interplanetary mission, Mariner 2 to Venus.

1963. Soviets put first woman, Valentina Tereshkova, in space.

1965. U.S. launches first 2-man mission, March 23. First space walk by cosmonaut Alexey Leonov. Early Bird, first commercial communications satellite, links U.S. and Europe.

1966. Venera 3 lands on Venus, first man-made object to reach another planet.

1969. U.S. lands first men on moon, July 16.

1971. Russia's Salyut 1 becomes first space station in Earth's orbit.

1972. President Nixon authorizes space shuttle, Jan. 5. Last Apollo mission, Dec. 7-19.

1973. First Skylab crew launched May 26.

1974. Skylab 4 crew aloft 84 days, a record. Mariner 10 conducts first probe of Mercury.

1975. Apollo-Soyez projects links U.S.-Soviet crews in space, in July.

1981. Space shuttle makes first of test flight, April 12.

1982. Shuttle's first operational mission, Nov. 11.

kamer reported, predicting that the figure would be several times greater by the mid-1980s.

Communication satellites receive signals from a ground station and retransmit them over a very broad area, eliminating the need for telephone and telegraph lines, cables and other surface means of communication. American Telephone & Telegraph Co. put up the first working communication satellite, Telstar, on July 20, 1962, to transmit telephone calls and some television signals across the Atlantic Ocean. Though disabled the next year, Telstar was followed by a procession of others.

Commercial interest in satellites was so strong that in 1962 Congress authorized the creation of the Communication Satellite Corp. (Comsat), jointly controlled by private industry and the federal government.[4] Comsat arranged with NASA to launch scores of satellites for communications purposes. There also have been dozens of satellites for weather observations, navigation, traffic control, mapping and surveying.

Spawning the Communications Economy

Social forecaster John Naisbitt makes the point that today's shuttle can orbit a 65,000-pound payload vastly greater than the

---

[4] See Congressional Quarterly's *Congress and the Nation*, Vol. I (1965), pp. 320, 326.

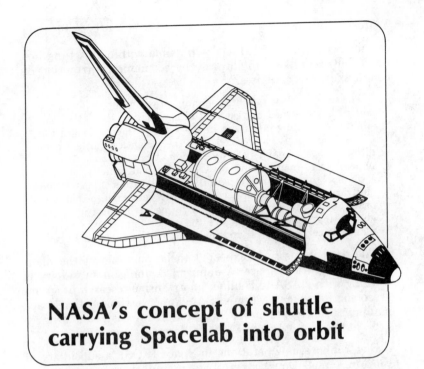

NASA's concept of shuttle carrying Spacelab into orbit

182-pound Sputnik, "and many, many times more sophisticated." In the past, the complex parts of a satellite system had to be in a ground station. "But the new shuttle ... can launch larger satellites that incorporate ground station functions...."

For all that "the space shuttle has a lot more to do with the globalized information economy than it will ever have to do — in our lifetimes — with space exploration." he added. "I do not want to minimize the importance of *Sputnik* and *Columbia* in opening up the heavens to us. But what has not been stressed enough is the way satellites transformed the Earth into what Marshall McLuhan called a global village."[5]

"No one looking at space a quarter century ago foresaw all ways in which space systems have altered human life," writes Daniel Deudney, a senior researcher with Worldwatch Institute, "and no one today predicting space activities over the next 50 to 100 years is likely to predict all the uses to which satellites will be put. Yet enough is known about the potential of space and the needs of earth that some ideas — large-scale space colonies, solar power satellites and asteroid mining — can be eliminated as practical and desirable goals. A modest industry producing

---

[5] John Naisbitt, *Megatrends*, Warner Books, 1982, pp. 12, 58. Naisbitt is publisher of the quarterly *Trend Report* and chairman of the Naisbitt Group, a research and consulting firm, in Washington, D.C. McLuhan, a Canadian professor-author, has been called the guru of the age of television. He is perhaps best known for his book *The Medium is the Massage* — or message.

certain high quality products is possible within this time horizon, but is unlikely to surpass the economic contribution of communications satellites." [6]

The success of the satellite communications industry [Deudney added] has spawned a great deal of speculation about the possibility of building industries in space. Experiments aboard the U.S. *Skylab* in 1974 revealed that the weightless, airless conditions of space enabled the production of certain goods that are impossible to manufacture on Earth. Without gravity, crystals form much more regularly, permitting the creation of glasses and electrical devices that have vastly higher performance than any others. And the products can be formed without containers, eliminating impurities that are the major limit to the performance of certain optical and metallurgical products on Earth. [7]

The drug industry is expected to become one of the main users of weightless space. A Johnson & Johnson subsidiary is working with NASA to conduct an extensive research program. Jesco von Puttakamer, the NASA planner, estimates that space manufacturing could lower the production cost of a drug to prevent blood clots from $1,200 a dose to about $100.

Electrophoresus Operations in Space (EOS), a subsidiary of the McDonnell Douglas aerospace manufacturing company, is reported to be experimenting extensively with producing pharmaceuticals and other materials in space. An official of the company said it was investing "millions of dollars" in materials research to determine what products could benefit from production in space. The results so far show that "hundreds" of new or improved products could be produced there.

NASA has predicted that it will not have enough launch facilities to meet the demand once big businesses become actively engaged in space manufacturing. Some companies are reported to be considering ways of establishing their own space transportation systems and bypassing the shuttle. One company, Space Services Inc. of Houston, went a step further last September by launching a small spacecraft made of surplus parts and carrying a mock payload of 40 gallons of water. It soared to 52.9 miles and plunged into the Gulf of Mexico, 326 miles from the Matagorda Island launch site in Texas. The test was part of the company's plan eventually to sell "low-cost, market-oriented" space services to customers, according to David H. Hannah Jr., the company chairman. [8]

The main problem facing a company that wants to go into

---

[6] Daniel Deudney, "Space: The High Frontier — Worldwatch Paper 50," August 1982, p. 39. It was published by the Worldwatch Institute, 1776 Massachusetts Ave., N.W., Washington, D.C. 20036.

[7] *Ibid*, p. 39. Also see Henry Cooper's 2-part articles "Shuttle I" and "Shuttle II" in *The New Yorker*, Feb. 9 and 16, 1981.

[8] Quoted in *The New York Times*, Sept. 10, 1982.

space transportation is finding a competitive alternative to NASA's shuttle. It conceivably could purchase boosters that the space agency no longer uses. Possibly a well-financed company could build its own shuttle, or buy one of NASA's — as the Space Transportation Co. of Princeton, N.J., has been attempting to do for an offering price reported to be about $1 billion.

Fairchild Industries at Germantown, Md., is spending more than $100 million to study the feasibility of building a series of "spacecraft buses," a company official said. Each "bus" would be launched into low orbit by NASA's space shuttle and then use onboard propulsion to move into higher orbit. Fairchild envisions leasing all or some of its "buses" to other companies.

While large companies such as Fairchild and McDonnell Douglas may need no further encouragement to invest in space research, many smaller ones remain skeptical that such ventures will be profitable. NASA's Customer Services office is developing pricing policies to persuade them to become shuttle users. However, the U.S. General Accounting Office has recommended to Congress that NASA charge more for use of the shuttle and gradually abandon its low-pricing policy.[9] NASA is technically a research and development agency and thus is not supposed to market its activities. This fact has led the agency to consider handing its shuttle operations over to a private company. NASA Administrator James M. Beggs is expected to make a decision this year on such a transfer.

Rising Competition in Europe and Japan

As the United States tries to find the right combination of government and industry involvement in the commercialization of space, several foreign countries are swiftly becoming competitive. The congressional Office of Technology Assessment recently advised the lawmakers that "increased foreign competition and stringent fiscal restraints" in the United States could diminish the U.S. lead in satellite communications, land-remote sensing, transportation and materials processing in space.[10]

Phil Culbertson, NASA associate deputy administrator, has said that the Japanese "have made major inroads in communications technology, and the Europeans are now vigorously marketing a launch system."[11] The European Space Agency's three-stage launch rocket, *Ariane*, already has lured commercial users away from the U.S. shuttle.[12] *Ariane's* American customers include Western Union, which has booked

[9] General Accounting Office, "NASA Must Reconsider Operations Pricing Policy for Cost Growth on the Space Transportation System," report to Congress by the Comptroller General, Feb. 23, 1982.
[10] "Civilian Space Policy and Applications," OTA report to Congress, June 15, 1982; Government Printing Office, Washington, D.C. 20402.
[11] Quoted in *Congressional Quarterly Weekly Report*, June 24, 1982, p. 1764.
[12] See *Aviation Week & Space Technology*, Oct. 4, 1982, p. 22.

its Westar satellite for launching this year, and Southern Pacific Communications of California. But unlike the shuttle, the unmanned Ariane cannot retrieve satellites or carry astronauts aboard to repair and replace damaged satellites.

Militarization of Space

W HILE the United States was developing the space shuttle, the Soviet Union was creating and launching *Salyut* space stations. The first one, in 1971, and subsequent ones in 1972, 1973, 1975 and 1977 have been characterized by James E. Oberg, a Soviet affairs specialist at NASA, as of the "civilian" variety. But he said others that were launched in 1973, 1974 and 1976 were essentially for military purposes.[13] However, it is often difficult to separate military purposes from the scientific—since any number of scientific advances in space can be adapted to military uses.

It is no secret that both the United States and Russia eye each other's space efforts warily, and often accuse the other of being obsessed with the military applications of space technology. According to the Department of Defense, the Soviet Union spends about 70 percent of its space budget on military-oriented missions, and an additional 15 percent on combined military and civilian activities.[14] About 20 percent of NASA's $6.6 billion budget in this fiscal year is allocated to military missions. However, there is an additional $8.3 billion in the Defense budget for military space activities, bringing America's military share of its total $14.9 billion space budget close to 70 percent also.

"Space in military terms is big, important business and getting more so," *Air Force Magazine* observed last summer.[15] Among the military services, the Air Force gets the lion's share of space money, some $7.2 billion in this fiscal year's budget, amounting to 9 percent of the Air Force's spending. The Air Force plans to use the space shuttle as a launching pad for spy satellites and for satellite service, repair and modification. Eventually it would like to use the shuttle as a base for assembling a manned space station which, among other things, could launch spacecraft to higher orbits for longer duration.

---

[13] See Oberg's book, *Red Star in Orbit* (1981).
[14] See "Soviet Military Power," publication released by the Public Correspondence Division, Office of Assistant Secretary of Defense for Public Affairs, 1982.
[15] *Air Force Magazine*, August 1982, p. 49. The magazine, published by the Air Force Association, does not officially speak for the Air Force but usually reflects its views.

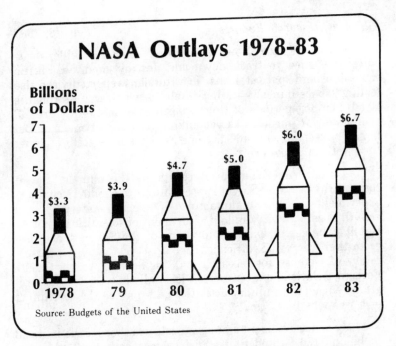

NASA Outlays 1978-83

Billions of Dollars

- 1978: $3.3
- 79: $3.9
- 80: $4.7
- 81: $5.0
- 82: $6.0
- 83: $6.7

Source: Budgets of the United States

Of the 234 shuttle flights scheduled through 1994, according to the General Accounting Office, 114 (48 percent) are military related; 13 of the initial 44 flights through 1986 are specifically military. NASA officials say that most of the shuttle's current military missions are "passive" — they involve such things as weather predictions, surveillance (spy satellites), navigation and communications. But the shuttle also is equipped to launch satellites that would give early warning of missile attacks, and would provide advanced and improved navigation for warships, warplanes and military vehicles.

Fear of Soviets Holding 'High Ground'

While "militarization of space" has been decried in Congress and in the press, Defense officials argue that the alternative is to let Russia gain uncontested control of "the high ground" and thus threaten U.S. security. They point to Soviet cosmonauts repeatedly setting records for length of time in orbit, currently up to 211 consecutive days, and note that Russia launches more satellites than the United States does. In June 1982, the Soviets established a new record by placing 15 satellites in orbit, about the same number this country launched in all of 1981. During that entire year, according to U.S. calculations, the Russians launched 858 military and 392 civilian satellites.

Some of the satellites conduct routine military tasks such as communications, mapping and reconnaissance. Like other nations with satellites in orbit, they are used to monitor world grain crops. Other satellites are more worrisome. U.S. sources say the Soviets have flown and tested about 20 "killer" satellites, designed to track down and destroy enemy satellites, spaceships and space stations. The Russians reportedly are also testing "space mines" — killer satellites which would orbit the Earth for long periods of time, awaiting detonation by ground command, for purposes as yet unknown. A Department of Defense spokesman said at least one Soviet killer satellite circles the Earth in a low orbit.

Like their American counterparts in the shuttle, Soviet cosmonauts use their Salyut space stations to conduct "civilian" experiments — the manufacture of special materials, seed growth in zero gravity, and an assortment of scientific activities. But it's the secret, military missions of the Soviet space program that worry U.S. officials. Richard D. DeLauer, Undersecretary of Defense for research and engineering, told a Senate Foreign Relations subcommittee last fall that the Salyut program "engages in military activities and may be the forerunner of a weapons platform."[16]

There is disagreement among experts whether Russia is ahead or behind the United States in its space activity. The Soviet program presumably does not have a reusable craft such as the U.S. shuttle — but that is not certain. There is some belief that, although unadvertised, a reusable Soviet space vehicle is being developed. As for Russia having more satellite launchings, that may reveal weakness rather than strength. The Soviet satellites usually do not remain operational as long as American satellites, so more of them must be put into orbit.

Nevertheless, Soviet space operations have been impressive to many. Oberg, for instance, believes Russia is developing the Salyut as a small basic space station in order to acquire long-term experience in space operations. Already, Soviet cosmonauts have spent more than twice as much time in orbit than have American astronauts. Valeriy Ryumin, the most experienced civilian engineer-cosmonaut, accumulated 362 days of space flight on three missions in 1977, 1979 and 1980.

While U.S. experts predict the Russians will continue to use expendable boosters and capsules in the near future, it is likely that at the same time they are developing a permanent space station to be manned by three or four cosmonauts for as long as a year at a time. It is envisioned that later in the 1980s or in the 1990s, Soviet space stations would be able to accommodate up to six crewmen. Boris Petrov, chairman of the Soviet Interkosmos Council, has been quoted as saying "scientists are already busy designing large stations for a crew of 12 to 20, with

---

[16] Testimony before the Subcommittee on Arms Control, Oceans, International Operations and Environment, Sept. 20, 1982.

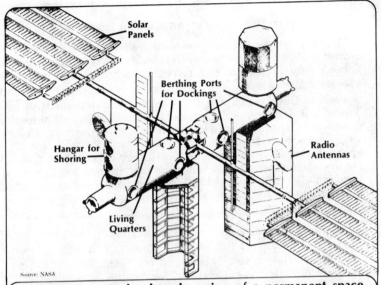

Solar Panels

Berthing Ports for Dockings

Hangar for Shoring

Radio Antennas

Living Quarters

Source: NASA

Space Station. A developed version of a permanent space station. Included is a scientific space laboratory, a materials-processing factory, a module for servicing payloads and another for fabrication of large space systems.

a life span of up to 10 years, which would replace the present small stations."[17] Soviet scientists also have predicted the appearance of "space towns" by the end of the century.

Permanent Bases Aloft; Killer Satellites

American space buffs, too, are enthusiastic about the idea of a space station. NASA Administrator Beggs has called a manned space station "the next logical step" after the development of the shuttle. He envisions it as the assembly point for manned and unmanned missions to Mars and other planets.[18] The space agency has contracted with eight aerospace companies[19] to study the potential commercial, military and scientific uses of a space station. The study results are expected in April.

Although President Reagan issued a national space policy statement last July 4, he stopped short of backing a big new project, such as a manned space station. His statement instead included a general endorsement of the space program and a commitment to the use of space for commercial and national security purposes. Reagan set out a number of civilian objec-

---

[17] James Oberg, *op. cit.*, p. 232.
[18] His views were outlined in a speech to the Detroit Economic Club and the Detroit Engineering Society, June 23, 1982.
[19] Boeing Aerospace Co., Seattle; General Dynamics Corp., Convair Division, San Diego; Grumman Aerospace Corp., Bethpage, N.Y.; Lockheed Missile and Space Co., Sunnyvale, Calif.; Martin Marietta Aerospace, Denver Aerospace, Denver; McDonnell Douglas Astronautics Co., Huntington Beach, Calif.; Rockwell International, Space Operations/Integration and Satellite Systems Division, Downey, Calif.; and TRW Inc., Defense and Space Systems Groups, Redondo Beach, Calif.

International Law and Outer Space

The main international agreement governing outer space was drafted in 1967 by a U.N. body and is known today as the Outer Space Treaty. It has been signed by 107 countries, including all that are active in space.

A second U.N.-sponsored space agreement, known as the Moon Treaty, was drafted in 1979 but has been ratified by only three countries, of which only one (France) has a space program. The 1967 treaty holds that outer space is not subject to national appropriation while the later one goes a step further, saying that the moon and other celestial bodies are the "common heritage of mankind" — a concept promoted by Third World countries but resisted by both the industrial West and Russia.

tives, including research and experimentation in the origin and evolution of the universe and solar system, the Earth's environment and its relation to the sun, and the technology of permanent space facilities. He also called for "a climate conductive to expanded private sector investment and involvement in space activities."

For national security aspects of space, the policy stated that the United States will proceed with development of an anti-satellite capability to deter threats to U.S. space systems. The statement added that the United States would develop an attack warning, notification and verification capability to detect and react to threats to the United States in space. A Fact Sheet issued by the White House describing the policy noted that it grew out of a National Security Council study, which explains its emphasis on defense issues, analysts said.

Scarcely more than a month after Reagan issued his policy statement emphasizing military aspects of space, the secretary general of the United Nations, Javier Perez de Cuellar, opened a U.N.-sponsored conference in Vienna on the future of outer space by warning that an arms race in space holds the "potential for confrontation."[20]

Russia and the United States negotiated off and on during the 1970s to control anti-satellite weapons, but the talks broke off at the end of the decade when Russia invaded Afghanistan. One immense barrier to agreement was Russia's insistence that the space shuttle be considered an anti-satellite system since it had the capability of intercepting and destroying Soviet satellites. The United States argued that shuttles are too expensive ever to become numerous[21] and, moreover, are not feasible anti-satellite weapons.

---

[20] Statement to the Unispace '82 Conference, Second United Nations Conference on the Exploration and Peaceful Uses of Outer Space, Aug. 9, 1982.
[21] Costs run to about $1 billion apiece; the United States currently expects to build only four.

Both the United States and Russia are known to be trying to build an even more futuristic weapon using laser beams. As envisioned, powerful lasers in orbit would intercept and destroy intercontinental ballistics missiles in flight as they arc above the Earth. However, it has been estimated that a laser ray system capable of providing the United States protection from Soviet ICBMs might cost $1 trillion or more. There is an even greater drawback. "Using space-based lasers as a ballistic missile defense suffers from the same problems — in spades — that led the U.S. and U.S.S.R. to agree by treaty to abandon all anti-ballistic missiles a decade ago," Daniel Deudney writes. "The central problem of all anti-ballistic missile systems is the ease with which the highly sensitive radars that track oncoming missiles can be utterly blinded."[22]

The American public appears about evenly divided on whether the U.S. space program should focus primarily on national defense or scientific exploration. In an NBC/Associated Press poll conducted in 1981, 47 percent of the people questioned favored a military emphasis while 43 percent said scientific aspects should be emphasized. The remaining 10 percent wanted an equal emphasis on both.

Directions of Space Science

MILITARY and commercial endeavors in space are possible only because gigantic strides have been made in space science and technology during the past quarter-century. Space science can be divided into two types: that which looks inward for a better understanding of our own planet and that which looks outward for a better understanding of the universe. A comparison of the NASA Space Science Program budgets in 1965 and 1983 indicates that today outer space is taking a back seat to the shuttle and Earth satellite programs. The 1983 figure is $697.8 million, less than half of the 1965 outlay in terms of constant dollars — without the effects of inflation. NASA's planetary missions make up only about 5 percent of the space agency's current budget.

The commitment to the shuttle and Earth satellites has led to the cancellation of postponement of several scientific projects. NASA's Office of Space Science has only two major missions in this decade, putting the Space Telescope *(see p. 166)* in orbit and sending another spacecraft to Jupiter. In contrast, there were 24 missions in the 1970s. NASA also postponed to 1987-88

---

[22] Daniel Deudney, *op. cit.*, p. 25.

Nuclear-Powered Satellites

Since a nuclear reactor can generate much more power for a satellite than the usual array of solar panels, they are favored for "supersatellites" of the future — especially for military purposes. Already the United States has one aloft and Russia has launched 18. One was Cosmos 1402, which plunged into the Indian Ocean Jan. 23 — except for fiery fragments of final piece which came down in the South Atlantic Feb. 7. They landed far from human habitation but caused concern over a cloud of radioactive dust the satellite's reaction left in the upper atmosphere.

Another nuclear-powered Cosmos crashed into a remote area of northern Canada in 1978. In that case the reactor's uranium fuel burned up high in the atmosphere and apparently spared the impact area of radioactive contamination. American space officials say that Russia has put up 18 nuclear-powered satellites during the past several years. The United States launched one such satellite in 1965 which is still operating in orbit. Defense officials are reported to be considering adding others.

a Gamma Ray Observatory to help astronomers study the universe at very high frequencies. The project Venus Orbiting Imaging Radar, which would study the cloud-covered Venusian surface in detail, also has been delayed.

Carl Sagan, the astronomer-author, has said that future knowledge of "deep" space is being denied by present-day cancellations and postponements. "We are the beneficiaries of decisions made in the 1960s and the 1970s," he said. "There are no new starts in this decade, with the single exception of Galileo . . . and that worries me greatly."[23]

American scientists are especially upset that NASA has decided not to sponsor a space probe to enter and investigate the great swath of ice, frozen gases and other celestial debris that make up Halley's Comet when it reappears in the Earth's view in the winter of 1985-86. The Office of Technology has said that the space agency's lack of interest in a comet mission "puts U.S. scientists at a clear disadvantage with respect to the Europeans and the Soviets, both of whom will be flying such missions." Sagan has said: "There is the ominous and very real prospect that American leadership in planetary exploration will come to an abrupt end."[24]

Reflecting the rising interest in Halley's Comet, the Library of Congress recently published a listing of books and articles that already have appeared on the subject. The listing run to seven printed pages. There is even a *Halley's Comet Watch*

---

[23] Remarks in an interview broadcast on "The MacNeil-Lehrer Report," PBS-TV, Nov. 4, 1981.
[24] Quoted in *The New York Times*, July 19, 1981.

Newsletter.[25] The comet's sighting occurs every 75 years when it approaches the sun on its journey back from the outer reaches of our solar system. The Soviet Union, in partnership with France, is sending out two spacecraft, the Venera Halley 1 and 2, to witness the event at close range.

In December 1984 the spacecraft should come within 6,000 miles of the comet's solid nucleus and spend hours taking pictures and gathering data. In July 1985 the European Space Agency will launch the Giotto, which will fly within 100 miles of the comet. A Japanese spacecraft, the Planet A, will be launched the following month on the same mission.

Past Leadership in Planetary Research

The U.S. space program has long been the pioneer in scientific ventures. There have been dozens of unmanned exploratory probes over the years. In 1959, the Mariner 1 and 2 spacecraft circled Venus. The Pioneer series continued the space quest among the planets in the 1960s and 1970s. Pioneer 10 and 11, launched in 1972 and 1973, were the first spacecraft to visit Jupiter. Pioneer 11 went on to Saturn and in September 1979 returned the first close-up images of that planet.

Since 1979, the Pioneer Venus Orbiter has been circling Venus, studying its atmosphere, taking hundreds of ultraviolet pictures and radar-mapping its surface. Five Pioneer Venus probes have descended by parachute through the planet's atmosphere, sending data back to Earth for over an hour. From that information scientists confirmed their suspicion that Venus is a "hellish" planet, with a surface temperature about 900 degrees Fahrenheit, hot enough to melt lead. Pioneer Venus Orbiter will continue to operate through 1985, changing orbital paths.[26] Pioneer spacecraft operations and data analysis activities were terminated in September 1983, although limited operations necessary to the survival of the spacecraft were performed. In October 1986, Pioneer will become the first space probe to leave to solar system and travel into eternity.

Voyager 2, following its sister ship Voyager 1 to Saturn by a different trajectory, discovered in a region surrounding Saturn the hottest gas yet detected in the solar system. Voyager's instruments showed temperatures ranging from 600 million to

---

[25] The listing appears in the *LC* [Library of Congress] *Information Bulletin,* Nov. 26, 1982, compiled by Ruth S. Freitag of the Library's Science and Technology Division. The newsletter describes itself as the "official publication of Halley's Comet Watch '86 ... an international organization dedicated to the historical, scientific study of ... Halley's Comet." Its address is Box 188, Vincetown, N.J. 08088.

[26] The Soviet Union also has sent probes to Venus. On Feb. 28 and March 5, 1982, two Soviet spacecraft landed on Venus, the seventh and eighth the Russians have landed on the planet.

more than one billion degrees Fahrenheit, about 330 degrees hotter than the Sun's corona. Like Voyager 1, Voyager 2 concentrated on Saturn's rings, but the spacecraft also studied Saturn's moons. It is now destined to reach Uranus in 1986 and Neptune in 1989 unless NASA decides to cancel those two visits.

NASA, in cooperation with West Germany, will launch the survey spacecraft Galileo toward Jupiter in 1985. Galileo initially was scheduled to go into orbit around Jupiter in 1987, but budget austerity will slow its flight. It won't reach the planet until 1989. A conventional upper-stage engine will be used to fire the spacecraft instead of the new, more powerful, hydrogen-fueled, high-energy Centaur engine, which would have enabled Galileo to fly a more direct path to Jupiter.

Telescope in Orbit and Earth Projects

Mankind will be able to peer farther into space than ever before when a gigantic telescope is sent above the Earth's atmosphere aboard a space shuttle and then placed in orbit. This log-shaped Space Telescope, 43 feet long and 14 feet wide and weighing 12 tons *(see illustration),* is expected to remain operable well into the 21st century. With a view unhindered by the Earth's atmosphere, astronomers expect to see stars created 14 billions years ago, about the time of the creation of the universe, according to some scientific thinking.

The telescope's first important assignment will include observations of Uranus to help plan the course of the Voyager 2 flyby of Uranus in January 1986. The telescope will also help astronomers study Halley's comet, though from a greater distance that the European and Japanese probes. Some scientists predict that one of the first discoveries with the telescope will be that of another planetary system.

For all of the fascination with planets and other celestial bodies, the space program's focus these days is essentially upon the Earth and its immediate surroundings. A decade ago on July 23, 1972, NASA inaugurated its Landsat satellite program to collect information about Earth's resources by means of remote sensing instruments placed on a platform in space. The Landsat 1 satellite was followed by 2 in 1975 and 3 in 1978, both of which are still in service. Last July 16, NASA launched Landsat 4, equipped with high advanced scanning devices that provide greater clarity of detail.

The space agency plans soon to hook a device called SARSAT — Satellite-aided Search and Rescue System — onto a satellite so that distress signals from ships and aircraft radio beacons can be monitored. The monitoring will be conducted by the National Oceanic and Atmospheric Administration.

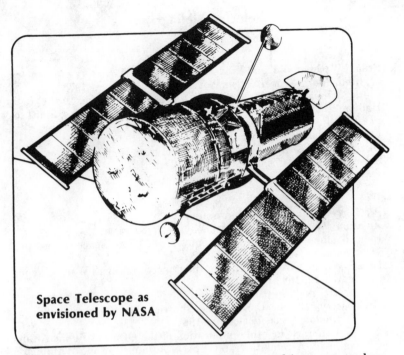

Space Telescope as envisioned by NASA

One futuristic concept on the drawing board is a space solar-power satellite. It would collect solar energy and beam it to Earth for conversion into electricity. But as-yet-unsolved technical problems and cost estimates that range between $1.5 trillion and $3 trillion have led the National Academy of Sciences to recommend that no funding be allocated to the satellite's development until the 21st century.

Envisioning 21st Century Space Colonies

By then, according to some of the more visionary notions of what lies ahead, may come mankind's first feeble efforts to establish colonies in space — until now only the stuff of science fiction. By the early 1970s Princeton University physicist Gerard O'Neill was seriously proposing that the world embark on a plan to place facilities in orbit capable of sustaining life for 10,000 — eventually one million — people. As portrayed in his 1977 book *The High Frontier: Human Colonies in Space,* these would be idyllic, spacious settings covered by transparent domes.

There are other scenarios which today seem far-fetched if no absurd. Yet considering how many of Jules Verne's 19th century insights became reality in the 20th century, people living in the last quarter of this century dare not scoff at predictions of what the next may bring. More than artistic achievement may account for the moviegoing popularity of "ET" and the readership of Arthur Clarke's *2010: Odyssey Two.*

167

Selected Bibliography

Books

Braun, Werhner von, and Frederick I. Ordway III, *History of Rocketry and Space Travel,* Thomas Y. Crowell Publisher, 1975.

Clark, Arthur C., *2010: Odyssey Two,* Ballantine Books, 1982.

Hallion, Richard, *Apollo: Ten Years Since Tranquility Base,* Smithsonian Institution Press, 1981.

Michener, James A., *Space,* Random House, 1982.

Oberg, James E. *Red Star in Space,* Random House, 1981.

Sagan, Carl, *The Cosmic Connection,* Dell, 1973.

Articles

Air Force Magazine, selected issues.

Aviation Week & Space Technology, selected issues.

Bahcall, John N., and Lyman Spitzer Jr., "The Space Telescope," *Scientific American,* July 1982.

Broad, William, "A Fatal Flaw in the Concept of Space War," *Science,* March 12, 1982.

Cooper, Henry, "Shuttle" (2 parts), *The New Yorker,* Feb. 9, 16, 1981.

Grey, Jerry, "Implications of the Shuttle: Our Business in Space," *Technology Review,* October 1981.

NASA Activities (monthly publication of the Office of Public Affairs, National Aeronautics and Space Administration, Washington, D.C.), selected issues.

Granat, Diane, "Space Issues Before Congress Involve Setting New Projects, Meeting Foreign Challenge," *Congressional Quarterly Weekly Report,* July 24, 1982.

Kidger, Neville, "Japanese Space Plans for 1982-85," *Spaceflight,* May 1982.

Sheldon, Charles, "Military Space in Transition," *Astronautics & Aeronautics,* October 1981.

von Puttkamer, Jesco, "The Industrialization of Space," *The Futurist,* June 1979.

Reports and Studies

Deudney, Daniel, "Space: The High Frontier in Perspective — Worldwatch Paper 50," Worldwatch Institute, 1776 Massachusetts Ave. N.W., Washington, D.C. 20036.

Editorial Research Reports: "Changing U.S. Space Policy," 1978 Vol. II, p. 823; "Space Shuttle Controversy," 1972 Vol. I, p. 211.

Office of Technolology Assessment, "Space Science Research in the United States," technical memorandum, Sept. 23, 1982; Government Printing Office, Washington, D.C. 20401.

Office of the White House Press Secretary, "National Space Policy," July 4, 1982.

Sheldon, Charles, and Marcia Smith, "Space Activities of the United States, Soviet Union, and Other Launching Countries/ Organizations," Congressional Research Service, U.S. Congress.

Research assistance by Marc Stencel.

Illustrations on cover and pp. 153, 159, 161, 167 by Staff Artist Robert Redding.

TROUBLED AIR TRANSPORT INDUSTRY

by

Richard C. Schroeder

Nov. 26
1 9 8 2

TROUBLED AIR TRANSPORT INDUSTRY

THE friendly skies have become increasingly troubled for commercial aviation in the United States and throughout the world. Depressed economic conditions have cut into airline traffic while operating costs have spiraled upward. For the past two years, airlines have been awash in red ink, and industry experts see little hope for a dramatic upturn in the near future. Two big international airlines have gone belly up this year alone. British-based Laker Airways folded early in the year, followed in May by the spectacular collapse of Braniff International.

Airline troubles have spilled over into the aircraft manufacturing industry as well. Shrinking airline profits and high interest rates have cut into sales of both new and used aircraft by the two remaining U.S. commercial jet airplane makers, Boeing and McDonnell Douglas, and by their competitor, Airbus Industrie, a multinational European airframe consortium. Declining aircraft sales could have a serious impact on the U.S. balance of trade. Exports of civil aircraft, engines and parts reached $13.9 billion last year, out of total aerospace exports of $18.1 billion, and exports represented 72 percent of industry sales. While not as significant as exports of agricultural products, which topped $40 billion, aerospace exports racked up a healthy $13.1 billion trade surplus in 1981.

Mounting Losses of Commercial Carriers

U.S. scheduled airline members of the Air Transport Association, the domestic airlines' trade association, suffered losses of $222 million in 1980 and $421 million in 1981.[1] In the first quarter of 1982, the 11 major airlines (see box, p. 173) — those with annual revenues of more than $1 billion — posted the worst performance in U.S. aviation history. Their net losses amounted to $583.3 million for the January-March period. A leading aviation trade journal headlined an editorial "Carnage in the First Quarter," noting that the losers included Delta Air

---

[1] See *Air Transport 1982*, Annual Report of the U.S. Scheduled Airline Industry. Among the big losers were Pan American World Airways, with an operating loss of $377 million in 1981, and United Airlines, the nation's largest carrier in terms of passenger miles flown, with an operating loss of $146 million. Pan American eased the pain by selling some of its non-airline properties, including the Pan American building in New York City and the profitable Intercontinental Hotel chain, bringing its net loss for the year to under $19 million. United, with no such ancillary transaction on the books, finished the year with a net loss of $105 million.

Lines which "had not shown a loss in 25 years." [2] In the second quarter, losses were smaller ($34.9 million) but still substantial.

In July, August and September the 11 majors reported profits of $147.8 million. But this performance did not generate much optimism because the industry is always strong at this season of vacation travel. It has never posted a loss in the third quarter, according to Dr. George James, senior vice president for economics and finance at the Air Transport Association. Not only did this year's third quarter profits appear disappointingly small, but virtually all analysts expect losses to reappear in the fourth quarter. Dr. James forecasts year-end red ink of $500 million, and *The Wall Street Journal* reported that "the year could be the worst ever for the industry." [3]

The picture is much the same the world over. For fiscal year 1982, which ended in March for British Airways, the company reported the largest financial loss ever sustained by an airline in a single year — 544.8 million British pounds, equivalent to about $923 million. The 1981 edition of *World Air Transport Statistics,* published by the International Air Transport Association (IATA), an organization of 120 international airlines, declared that "1981 set a new unwelcome record of the lowest rate of growth in traffic since records began in 1929." In terms of "ton miles" — the amount of weight times distance — scheduled traffic increased by less than 3 percent.

Following record losses in 1980, the scheduled airlines of the member countries of the International Civil Aviation Organization (ICAO), an intergovernmental specialized agency of the United Nations, posted even larger deficits in 1981. The overall losses were $1.1 billion in 1980 and $1.2 billion in 1981. The two years marked the first time since record keeping began in 1947 that world airlines recorded losses *before* taking into account such factors as interest and money-losing operations of affiliated companies.[4]

Adding to the misery of the airlines, an unusual number of fatal airplane crashes have taken place in 1982. Normally, airplanes are among the safest modes of transportation. There were no fatal accidents involving scheduled airlines in the United States in 1980 and only four in 1981.[5] This year was a different story. In the first five days of the year, six persons died

---

[2] *Aviation Week & Space Technology,* May 3, 1982, p. 7.
[3] Harlan S. Byrne, *The Wall Street Journal,* Oct. 27, 1982. Dr. James' views were reported by Anita Schrodt in *The Journal of Commerce,* Nov. 3, 1982.
[4] See *World Air Transport Statistics,* 26th edition, and *The State of the Air Transport Industry,* Annual Report of IATA, 1981, p. 5.
[5] *Flight Safety Digest,* published by the Flight Safety Foundation, January 1982, p. 3.

Major U.S. Airlines

Revenue Passenger Miles Flown: (add 000)		Total Operating Revenues: (add 000)	
1. United Airlines	34,340,808	1. United	$4,470,312
2. Pan American World Airways	28,909,490	2. American	3,911,109
		3. Eastern	3,727,093
3. American Airlines	27,798,062	4. Delta	3,644,209
4. Eastern Air Lines	26,069,890	5. Pan Am	3,585,584
5. Trans World Airlines	25,727,012	6. TWA	3,395,419
6. Delta Air Lines	24,245,068	7. Northwest	1,844,988
7. Northwest Airlines	14,251,932	8. Republic	1,448,416
8. Western Airlines	8,532,779	9. USAir	1,110,491
9. Continental Airlines	7,915,677	10. Continental	1,075,114
10. Republic Airlines	7,554,865	11. Western	1,059,841
11. USAir	5,423,605		

Source: Air Transport Association of America

in three air crashes. Then on Jan. 13, an Air Florida flight plunged into the frigid waters of the Potomac River during takeoff from Washington's National Airport, with a loss of 78 lives. In July, 154 persons died in the crash of a Pan American World Airways jet in suburban New Orleans. Two foreign crashes had meanwhile occurred in March, leaving 49 dead. And in September 55 persons were killed in the crash of a charter flight taking off from Malaga, Spain for New York.

Less Passenger Traffic and Higher Costs

The plight of the airlines is one familiar to businesses everywhere that have been hit by recession, high interest rates and huge fuel bills. Customers are fewer and costs are rising. Excess capacity, built up by optimistic managers during the booming 1970s, adds to competitive pressures and has led to a wave of business failures and corporate mergers, such as the takeover of National Airlines by Pan American two years ago.

Airline passenger volume hit a peak in 1979 and has been declining ever since (see graph, p. 174). Nearly 317 million passengers boarded U.S. scheduled airlines that year. In 1980, the number dwindled to 296 million and dropped again to 287 million last year. Passenger miles flown followed a similar down curve, falling from 262 billion in 1979 to 255 billion in 1980 and 249 million in 1981. In the same period, airline capacity was rising from 416 billion "seat miles" in 1979 to 425 billion last year. As a result, the load factor, the percentage of capacity

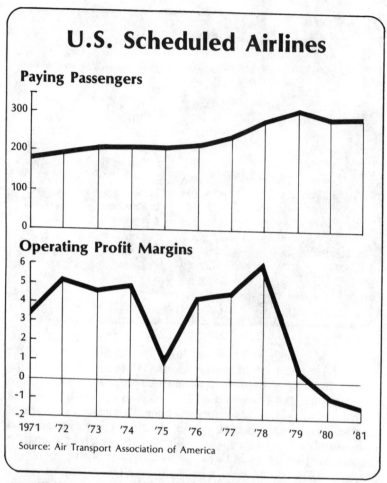

U.S. Scheduled Airlines

Paying Passengers

Operating Profit Margins

1971 '72 '73 '74 '75 '76 '77 '78 '79 '80 '81

Source: Air Transport Association of America

actually used, slipped from 63 percent in 1979 to 58 in 1981. Many experts think the 1982 load factor will be even lower.

Passenger revenues have been rising slowly, as airlines have made selective fare adjustments on various routes. Passenger revenues of scheduled airline members of the ATA rose from $22.8 billion in 1979 to $30.6 billion in 1981, a 34 percent improvement. In the past 10 years, total revenues, including freight and other operations, have more than tripled, rising from $10 billion in 1971 to $36.5 billion in 1981. But the real story is told in the other side of the coin — expenses — which have gone from $9.7 billion in 1971 (producing an operating profit of more than $300 million) to $36.9 billion last year (leaving an operating deficit of more than $400 million).

The most important cost factor for airlines today is the price of fuel. According to the Air Transport Association, the average cost of a gallon of aviation fuel rose from 11.3 cents in 1971 to $1.04 last year. In 1971, fuel represented only 12.6 percent of all airline operating costs, while in 1981 it amounted to 30.4 percent — even though fuel consumption was actually less than a decade earlier.

By contrast, the number of U.S. airline employees rose from 292,000 in 1971 to 318,000 in 1981, but labor's percentage of total operating expenses declined from 46.1 to 35.5. In similar fashion, interest payments on airline debts more than tripled, growing to $1.2 billion in 1981. Yet debt service as a percentage of operating expenses actually dropped from 4.1 to 3.5 percent. In fact, virtually every expense category — including passenger meals, aircraft maintenance materials, landing fees and advertising and promotion — declined as a percentage of operating costs even though they rose in absolute volume.

Internationally, the record is spotty. Domestic operations of IATA member airlines are down, but international traffic was up by 5 percent in 1981. In some parts of the world, particularly Africa, Asia and the Middle East, vigorous growth is the norm. But traffic is down all over the Western Hemisphere and in transoceanic crossings. In its 1982 annual report, IATA predicts a deficit of $1.9 billion for all of its member airlines this year and adds that the loss could rise to $2.1 billion in 1983. According to IATA Director-General Knut Hammarskjold, the world's airlines could reach an industry position of "negative net worth" by the end of next year.

The international scene is not directly analogous to that in the United States. Only in this country is private ownership of commercial airlines the general rule. In most other countries, airlines are predominantly government-owned, and looked on as a public utility rather than as a purely profit-making venture. One exception is Air Canada, which is government-owned but operates under legislation requiring it to function as a "profit center," competing in the marketplace. Air Canada is, by industry consensus, one of the better managed airlines. Though consistently profitable, it too has been hurt by depressed economic conditions and may be forced to cut back operations and personnel, according to company officials. Elsewhere, a large number of state-owned air transport companies are being kept alive largely through subsidies and protectionist laws and rules.

Airline Deregulation's Disputed Aftereffect

The depressed state of the economy is the root cause of the problems of all airlines, but another factor — airline deregulation — has arguably worsened the situation for U.S. carriers. There is no consensus on the impact of deregulation; in fact, it remains, four years after taking effect, one of the most controversial issues in the air transport field. Some airline executives praise deregulation; others say it is the principal reason for a wave of bankruptcies and mergers that have overtaken the industry. Airline pilots denounce it on safety grounds, while consumer advocates generally say it has brought lower air fares and improved airline productivity.

Deregulation certainly has brought ruinous rate-cutting wars among major trunk line carriers — those flying the most-traveled routes between big cities — precisely when airlines cannot afford to lose a penny in passenger revenues.[6] New companies, called "cream-skimmers," have flocked to provide cut-rate service on the most lucrative short-hop routes. As observed in the magazine of the Air Line Pilots Association (ALPA):

> . . . [T]he airline game has turned into a brawl. There have been mergers and shutdowns. Intrastate airlines have gone interstate. New airlines have sprung up with startling alacrity. Commuter airlines, operating at a lower level of safety under the permissive rules of the Federal Aviation Administration, have proliferated. Fare wars take place daily as the upstart airlines fight for their place in the sun and the established carriers try to play stayupmanship.[7]

The Airline Deregulation Act was signed by President Carter on Oct. 24, 1978, replacing the Federal Aviation Act of 1958.[8] Shortly after the act became law, *Consumer Reports* magazine noted admiringly, "Where the old law treated the airline industry like a giant public utility to be protected from the hazards of the marketplace, the new law encourages competition as the source of efficiency, innovation, low prices, and a greater variety of service, while allowing reasonable profits for the airlines."[9]

The act provided for the abolition of the Civil Aeronautics Board on Jan. 1, 1985. In the meantime, the CAB's authority over airline routes and air fares would be gradually phased out. The board relinquished control over routes at the end of 1981, and will terminate its authority over rates and fares, airline mergers and acquisitions at the end of this year. When the CAB is abolished, the Department of Transportation will take over its subsidy program. Its foreign air transportation authority will be transferred to the Departments of Justice and Transportation.

Regulations written to implement the Airline Deregulation Act were even looser than the act itself. Established airlines set up hundreds of new routes and discontinued service on many others. Smaller cities faced severe cutbacks in service, while competition intensified and fares plummeted in service to lucrative "hub" cities around the country. "At the same time,"

---

[6] See "The Carriers' Kamikaze Attack on Air Fares," *Business Week*, Oct. 18, 1982, pp. 46-47.
[7] C. V. Glines, "The Escalating Threat," *Air Line Pilot*, June 1981.
[8] For background, see "Deregulating Transportation," *E.R.R.*, 1979 Vol. I, pp. 441-460.
[9] "Where Deregulation Works," *Consumer Reports*, May 1979, p. 284.

wrote veteran air transport reporter Stuart Nixon, "new airlines began to appear; Midway Airlines started service in November 1979, followed a year later by New York Air."

A wave of mergers [he continued] also got under way: North Central and Southern joined forces in July 1979 to become Republic; then Pan American won a bitter fight with Texas International for the chance to buy National. Tiger International, parent company of the Flying Tiger Line (FTL), went after Seaboard in hopes of combining it with FTL (the merger was completed in 1980) and Summa Corporation, owner of Hughes Airwest, decided to sell its airline holdings, talking initially to Allegheny (which was in the process of changing its name to USAir) and then to Republic, the eventual buyer.[10]

R. S. Maurer, vice chairman of Delta, is an airline executive who favors deregulation. "There is a lot more flexibility of being able to marshal assets and put them where you have the best opportunity to make a profit," he said. On the other hand, Gordon Autry, president of Rocky Mountain Airways, advocates a return to federal control. "We took an industry that has been regulated for some degree for about 50 years, and heavily regulated for 40 years, and virtually overnight thrust it into a total free-for-all."[11]

The Air Line Pilots Association also wants a return to federal supervision of airline operations. ALPA President J. J. O'Donnell fears that cost-conscious airline managers may stint on maintenance and raise the risk of accidents. "Aviation safety is a very delicate cord, easily severed when placed at the mercy of razor-sharp competition," he wrote in a letter to *The Wall Street Journal*, dated April 27, 1982. ALPA is also unhappy that, in the relaxed environment of deregulation, some newer airlines are employing non-union personnel at wages below union scale.

Cost-Cutting and Promotional Gimmickry

The major airlines have been doing everything they can think of to reduce costs and boost passenger revenues. In the wake of deregulation, many companies cut back their management staffs and placed greater emphasis on marketing. A CAB spokesman said of airline management: "Those boys are finally being forced to work for their money."

Cost-cutting extends from such obvious efforts as purchasing more fuel-efficient planes and engines, to minuscule weight-reduction details. The uniforms of cabin personnel are made of lighter materials and crews are limited in the amount of per-

---

[10] Stuart Nixon, "Turbulent Times for Airlines," *Air Line Pilot*, May 1982.

[11] Maurer was quoted by Agis Salpukas in *The New York Times*, May 8, 1982; Autry by Hobart Rowen in *The Washington Post*, Oct. 31, 1982. Rowen, a senior economics and business writer at the Post, has frequently opposed deregulation in his columns.

sonal luggage they can carry aboard. Passenger seats are smaller and lighter. The April 1982 issue of *Airline Executive* magazine ran an advertisement for a new line of aircraft seats touted as the "Undercover Fuel Saver." Eastern Airlines has sanded the paint off some of its planes, leaving the bare aluminum skin, to reduce drag while in flight. United Airlines took the radical step — radical at least to enologists — of serving wine in cans because they are lighter than bottles.

To attract more passengers, rate-cutting is widespread on heavily traveled routes. Last summer, the standard round-trip fare for the New York-Los Angeles run was $378. By mid-October it was down as low as $218 on some lines. It will rise again during the busy holiday season, and then taper off as the winter doldrums set in. Rate-cutting, in fact, is done on a selective basis that borders on the bizarre. There are discounts for families, discounts for frequent travelers, discounts for flying within a specific period of time, for flying on weekdays on some routes and for flying on weekends on some others. Arturo Valle, operator of a travel agency in Washington, D.C., said his newly installed computers are of little help in determining discount fares. "They change too quickly. I have to use the telephone to get the best deal for my customers."

Promotional devices are equally lurid. Pan American's "two-fer" offer — take a flight on Pan Am and receive a certificate entitling you to two tickets for the price of one the next time you fly with your spouse — is relatively staid compared to some offers. One airline, opening a new route, offered tickets "for a kiss," and then stationed pretty models at ticket counters to make good on the offer. Another gave round-trip tickets to anyone who showed up with 50 of any number of items. One passenger claimed his ticket by presenting 50 hot peppers, 50 peanuts and a 50-foot chain of paper clips.

For all the hoopla, the prospects remain bleak for many airlines. Stuart Nixon said the condition of airlines is such that "what was once an unthinkable scenario — multiple bank-ruptcies among U.S. carriers — [is] a real possibility.... What will be left when all the dust clears may be the core of the old industry, with the most efficient incumbents surviving, plus a large number of new carriers that are structured in un-traditional ways."

Commuters and Freight: Two Bright Spots

The same deregulation process that has hurt the big commercial airlines has promoted a boom in smaller operations, particularly "commuter" airlines, now the fastest growing segment of the air transport industry. Commuter lines fly relatively short distances and use airplanes with fewer than 50 seats, serving markets too small to attract the majors.

According to the Air Transport Association, there are 214,300 airplanes operating in general aviation, a category that includes corporate and pleasure aircraft as well as commuter planes. Airplanes in general aviation account for 98.7 percent of all passenger aircraft in the United States. By contrast, scheduled airlines operate only 2,808 planes, all but 59 of them jet-powered. More than 195,000 general aviation planes are piston driven.

So rapid has been the expansion of general aviation that U.S. aircraft makers have been hard-pressed to keep up with the demand for new equipment. Foreign manufacturers increasingly have been invading the U.S. market. Recently, Fairchild-Swearingen, the U.S. producer of the Metro, a 19-seat turbo-prop commuter plane, filed a complaint with the federal government charging that it was losing business to the Bandeirante, an 18-seat turboprop manufactured by Embraer, a Brazilian corporation controlled by the Brazilian government.

Although Embraer has sold 85 of its Bandeirantes in the United States since 1978, the U.S. International Trade Commission rejected Fairchild-Swearingen's charges that it was being hurt by the sale of subsidized Brazilian aircraft. Fairchild-Swearingen itself is in partnership with a foreign manufacturer, Saab-Scandia of Sweden, in the production of a new, larger commuter aircraft, the 34-passenger twin-engine turboprop Saab-Fairchild 340.

Another exception to the general picture of gloom around the airlines is in air freight, especially the overnight delivery of small packages. Overall freight operations have declined in the past three years, but less rapidly than passenger traffic, and revenues have increased despite the drop in volume. The small-package business — a highly lucrative operation yielding as much as $4 a pound compared to $1 a pound for conventional air freight — has taken off like a rocket. Its revenues are now estimated at $2 billion a year, and industry executives foresee growth rates of 15 to 25 percent a year for the next five years.[12]

Overnight freight firms offer door-to-door delivery service and, in most cases, on-time delivery guarantees. Experts say the business has grown swiftly because of (1) lack of reliable first-class mail service, (2) expansion of high-technology and professional fields demanding fast communication services, and (3) a change of inventory-distribution patterns. Automobile dealers, for example, are beginning to use overnight services as

---

[12] See Don Knoles, "Boom in U.S. Overnight Service Highlights World Air Freight Market," *Airline Executive*, July 1982, p. 19.

"flying warehouses," reducing the number of parts held in inventory, and relying on express delivery of parts ordered through a computerized telecommunications network.

Federal Express, a private company that pioneered overnight delivery, operates out of a central "hub" in Memphis, Tenn. Each night, a Federal Express fleet of 29 727-100s, 32 Falcons and four DC-10s flies to Memphis from points around the country, carrying between 130,000 and 180,000 packages. The planes are unloaded, packages are sorted according to destination and the planes are reloaded and airborne within three hours. Federal Express officials say they expect to be able to handle 400,000 packages a night by 1984, with an average turnaround time of only two hours. The success of Federal Express has drawn competition, ranging from the Flying Tigers, the biggest conventional air freight firm in the United States,[13] to the U.S. Postal Service which has inaugurated Express Mail, promising next day delivery between major cities.

Outlook for Plane Makers

AIRLINE troubles are reflected in sales slumps in aircraft and engine manufacturing industries. The number of makers of large commercial jets outside of the Soviet bloc has dwindled to just three: the Boeing Corp., based at Seattle; Airbus Industrie, a European consortium of public and privately owned airframe manufacturers in Britain, France, Spain and West Germany; and McDonnell Douglas Corp. , based at St. Louis, a longtime producer of both civil and military aircraft. The Lockheed Corp. at Burbank, Calif., maker of the wide-body Tristar jet, recently announced it would fill 17 more orders for the Tristar and would then close down commercial operations to concentrate on military sales.

Both Boeing and Airbus have introduced new model aircraft on the commercial market. McDonnell Douglas has not come out with a wholly new model in several years, but recently won an order for more than $1 billion from Alitalia, Italy's national airline, for 30 DC-9 Super 80 twin-engine jets. Before that order was announced, some industry analysts thought McDonnell Douglas would follow Lockheed, filling the remaining 45 orders on its books and withdrawing from the commercial market.

As aircraft have grown larger, more complex and much more expensive, the number of aircraft manufacturers has steadily

---

[13] Worldwide, Flying Tigers is second only to Aeroflot, the Soviet airline, on a ton-mile volume basis.

diminished. In the early days of aviation, there was a plethora of companies offering an assortment of commercial aircraft. One famous name from that time was the Ford Motor Co., which produced the Ford Trimotor, a workhorse of many airline fleets. Ford has long since withdrawn from aviation, although it is still in aerospace as the prime contractor on Intelsat V, a communications satellite operated by Communications Satellite Corp.

Enormous Financial Investment and Risk

The reason why there are so few manufacturers of big commercial jet aircraft is the enormous capital outlays required for developing and producing new models. In a book published this year, *The Sporty Game*, author John Newhouse observes that a plane manufacturer "is literally betting the company" in deciding to build a new airliner, "because the size of the investment may exceed the company's entire net worth." According to Newhouse, a new airplane program will devour $2 billion long before deliveries begin. Then, too, there is no guarantee that even a best-selling plane will make money.

Starting in 1952 with Britain's de Haviland Comet [Newhouse wrote], an airplane prone to metal fatigue and hence disaster (two of them fell apart in the air), there have been twenty-two commercial jet-powered transports, of which only two, thus far, are believed to have made any money. These are the Boeing Company's first two entries, its long-range 707 and the medium-range 727, the industry's biggest seller.

Boeing's largest airplane, the 747, may one day be judged to have crossed the break-even point, whereas the company's smallest, the 737, although it may eventually approach the 727 in sales, is not likely to cross the break-even line.

The McDonnell Douglas Corporation's DC-8 would probably have been profitable but for some questionable decisions by management, especially the decision to kill it in favor of the DC-10; the firm's small two-engine DC-9, which preceded its chief rival, Boeing's 737, is unlikely to make any money.

Lockheed's L-1011 — an airplane that is more admired within the industry than most others, including its rival, the DC-10 — had lost $2,500 million [$2.5 billion] by the time it was cancelled.[14]

---

[14] John Newhouse, *The Sporty Game* (1982), pp. 1-2. The book's material appeared first as a series of articles in *The New Yorker* magazine.

With so much at stake, and such heavy odds against success, it is small wonder that few are willing — or able — to enter the field. Not surprisingly, the chief rival of Boeing and McDonnell Douglas is a multinational group made up of companies that are wholly or partly owned by European governments. It is called Airbus Industrie, which was formally constituted in December 1970.[15] Airbus Industrie's first plane, the A300, a short-to-medium-range twin-engine wide-body transport, went into service in May 1974. Until now, that plane, in various versions carrying between 220 and 345 passengers, has been the only operating Airbus model. However, a smaller Airbus, the A310, is scheduled for delivery to customers in the spring of 1983.

Boeing's newest planes are both twin-engine jetliners with new, fuel-efficient power plants. The 767, a twin-aisle wide-body of smaller dimensions than the 747, went into operation on U.S. domestic airlines in September. With seven seats across, it has a capacity of 211 passengers. The 757, currently being air-tested, is a short-to-medium range jetliner, capable of carrying 186 passengers. Deliveries of the 757 are due to start next year, with the first models going to British Airways in January.[16] Boeing and Airbus are bucking traditional resistance to the use of two-engine planes in transoceanic traffic. FAA regulations, currently under review, prevent two-engine planes from flying passengers between the West Coast and Hawaii, and on routes in the North Pacific, as well as on long trans-Atlantic routes.

Boeing and Airbus are both working on a still smaller plane, in the 150-passenger range, a capacity which marketing specialists say will fit a "hole in the market." This is a size desired by airlines for its fuel economy but not yet available. Airbus has already released preliminary details of the technology and configuration of its A320. Boeing is not yet ready to talk about its plane, which so far has no numbered designation. McDonnell Douglas' plans are not known, but industry experts believe the company intends for the present to emphasize its improved DC-8 Super 80 twinjet.

Just as only three companies supply the aircraft market in the free world, production of aircraft engines is limited to three companies: Pratt & Whitney and General Electric in the United States, and Rolls Royce of Britain, a government-owned cor-

---

[15] Members are Aerospatiale of France (37.9 ownership), Deutsche Airbus of Germany (37.9 percent), British Aerospace (20 percent), and Construcciones Aeronauticas of Spain (CASA) (4.2 percent). The French government owns more than 97 percent of Aerospatiale, while the British government holds 48.3 percent of British Aerospace's shares, with the rest in private hands. CASA is wholly owned by the Spanish government and Deutsche Airbus is a subsidiary of Messerschmitt-Bolkow-Blohm and VFW, two commercial companies that are in the process of merging. See *Airbus Industrie Briefing,* pamphlet published in April 1982.

[16] See *Background Information: Boeing 757,* Boeing Commercial Airplane Co. [a division of the parent Boeing Corp.], April 1982, and *Background Information: The Boeing 767 Twinjet,* June 1982.

Ten Leading Exporting Companies

Rank	Company	Total Sales*	Exports*	Percentage of Sales
		(in billions)		
1	Boeing	$ 9.78	$6.10	62.4%
2	General Motors	62.69	5.72	9.1
3	General Electric	27.24	4.34	15.9
4	Ford Motor	38.24	3.74	9.8
5	Caterpillar Tractor	9.15	3.51	38.3
6	McDonnell Douglas	7.38	2.76	37.5
7	E.I. du Pont de Nemours	22.81	2.64	11.6
8	United Technologies	13.66	2.63	19.2
9	IBM	29.07	1.85	6.3
10	Eastman Kodak	10.33	1.80	17.4

*For 1981, as reported by *Fortune*, Aug. 9, 1982, p. 68.

Underline denotes companies that are engaged wholly or partly in aircraft manufacture.

poration. A large number of companies in the United States, Europe and Japan make parts for commercial jet planes, and aerospace giants such as General Dynamics, Martin Marietta, North American Aviation and Northrop are prime contractors for military aircraft and aerospace equipment,[17] but the civilian jet market belongs essentially to one British and two American companies.

Government Roles in Foreign Competition

Competition between Boeing and Airbus is already keen and is expected to become intense if the battle for the 150-seat market begins. Each company has complained that the other enjoys unfair marketing advantages. Boeing says that Airbus is subsidized by the participating governments and thus is able to arrange preferential financing through the governments for potential customers. Moreover, Boeing contends there is a natural preference among nationally owned airlines in the owner countries for Airbus planes — a claim which Airbus says is refuted by the sale of the 757 to British Airways. Airbus, in turn, charges that aerospace research undertaken by the U.S. National Aeronautics and Space Administration (NASA), and made available to American manufacturers, is a hidden subsidy for U.S. companies. Airbus further asserts that the U.S. Export-Import Bank devotes an inordinate amount of its resources to financing Boeing sales overseas — which are the largest of any American company *(see box above)*.

---

[17] There are also sizable U.S. manufacturers of general aviation craft, including Fairchild, Cessna Aircraft Co., Piper Aircraft Corp. and Gates Learjet Corp.

— Boeing 727 and 737 production at Renton, Wash.

On a recent television appearance with representatives of the Export-Import Bank and Airbus Industrie, Boeing President Malcolm T. Stampler said Ex-Im Bank support for Boeing has been exaggerated.[18] Stampler said, "[T]hey [the Ex-Im Bank] do not give direct credits on 747s, 737-200s, 727s; they insist upon a competitive offer from Airbus before they will grant any kind of a direct credit. They won't give direct credits to developed countries. They charge a 2 percent extra fee. All of this has exacerbated the problem of trying to get sales. . . ."

Despite Stampler's disclaimer, the importance of government financing in multimillion-dollar aircraft deals was shown in the terms extended by the Ex-Im Bank in the sale of 30 McDonnell Douglas DS-8 Super 80s to Alitalia. According to *The Journal of Commerce* on Nov. 8, the bank made a direct loan commitment covering 42.5 percent of the purchase at 12 percent interest, and gave Alitalia the option of raising the bank's commitment to 62.5 percent of the sale. Bank officials said the same financing terms would have been available to Boeing had Alitalia decided to buy the 757 instead of the McDonnell Douglas plane.

Despite government assistance on both sides of the Atlantic, aircraft makers are feeling the effects of the slump in airline business. Commercial banks are increasingly reluctant to finance new equipment for airlines deep in the red. Adam Thomson, chairman of the British-based Caledonian Aviation Group,

---

[18] Stampler appeared on public television's "MacNeil-Lehrer Report," Oct. 19, 1982, along with Alan Boyd, president of Airbus Industries of North America, and William H. Draper, chairman of the Ex-Im Bank.

remarked: "I think airlines that are in a weak position will find it very difficult to finance airplanes at all." [19]

There is an unknown factor in the competiton between European and American plane manufacturers that makes both sides nervous. That is the possibility Japan may decide to enter their field, one of the few high technologies in which that country is not yet firmly implanted. Japanese companies have been easing into aircraft production in recent years by subcontracting to make component parts for both Boeing and Airbus. In 1981, Japan had aircraft industry sales of $1.3 billion.

A joint Japanese-British project for the development of a new aircraft engine is under way, as are talks between Boeing and Japanese firms on the possibility of collaboration on the 150-seat airliner. But on both sides of the Atlantic there is suspicion that the eventual goal of the Japanese Ministry of International Trade and Industry is a fully integrated Japanese aircraft industry, turning out out a wholly Japanese product.

Aviation Technology's Expensive Advances

The idea of 350 tons of metal and plastic hurtling through the air with 400 human beings aboard at or above the speed of sound seems, on the face of it, absurd. In the beginning days of aviation, one man wrote:

> It is a bare possibility that a one-man machine without a float and favored by a wind of, say, 15 miles an hour, might succeed in getting across the Atlantic. But such an attempt would be the height of folly. When one comes to increase the size of the craft, the possibility rapidly fades away. This is because of the difficulties of carrying sufficient fuel. It will be readily seen, therefore, why the Atlantic flight is out of the question. [20]

The writer was Orville Wright, one of the inventors of the airplane, and the year was 1913, ten years after he made the first heavier-than-air flight at Kitty Hawk, N.C.

Orville Wright may be forgiven his lack of foresight, for in the short span of a few decades technology was to accomplish wonders impossible to foresee. A modern commercial jet is a blend of dozens of high technologies, ranging from high-stress metal alloy research to aerodynamic design and digital computers. The air transport industry is one of the most technologically advanced of all. Research is being done — much of it by NASA[21] — to improve aircraft and engine safety and efficiency. The

---

[19] Quoted by Chris Barnett in *The Journal of Commerce,* June 8, 1982.
[20] Quoted by Robert J. Sterling in "Wrights to Wide-Bodies: The First 75 Years," pamphlet published by the Air Transport Association of America, April 1978.
[21] See *NASA Aeronautics,* publication EP-85, published by the National Aeronautics and Space Administration, Washington, D.C.

latest jetliners rely heavily on advances in microcomputers, telecommunications and light wave information transmittal.

Flight instrument systems are fully electronic. Flight management computers monitor all phases of aircraft operation, including fuel consumption, and make automatic adjustments when needed. Navigation systems use digital technology as do modern weather radar devices. A new generation landing aid, called the Microwave Landing System (MLS), will soon replace the Instrument Landing System in current use. With MLS, landings will be controlled by interacting computers in the cockpit and on the ground.

The newest airliners are designed and built for "worst case" circumstances. Most of those now in service have a number of "redundant" systems — two or more backup systems that swing into action automatically if the primary system fails. Three or four hydraulic, electrical, communications and guidance systems are the rule in modern jets.

While this kind of aircraft design achieves a high level of safety and efficiency, it may be pricing future aircraft out of the market. A new study by the Office of Technology Assessment,[22] a congressional agency, indicates that the next generation of airplanes may be so expensive that their design and production could be undertaken only by a joint effort of several companies, or underwritten by the government. The study estimates that the development cost of a single new model using advances in propulsion systems, aerodynamic design and computer technology would be no less than $6 billion and could possibly exceed $11 billion.

To the cost of airplanes themselves must be added the huge investment required to upgrade existing ground control systems. The Federal Aviation Administration recently announced a National Airspace System Plan, a comprehensive 20-year plan to modernize the U.S. Air Traffic Control and Air Navigation Systems. Current cost estimates for new equipment and construction are in the $10 billion to $14 billion range. The plan proposes to consolidate existing ground control facilities from 200 to 60 and provide an integrated national telecommunications network. Existing vacuum-tube systems would be replaced by modern solid-state digital equipment. When the system is finally in place, there would be constant, automatic monitoring of aircraft performance, weather, and air traffic by computers in the cockpit and on the ground.[23]

[22] "Financing and Program Alternatives for Advanced High-speed Aircraft," released October 1982. It forms the fourth part of a larger study, *The Impact of Advanced Air Transport Technology.*

[23] The National Airspace System Plan is outlined in a 450-page document, available at $9.75 a copy from the Federal Aviation Administration, 800 Independence Ave. S.W., Washington, D.C. 20591.

Constraints to Growth

I N addition to its financial distress, the air transport industry faces numerous longer-range problems affecting future growth. The biggest is congestion, both in the air and on the ground. This is due partly to the rapid growth of airlines in the 1960s and 1970s, and the purchase of newer and larger jetliners while the air transport industry was still healthy. But there are other factors as well. The airlines share the skies with the bourgeoning fleets of general aviation operators, and also with military aircraft. In the United States, military operations are not a serious problem for scheduled airlines, but in parts of Europe and Japan, large blocks of airspace are reserved for military flights and are off-limits to civil aviation. This requires wide detours in air routes, adding to flying time and fuel costs.[24]

A more serious problem in the United States results from the growth of general aviation. During the air controllers' strike in 1981,[25] the Federal Aviation Administration cut back the number of "slots," or landing rights, at 22 of the nation's busiest airports. In a few cases, landing slots had already been limited at airports that were operating at capacity levels. During a six-week period last spring, the FAA permitted airlines to buy or trade landing slots at controlled airports. In that time, People's Express Airlines paid a record $1.75 million for five landing slots at Washington's crowded National Airport. The seller, Altair Airlines, also received from People's Express three slots at Logan Airport in Boston. The FAA ended the experimental program on June 24.

Airport operators have criticized the FAA's National Airspace System Plan for paying insufficient attention to the need for expansion and modernization of airports and ground facilities. In congressional testimony last March,[26] the operators said that 41 U.S. airports will have severe airside congestion by 1990 and as many as 91 airports by the year 2000. The operators said the government was accepting as inevitable a need to impose quotas and flow-control restrictions at the affected airports. "We are concerned," their statement read, "that the FAA is so smitten with its National *Airspace* System Plan that it has forgotten it

[24] See "Long-term Technical Constraints to Industry Growth," *World Airline Cooperation Review,* published by the International Air Transport Association, July-September 1982, p. 11.
[25] The 15,000-member Professional Air Traffic Controllers Organization struck Aug. 3, 1981, demanding higher pay and benefits from the government, which declared the strike illegal and decertified — banned — the union. The 11,500 controllers who struck were dismissed from their jobs.
[26] Joint testimony of the Airport Operators Council International and the American Association of Airport Executives on the proposal of the Federal Aviation Administration for modernization of the air traffic control system before the Subcommittee on Aviation, House Committee on Public Works and Transportation, March 23, 1982.

A Traveler's Tale

The emergency plan is taken seriously by ATA and IATA member airlines. I was at Miami Airport the afternoon of May 12, when Braniff folded without advanced warning. I spent some time with the station manager of Varig, a Brazilian airline, who worked feverishly all afternoon to bring in extra airplanes from Brazil to accommodate the passenger overflow. My flight to Panama via Pan American, which had been considerably underbooked, was filled by flight time with standbys from Braniff. — Richard C. Schroeder.

also has a National *Airport* System Plan that, when last updated, projected a $36 billion airport program for the decade ahead."

Even with adequate federal support and financing, the necessary airport expansion or construction of new facilities could be hampered by opposition from environmental groups. Japan experienced prolonged delays in opening its new Tokyo/Narita airport because of environmentalists' protests and has all but abandoned plans for further development at Osaka airport. In this country, environmental considerations — noise in particular — have dictated the construction of new airports at considerable distances from major cities. Airports adjacent to cities operate under elaborate noise abatement procedures. Planes landing or taking off at National Airport, for example, must follow a snaky route over the Potomac River to keep noise to a minimum, a procedure pilots say is difficult, if not hazardous.

Travel Agents' Influence; Computer 'Bias'

In the present depressed airline environment, travel agents can make or break a troubled carrier. Agents sell more than 60 percent of all airline tickets in the United States. Fewer than 20 percent of their clients express a specific preference for one airline over another, giving the agents extraordinary power to decide which carriers get the lion's share of travelers. Increasingly, agents have been showing reluctance to book their customers on airlines in danger of failure. As Braniff showed signs of weakening earlier this year, ticket sales by travel agents dropped off by 40 to 50 percent, according to Braniff executives, and that was a prime factor in causing the airline to file for bankrupcy.[27]

The Air Transport Association operates an emergency plan for situations such as the Braniff collapse *(see box above)*. All ticket holders have the option to transfer to other airlines, but on a standby basis. Delays, however, are inevitable. Tickets are

[27] Reported by Agis Salpukas in *The New York Times*, May 21, 1982.

also refundable from a central ATA contingency fund. The tendency among agents is to avoid risking inconvenience for their customers, though. Some agents make it a point to advise clients of the possibility of sudden failure by a weak carrier.

Rumors of bankruptcy can be extremely damaging to an airline that is perceived to be in trouble. "Talk of bankruptcy is a touchy subject," *The Wall Street Journal* reported Oct. 27. "Airlines suspect that competitors start rumors of bankruptcy to draw away business. Air Florida recently charged Pan American with starting bankruptcy rumors, while Pan American accused Trans World and United of starting rumors about Pan

World's Busiest Airports

Passengers		Freight/mail (metric tons)	
1. O'Hare, Chicago	37,992,151	1. Kennedy	1,206,173
2. Hartsfield, Atlanta	37,594,073	2. Los Angeles	819,551
3. Los Angeles	32,722,534	3. O'Hare	751,472
4. Heathrow, London	27,512,945	4. Frankfurt/Main	696,565
5. Kennedy, New York	25,752,719	5. Miami	573,326
		6. Heathrow	524,810
6. Dallas/Fort Worth	25,533,929	7. Hartsfield	512,468
7. Stapleton, Denver	22,601,877	8. Tokyo Narita	493,245
8. Tokyo Haneda	21,235,185	9. Charles de Gaulle, Paris	468,042
9. Miami	19,848,593		
10. San Francisco	19,848,491	10. San Francisco	423,031

Source: Airport Operators Council International

Am. The airlines have denied starting such rumors." Airlines that are the subject of bankruptcy talk make special efforts to reassure travel agents that they intend to stay in business, and some mount elaborate entertainment efforts at travel agents' conventions.

Computerization of airline reservation systems has also contributed to the woes of some carriers. More than 80 percent of all travel agents are expected to have computers by the end of this year. The three major computer systems that have been developed by airline companies contain a built-in "bias" for the owner-company's flights, which are listed first. These are followed by the flights of other airlines willing to pay a fee for listing in the computer. Airlines that do not pay the fee are not listed. Delta Air Lines is preparing a "bias-free" computer system in which flights will be listed exactly as they are printed in the Official Airlines Guide. Delta hopes not only to reap a publicity dividend, but also to attract the business of travel agents who are annoyed or confused by the biased systems.

Needs Beyond Reach of Better Economy

Recovery of the troubled air transport industry clearly depends on a resurgence of the economy. Lower interest rates, more plentiful sources of loans and capital, more money in the pocketbooks of businessmen and consumers, are all essential to the near-term health of airlines and aircraft manufacturers. But experts point out that there are a number of more fundamental problems that simply will not go away with the return of relative prosperity.

An IATA Technical Committee recently declared that "There are no purely physical limitations to the growth of civil air transport up to 1995." [28] But the committee cited a number of political disputes that have disrupted air route structures, and have led to inefficiency in the use of airspace. To these must be added the mounting problems associated with subsidization of airline operations by several national governments, and the subsequent distortion of airline fare structures.

There are also nascent problems in airline insurance and liability. In the wake of recent crashes, insurance rates for major airlines have risen by between 13 and 29 percent. In addition, a U.S. appeals court recently ruled invalid the Warsaw Convention on the limits of airline liability for losses and accidents.[29] If

[28] *World Airline Cooperation Review, op. cit.,* p. 9.
[29] The Warsaw Convention, drawn up in 1929, established a maximum level of airline liability to protect the airlines from huge damage suits and extremely high insurance premiums in the event that baggage or freight is lost or destroyed. The amount of liability was increased in 1955, 1966, 1971 and 1975. In its recent ruling, the U.S. Court of Appeals for the 2nd Circuit (New York) said "there is no longer an internationally agreed upon unit of conversion" for determining maximum airline liability, and the Warsaw Convention is therefore unenforceable in the United States.

upheld on appeal, the ruling could throw the worldwide airline business into chaos and raise insurance rates beyond sustainable levels.

Further down the road is the specter of sharply reduced business travel, as more executives turn to "teleconferencing." Technological advances now permit the transmission of video and audio material via satellite between major cities in the United States, and such links will eventually be established worldwide. Where a businessman once had to contemplate several days of arduous travel, he can now walk down the hall to a teleconferencing facility and accomplish just as much in a few hours of discussion with colleagues thousands of miles away.

No one doubts the necessity of a healthy air transport industry for both passenger and freight traffic. Indeed, in some of the remoter parts of the world, the airplane is virtually the only transportation link available. But the experts grow cautious when asked to foretell the structure of the industry after it has emerged from its present series of crises. Change, they say, is the only constant in the troubled skies.

Selected Bibliography

Books

Newhouse, John, *The Sporty Game,* Alfred A. Knopf, 1982.
Bender, Marilyn, and Selig Altschul, *The Chosen Instrument: Pan Am, Juan Trippe, The Rise and Fall of an American Entrepreneur,* Simon & Shuster, 1982.

Articles

Aerospace (published by the Aerospace Industries Association), selected issues.
"Airline Avionics," *Airline Executive,* special report, April 1982.
Byrne, Harlan S., "The Outlook for Airlines Gets Bleaker," *Wall Street Journal,* Oct. 27, 1982.
Flight Safety Digest (published by the Flight Safety Foundation), selected issues.
Knoles, Don, "Boom in U.S. Overnight Service Highlights World Air Freight Market," *Airline Executive,* July 1982.
"Longer-term Technical Constraints to Industry Growth," *IATA Review,* July-September 1982, pp. 8-15.
Malkin, Edward, "Airports and Air Freight," special supplement of *The Journal of Commerce,* Sept. 27, 1982.
Nixon, Stuart, "Turbulent Times for Airlines," *Airline Pilot,* May 1982.
"The Carrier's Kamikaze Attack on Air Fares," *Business Week,* Oct. 18, 1982.
World (published by the Federal Aviation Administration), selected issues.

Reports and Studies

"Aerospace Facts and Figures, 1981/82," Aerospace Industries Association of America, July 1981.
"Boeing, Boeing, Gone," transcript of the "MacNeil-Lehrer Report," Oct. 19, 1982.
"Air Transport 1982," Annual Report of the U.S. Scheduled Airline Industy, Air Transport Association, June 1982.
"Annual Report of the Council," International Civil Aviation Organization, 1982.
Editorial Research Reports: "Deregulating Transportation," 1979 Vol. I, p. 41.
"14th Annual Report, Fiscal Year 1980," U.S. Department of Transportation, 1982.
"NASA Aeronautics," National Aeronautics and Space Administration (publication EP-85, undated).
"National Airspace Plan," Federal Aviation Administration, December 1981.
"The State of the Air Transport Industry," Annual Report of the International Air Transport Association, 1981 & 1982.
"World Air Transport Statistics," 26th Edition, 1981, International Air Transportation Association, June 1982.
"Worldwide Airport Traffic Report, Calendar Year 1981," Airport Operators Council International.

INDEX